"In the golden age of American newspapers, Warren Phillips was a giant. In his twenties, he was a star reporter for *The Wall Street Journal* in postwar Europe; in his thirties and forties he was the managing editor and executive editor of the *Journal*, which became the country's largest newspaper; in his fifties and sixties he was the CEO of Dow Jones, then the most respected news media company in the United States. He has written a poignant and perceptive story of his rise from a middle-class Queens neighborhood to the highest tier of the global news business. At times touching and humorous, Phillips offers fascinating insights about American business, politics, and journalism. He traveled in the circles of CEOs, U.S. presidents, prime ministers, and royalty; always at his core he was a reporter. That is the beauty of *Newspaperman*."

—VERNON E. JORDAN JR.
senior managing director, Lazard Freres & Company;
civil rights leader and former president, National Urban League;
author of the memoir Vernon Can Read!

"London bureau chief of *The Wall Street Journal* at twenty-three, foreign editor at twenty-five, managing editor at thirty, Warren Phillips rode the fast track, and *Newspaperman* takes readers along for his adventurous ride to the top of Dow Jones. The path wasn't always smooth or easy, but you arrive with him at his desk in the CEO's office knowing what a ride it was. Phillips fell in love with newspapers when he was a boy. He's still infatuated but he doesn't skip over his tough times or mistakes. That's what makes *Newspaperman* such a telling guide to the newsroom and to the top office in the executive suite."

—LOU BOCCARDI
president and chief executive, the Associated Press, 1985–2003,
and former chairman, Pulitzer Prize Board

"This lovely book recounts the life of a wise, thoughtful, and admired newspaper editor and publisher. The tiny *Wall Street Journal* Warren Phillips joined grew up to be a giant. *Newspaperman* tells that story; it also includes tough self-criticism and a surprising take on what happened at Dow Jones after Phillips left. A most winning love story is also included."

—DONALD E. GRAHAM
chairman and chief executive, The Washington Post Company

"This is the story of Warren Phillips, a precocious boy born in Brooklyn, a reporter, an editor, a publisher, a corporate executive, and now the author of a fascinating book. The focus of the book is his career of almost fifty years with Dow Jones, publisher of *The Wall Street Journal*—the world's best newspaper. Phillips was CEO of Dow Jones for fifteen years—a period of growth in revenues, circulation, and profits; a period of technological innovation that made it possible to produce a national newspaper that arrived at breakfast time in Seattle, Miami, Los Angeles, and Boston; a period that saw the paper circle the globe with two international editions as well as the creation of online publishing. This remarkable record was based on core principles—a commitment to editorial integrity and technological innovation and an editorial policy that supported free markets and free men. During Phillips's tenure there were Pulitzer Prizes and repeated recognition of Dow Jones as one of our most admired and respected institutions.

"How did he do it? Phillips attracted and promoted a diverse and talented group of executives—strong individuals with unique abilities. He encouraged each of them to develop his or her own special gifts and persona while working together to create a coherent enterprise. He did all this for a public company that was family controlled. Good communication with the family shareholders was essential to the success of the enterprise. Phillips earned the trust of the family and it in turn steadfastly supported professional standards and core principles. The result was the growth of one of the world's great brands—*The Wall Street Journal*."

—JAMES Q. RIORDAN
former vice chairman, Mobil Corporation

"Already an enthusiastic newspaperman at Queens College in New York City, the young Warren Phillips couldn't get hired by any major city paper, so he accepted a job as copyreader at the small *Wall Street Journal*, circulation one hundred thousand. There, his drive and initiative developed his career rapidly through ever-more responsible editorial positions, until he became CEO of Dow Jones, parent of *The Wall Street Journal*. Along the way, he met and reported on countless world leaders, visited exotic and remote countries, and selected and nurtured many colorful and capable colleagues, always supported by his attractive and loving family (led by the good judgment and occasional skepticism of his wife, Barbara).

"By constant devotion to the highest standards of quality and integrity, he built *The Wall Street Journal* circulation to two million and multiplied Dow Jones's revenues and earnings. In spite of a few hiccups, honestly related here, Dow Jones was rated by *Fortune* magazine as the second most-admired company in the United States, and so proved that an outstanding newspaperman can also achieve enormous success as a business builder and leader."

—HAMISH MAXWELL
former chairman and CEO, Philip Morris Companies Inc.

"This is the amazing life story of a young newspaperman, growing from employee of *The Wall Street Journal*, then a small financial paper in New York, to become foreign editor, editor, publisher, and CEO for fifteen years of the United States' highly respected and largest circulation newspaper, eventually expanded to include Far East and European editions. This is a story that would be useful to any executive responsible for guiding a business. An attractive family story is included, as are perceptive commentaries on Germany, Greece, Turkey, England, Spain, China, Russia, and the Middle East. All is told with modest good humor, but repeatedly emphasizes the need for integrity and high standards."

—GEORGE B. MUNROE
retired chairman and chief executive, Phelps Dodge Corporation

NEWSPAPERMAN

Inside the News Business
at *The Wall Street Journal*

Also by Warren H. Phillips

China: Behind the Mask (with Robert Keatley)

NEWSPAPERMAN

Inside the News Business
at *The Wall Street Journal*

WARREN H. PHILLIPS

New York   Chicago   San Francisco   Lisbon   London   Madrid   Mexico City
Milan   New Delhi   San Juan   Seoul   Singapore   Sydney   Toronto

Copyright © 2012 by Warren H. Phillips. All rights reserved. Printed in the United States of America. Except as permitted under the United States Copyright Act of 1976, no part of this publication may be reproduced or distributed in any form or by any means, or stored in a database or retrieval system, without the prior written permission of the publisher.

1 2 3 4 5 6 7 8 9 10 11 12 13 14 15 16   QFR/QFR   1 9 8 7 6 5 4 3 2 1

ISBN   978-0-07-177690-5
MHID   0-07-177690-7

e-ISBN   978-0-07-177691-2
e-MHID   0-07-177691-5

Library of Congress Cataloging-in-Publication Data

Phillips, Warren, 1926–
        Newspaperman : inside the news business at the Wall Street Journal / by Warren Phillips.
          p.   cm.
        Includes index.
        ISBN-13: 978-0-07-177690-5 (alk. paper)
        ISBN-10: 0-07-177690-7 (alk. paper)
        1. Phillips, Warren, 1926–.   2. Journalists—United States—Biography.
3. Newspaper editors—United States—Biography.   4. Newspaper publishers—United States—Biography.   5. Wall Street Journal—History.   I. Title.

PN4874.P48A3   2011
070.92—dc22
[B]   2011016239

McGraw-Hill books are available at special quantity discounts to use as premiums and sales promotions or for use in corporate training programs. To contact a representative, please e-mail us at bulksales@mcgraw-hill.com.

This book is printed on acid-free paper.

For Barbara,
who forged the keys to every kingdom I was blessed to enter.

And my father, Abraham Phillips,
who was gone before he could draw warmth
from bearing witness.

Contents

PART FOUR **PUBLISHER**

ACKNOWLEDGMENTS

I AM INDEBTED to my wife, Barbara Phillips, and to my late mother, Juliette Phillips Heller, for preserving correspondence, clippings, and other mementos. Without those records, this memoir would not have been possible.

I also owe much to Robin Siegel and to Bernard Friedlander, both cousins, and to my youngest daughter, Nina Phillips, for researching the family genealogy, including the passenger manifests of ships that brought my father and his family to the United States in the late nineteenth and early twentieth centuries.

My past administrative assistants—Karen Cuddy, Susan Chin, and Diane Scanlon—preserved, organized, and contributed to other records many years ago and these, too, proved helpful in preparing this book. More important, they kept me preserved and organized over the years and thus were indispensable partners in this story.

Several good friends urged me in past years to write a memoir. I thank them all for their interest and confidence. They included Michele Rubin, a tireless and talented agent at New York's Writers House literary agency; Salvatore Macri, my barber-philosopher for the past forty-three years; and Ivan R. Dee, a longtime Chicago publisher of quality books and a credit to his profession, a distinguished and model publisher. Most persuasive in getting me to embark on this undertaking was my wife, Barbara. Hers was the deciding voice, as in so many other things. I shall be forever grateful for her support and suggestions, and for those of our three daughters, Lisa, Leslie, and Nina.

I also am indebted to editor Stephanie Frerich and her colleagues at McGraw-Hill, my publisher, not only for their confidence, support, and hard work, but especially for their enthusiasm.

Lastly, the books listed in the Further Reading were helpful in refreshing and confirming certain memories, particularly dates, and in filling a few gaps in my recollections.

INTRODUCTION

THIS IS THE STORY of a lifelong love affair with journalism, of newspapers in their heyday and a boy who grew to manhood incurably intoxicated with everything about them. Few who have fallen under the spell of newsrooms at deadline and the sound of a newspaper's presses gathering speed, growing from a slow rumble to a thunderous roar, have ever been cured of that addiction. Certainly not I.

There also is a second, even more personal story here: that of how a skinny, timid, unathletic Jewish kid from Queens, New York, an immigrant's son, somehow eventually developed the poise and self-confidence to lead a Fortune 500 publishing company, with ten thousand employees producing daily newspapers and electronic news services around the globe.

The third story here, embedded in the others and more personal yet, is the role that family and pride in family played in this transition. It was an element, a glue, that made all else possible.

My passion for newspapers began at the age of eleven. My father took me on one of the guided tours that the *New York Daily News* conducted through its East Forty-Second Street building in those days. From the huge revolving globe in its lobby to its reporters hunched over typewriters to its mammoth presses, all were subtly seductive. So, too, were the Teletype machines in the ground-floor windows of the Associated Press headquarters at 50 Rockefeller Plaza. It was always worth a detour on trips into Manhattan to pause and watch them relentlessly type out news of oncoming war, train wrecks, and distant hurricanes.

At age twelve, while recuperating at home from pneumonia, I began keeping a diary of the daily news of the far-off beginnings of war. At the same time, I started a home newspaper, on a kid's typewriter, titled *The Snoopy Scoop.* Its juvenile masthead slogan was: "Everywhere we snoop, until we find a scoop." Later, I began visiting the German Information Office at 11 Battery Place, the British Information Office at Rockefeller Center, and the French Consulate, collecting the glossy magazines and other publications they were distributing in attempts to glorify their early wartime achievements.

When I finished my army tour in 1945, I worked as a copyboy at the *New York Herald Tribune,* first full-time and then part-time after I returned to college. The pay was sixteen dollars a week. It was an exhilarating time and place in the newspaper world of that era, a bustling and colorful newsroom that reignited and fueled a young man's passion. On finishing college in 1947, I sought a reporter's job at each of the ten general daily newspapers that existed in New York at that time. Each turned me down, as did the Columbia University Graduate School of Journalism. *The Wall Street Journal,* then a small financial paper with one hundred thousand circulation, hired me at forty dollars a week.

After that, I worked on copydesks, on rewrite, as a reporter in Germany and Britain and other lands, then as an editor in Chicago and New York. By age thirty I was managing editor of the *Journal.* Later I would become the *Journal*'s publisher, seeing its circulation pass two million, and simultaneously serve as the chief executive officer of its parent company, Dow Jones & Company. I would be elected president of the American Society of Newspaper Editors and would serve for ten years on the Pulitzer Prize Board, enjoying debates about our profession with some of the most respected editors of the day.

Some of the things I learned over these years have found their way into this book as an insider's reflections on the practice and profession of journalism as well as the personalities of some of its most colorful practitioners in the second half of the twentieth century.

After forty-five years at the *Journal* and Dow Jones, I retired from operating responsibilities there and in 1992, on the initiative of my wife, Barbara, a writer, editor, and teacher, we together formed Bridge Works Publishing Company to publish quality fiction and nonfiction books. We thus continued in the world of words, the world of ideas, and the world of writers and others with lively minds. *American Bookseller*, then the magazine of the American Booksellers Association, wrote in its November 1995 issue of Bridge Works's "amazing record," with "more than its share of winners."

Looking back over these years, I find myself lucky beyond belief to have been able to make my way, with the help of so many generous souls in and out of the profession, from the cocooned life of a sheltered only child, short on self-confidence, to a world in which I could converse with news makers and history makers—from Germany's Chancellor Konrad Adenauer, Russia's Mikhail Gorbachev, China's Premier Chou En-lai, and Britain's Margaret Thatcher to Ronald Reagan, Jimmy Carter, George H. W. Bush, and leaders of American industry and finance.

Because I was unwisely skipped by school officials through several elementary school grades, I graduated from high school at fourteen. The result was a child always much younger than his classmates, socially backward with the girls, not knowing such niceties as peeling and slicing an apple as a guest at dinner. Some may say that adds up to the picture of a precocious child. I would say it added up to the picture of a very immature, easily awed, and intimidated youth.

What formative experiences enable such a kid to mature and move among colleagues and among business, political, and media leaders who once would have left him tongue-tied and in awe? That is all part of this story.

Having a wife with smarts, ability, finely tuned antennae, and unerringly keen instincts certainly was a large part of it. Another part was taking to heart the advice I heard the *Journal*'s former Chicago Bureau chief, John McWethy, and the accomplished reporter Ray Vicker separately give to young reporters on many occasions: "When you go into a grand, sweeping office to interview a big-shot CEO, sitting behind a huge desk, just remember he puts his pants on one leg at a time just as you do." Only more often than not, they put it less elegantly and more earthily: "Just remember that when he goes to the bathroom, he sits down on the pot the same way you do." Those influences and additional experiences helped the kid transform himself into a reporter, editor, and executive with more confidence than his early years would have indicated.

I have encountered over the years many men and women addicted to name-dropping. I am always inwardly amused and think it a sign that they feel they must try to inflate their own importance by working into the conversation the names of celebrities they know and have recently encountered. The reader will notice that I have done my share of this above, and I will do so again at more than a few other points in this narrative. My excuse is this: It may be helpful—or at least that is my hope—in holding the reader's interest, in keeping him or her engaged. I am ever mindful of a remark I heard often from the late Barney Kilgore, who more than any other fashioned the modern *Wall Street Journal*. In advocating fast-paced, lively writing, he would continually caution: "The easiest thing for the reader to do is to stop reading."

Barney was a wise man. There was another homily he used often, attributing it to his father. "No tree grows to the sky," he would say. The ailments afflicting America's treasured newspapers today, in big city and small, coast to coast, are evidence that he wasn't wrong about that, either.

NEWSPAPERMAN

Inside the News Business
at *The Wall Street Journal*

PART ONE

YOUTH

CHAPTER 1

Early Boyhood

ON THE NIGHT I WAS BORN, my mother was dancing the Black Bottom, a step popular in that year, 1926. She jokingly maintained throughout her life that she had been a flapper, the Jazz Age term for young women of the carefree 1920s who were devoted to dancing, to parties, to frivolity. The term could have described the way they flapped their arms and legs wildly as they gyrated across the dance floor, imagining themselves characters from an F. Scott Fitzgerald novel.

On that late June evening, young Juliette Phillips was apparently determined not to let even the ninth month of pregnancy interfere with a good time. The Black Bottom had the predictable effect of inducing labor, and off to the hospital she went.

She and my father, who married in 1923, were living in Manhattan Beach, Brooklyn, an ocean-front community not far from Sheepshead Bay. She was almost twenty-seven, having been born September 3, 1899, at 280 Halsey Street, Brooklyn, the daughter of parents of German background. She had graduated from Girls High School in Brooklyn, worked as a volunteer for the navy in World War I and as a clerk in the New York public school system, then met and married my father, Abraham Phillips, whom everyone called Abe.

My father had been born Abram Figowski in 1895 in Bialystok, then in czarist Russia, today part of eastern Poland. At the age of four he, with four brothers and two sisters, were smuggled across the border in a hay cart, fleeing Russian pogroms. If the border guards had been more conscientious probing the hay with bayonets and pitchforks for contraband, this story would have had a different ending. More accurately, it never would have had a beginning.

My father's father, Wolf Figowski, born in 1862, had preceded his family to New York seven months before they crossed the Atlantic, changing and Americanizing the family name upon his arrival. His first wife, Hannah, my father's mother, died before she could leave Russia with her young children. The seven children were brought to America on the steamship *Albano* out of Hamburg, arriving July 19, 1900, in the care of a sixteen-year-old distant cousin of Hannah's, Theofilia "Tillie" Levski. Wolf subsequently married her and fathered three children with her.

Perhaps because of my father's young age when he arrived in New York, as well as his attendance at American schools, he spoke in adulthood without any trace of an accent. The same was true of his siblings. They lived in a fourth-floor, walk-up apartment on Manhattan's East Fourth Street, near First Avenue. They later moved to Brooklyn, in the Williamsburg district, and in 1922 my father's older, bachelor brother Joe, who became a school principal, bought the family a house on Bedford Avenue.

On Friday nights friends would join them to play music. My father had a fine voice, and as a boy, perhaps in his preteens or early teens, he traveled the country with a boys' choir. His love of music continued, and I recall during my boyhood that the radio on weekends was always tuned to the Metropolitan Opera. We even possessed a recording by the great Enrico Caruso.

My father became a naturalized U.S. citizen, worked in the business office of the storied New York evening newspaper, the *Sun*, then served in the Army Air Corps as an aerial gunner in World War I. After he returned to civilian life and subsequently met and courted my mother, they eloped to marry.

Returning to my maternal grandparents' home with news of their marriage, assuming they had saved my mother's parents much trouble and expense by eloping, they were met with the full fury of my grandfather Morris Rosenberg's wrath. He castigated the newlyweds for their lack of consideration, for Abe marrying their daughter without giving her parents a chance to be present, for denying them the chance to put on a big wedding for their sole surviving child. As the tirade went on and on, my father grew pale and ill, finally rushing into the bathroom to throw up. When he emerged, his new father-in-law, wracked by remorse, tearfully rushed to embrace him, threw his arms around him, and cried out: "My son, my son!"

These were among the stories I heard in my childhood. It was a childhood lived between two world wars that transformed a century. And three years after my birth came the crash of 1929 and the subsequent Great Depression, which likewise transformed the country and the century. Though I grew up in the Depression years, an only child, I was fortunate to have been sheltered from the hardship and deprivation that gripped the world around me.

My family moved before I reached school age to Forest Hills, in Queens, to the first floor of what was then called an "attached house" at 68–31 Dartmouth Street, a house that might today be called a town house, joined to many other brick houses on both sides. About two years later we moved to a two-story, six-room brick house at 69–49 Harrow Street, adjacent on the west to a small hill atop which sat an empty lot where the neighborhood kids could play. It was after the move to Dartmouth Street that my first episodic childhood memories began.

One of the first was of dressing up in a cowboy costume, complete with chaps, holster, and toy pistol, which I had received as a gift. Preparing to go outdoors, where it was raw and damp, my mother insisted that I bundle up in a windbreaker and don rubbers over my shoes. I recall how desolate I felt as I cried, "Cowboys don't wear rubbers."

Another vivid memory, one that perhaps spawned timidity, was of being punched in the face after we had moved to Harrow Street. Just before lunchtime, neighbors Stuie Nadelbach, Joel Rabin, and I were standing and admiring the newly poured concrete on the freshly repaved driveway of the Nadelbachs' corner house. Irrationally thinking it would be an amusing prank, I pushed Stuie into the wet cement. Emerging, and understandably provoked, he bloodied my nose, and I went home, humiliated, to eat my lunch and ponder the idiocy of mischief without purpose.

I recount such childhood episodes with a purpose in mind. These minor setbacks demonstrate the extent of the worst memories and traumas, if they could even be labeled such, that marked a mostly pleasant, insulated, trauma-free childhood while, in the Depression years, other families were enduring true trauma, anguish, and deprivation.

My father, who was by then working as a salesman for a company manufacturing women's lingerie, before starting up his own firm, never lost his job. This was in contrast to the widespread unemployment that characterized the 1930s, bringing strain and suffering to so many American families.

CHAPTER **2**

The Innocent Years

MY FIRST RECOLLECTION of attending elementary school at Public School 144 in Forest Hills, about six blocks south of our Harrow Street house, is of my pretty first-grade teacher giving me a kiss on the forehead. I had been promoted from grade 1A to 2A, skipping 1B, the second term of the school's first year. I subsequently was similarly skipped through the second half of the second, third, and fourth grades.

This was considered a recognition of good classroom performance, and my parents were pleased. In later years I realized it was not a good idea to have a pupil skip grades and wind up always younger and more immature than his classmates. This was how it was, however, as I proceeded from PS 144 to PS 171, also known as Abraham Lincoln Junior High School, and then Franklin K. Lane High School. I often was regarded as a class mascot. In a junior high school graduation souvenir memory book, in which classmates penned sometimes witty greetings and remembrances, one affectionately referred to me as "midget," another as "squirt."

Lincoln Junior High and Lane were close together, just off Jamaica Avenue on the border of Queens and Brooklyn, many miles from my home. I went there because my mother was an assistant to the principal of the junior high school, Samuel Moskowitz, and hence was able to drive me to and fro each day as she commuted by car to work. Forest Hills High School, not far from my home, was not built until the year I graduated from high school.

My school days and life at home were tranquil. I cannot claim to have been particularly perceptive or aware of the world outside the one in which I moved from day to day. My memories of those years are fragmented, kaleidoscopic. Here are some of them.

As I was growing up, there was always the exciting (to me) presence in a closet of the helmet my father brought home from World War I. It was steel, with worn leather head straps; it was big and it was heavy, very heavy, at least to a child. It was too large and heavy for me to wear.

I have often reflected in the years since on the fact that World War I ended only eight years before I was born, a time span so short that nowadays, when I think back on occurrences as recent as eight years ago, they seem like yesterday. But to a young person, anything that happened even a year or two before his or her birth seems as distant as the Middle Ages. Youths' sense of time and history seems destined always to start with their arrival on this earth.

Other mementos of the war that I often turned over in my child's hands were my father's Victory Medal, his dog tags, and a letter on Windsor Castle stationery, in King George V's handwritten script but obviously duplicated, welcoming the American troops to England. The letter, still preserved, reads:

> Soldiers of the United States, the people of the British Isles welcome you on your way to take your stand beside the Armies of many Nations now fighting in the Old World the great battle for human freedom.
>
> The Allies will gain new heart and spirit in your company. I wish that I could shake the hand of each one of you and bid you God speed on your mission.

It is signed "George R.I." and is dated April 1918. The R.I. stands for Rex Imperator, or King and Emperor (of India).

My father, after training at Camp Upton, Long Island, and at a Langley, Virginia, airfield, had been based in England as an aerial gunner, manning a Lewis machine gun from the rear cockpit of one of those two-seater, open-cockpit military planes of that early era in aviation history. He had seen his best friend decapitated there when he accidentally walked into a propeller. His unit did not see action in France before war's end.

Nowadays bookstores and magazine stands are filled with stories of dysfunctional families; mine was a functional, harmonious one. I have no memory of cross words ever being exchanged by my parents within my earshot. I remember only one occasion, when I was about eight, when my mother and father fought over some unknown issue and did not talk to each other for two days. I pleaded with them, as a mediator, to please make up. Even on that occasion, their argument did not take place in my presence. I mention this incident because it is the only husband-wife tension I can recall. It was unique in its break from the harmonious atmosphere that surrounded me at home. I did not realize at the time how fortunate I was in being spared the acrimony and conflict present in many other households.

My father commuted to work in Manhattan each day on the Long Island Rail Road. Forest Hills in those days was a suburb not yet served by New York's subway system. On summer evenings I would sometimes walk the eight or ten blocks to the station to meet his train, and I would be buoyed by his loving greeting.

He formed a company, Melody Lane Lingerie, making mostly women's slips, in partnership with a former colleague, Abe Sabeson. Their office and factory were on a loft floor on East Thirty-Third Street, on the south side of the street a few doors west of Park Avenue. My father would take me to work occasionally when I had a holiday, and he would take me around the corner to Schrafft's on Park Avenue for a chocolate sundae or to the nearby Longchamp for a fancy lunch.

I learned once that my father earned one hundred dollars a week, or five thousand dollars a year. That was big money in our eyes, especially in those days, when a dollar went much farther than it has since. A cup of coffee cost ten cents in a typical restaurant in 1935, a half-dozen clams thirty-five cents, and you could buy an eight-ounce box of Kellogg's cornflakes in the grocery store for eight cents. Until I reached adulthood, and maybe for a few years after that, my ambition was to some day earn what my father was then earning, and thus have a comfortable life. I considered that the point at which I would be a success.

Aside from my maternal grandparents, whom we saw frequently while they were alive, we visited often with my cousins, uncles, and aunts on my father's side—his brothers and sisters and their children. We saw much less frequently members of my mother's side of the family, aside from her parents, perhaps because she had no living siblings.

My mother had had an older sister, Mamie, who died in 1914 at age sixteen from food poisoning after eating polluted shellfish while visiting Atlantic City, New Jersey, in the company of her and my mother's Aunt Jennie. My mother also had had a younger brother, Henry, who drowned in 1919, also at age sixteen, while swimming off Howard Beach, Queens. My middle name is in remembrance of him.

My mother's parents, Morris and Eva Rosenberg, owned a two-story wooden house in Richmond Hill, Queens, about a twenty-minute drive from where we lived. My grandmother Eva was short, shy, and quiet and wore her wispy hair in a bun at the back, a chignon. Her husband, Moe, had a bushy, snow-white moustache and was usually in shirtsleeves. He had been born in 1856, had emigrated to the United States from Germany at age fourteen, and later owned a cigar factory at 80 Clinton Street in downtown Manhattan. He married Eva Friedlander in 1897. Her parents, after emigrating from Hamburg, Germany, about 1800, lived in Massachusetts, then Connecticut, before moving to New York. Eva was born in Connecticut in 1867.

I had many living aunts, uncles, and cousins in my father's family and, being an only child myself, felt close to them. I always looked forward to visiting them individually and, particularly, to the assembling of the entire extended family—for Passover and other holidays—at the Bedford Avenue, Brooklyn, house of our "Aunt Tillie" Phillips.

It was she who had married my father's father, Wolf Phillips, and become stepmother to my father and his siblings after Wolf's first wife, Hannah ("Helinka"), had died. Wolf is believed to have worked as a tailor, and he obviously earned enough to send for the children after he reached America. He died in 1924, two years before I was born.

Hannah's family had owned the Hotel Priluka in Bialystok. The Russian pogroms there in the late nineteenth and early twentieth centuries preceded by nearly half a century the Nazi Holocaust that wiped out virtually the entire once-sizable Jewish population of Bialystok. One of my father's sisters, the oldest of the children, had opted to stay behind when the others came to America. I never learned her fate.

CHAPTER **3**

Innocence Lost

IN THE 1930S, as I was growing up, Hitler came to power in Germany, and before he moved against the Rhineland, then Austria, then Czechoslovakia, then all of Europe, he moved against the Jews in Germany. My family followed closely the persecution of the Jews there and wondered where it would spread. My family was Jewish—not particularly religious, but certainly identifying ourselves closely with the Jewish community and its vulnerability.

One minor boyhood incident linked to the Nazis' faraway depredations arose, curiously enough, in connection with my having been given piano lessons. At a family gathering at our house, my parents proudly pushed me to play something I had learned, as parents are inclined to do. I took out the sheet music and began to play one of the pieces I had been taught, a seventeenth-century Austrian folk song with German lyrics, "Ach Du Lieber Augustin." One of my aunts interrupted and said sharply, "Can't we play something else!" I got the point.

My Uncle Joe, the bachelor school principal, traveled on vacation to Sweden and other parts of Europe outside the Nazi orbit many summers in the 1930s. I treasured the exotic stamps on the postcards he sent us from faraway places. The matching of stamps in a stamp album with countries and locations provided an early introduction to world geography.

My introduction to other worlds—the worlds of "the birds and the bees"—began, haltingly, in those years. My parents bought me a book, *Growing Up*, written to teach children tastefully the facts of life. My mother read it with me. It had a full-page illustration that consisted of a field of black with a pin-prick-size dot of white in the center. The text explained that the egg that was fertilized to begin the reader's life was a thousand times smaller than that dot.

A few months later, I was sitting in the back of a Latin class taught by Helen Nugent at Abraham Lincoln Junior High School, from which I was to graduate a year later, on June 21, 1938. I was sitting near my friends Janice Elliott and Ruth Greenberg and my best pal, William Treibel. He was older and considerably taller and heavier than I. Some pupils referred to us as Mutt and Jeff, after two similarly proportioned comic-page characters of the time. But it was two other comics characters of the era, Maggie and Jiggs, who were implanted in my memory in the back of the classroom that day. Someone passed around among the boys a small pornographic comic book featuring Maggie accommodating Jiggs.

In the car on the way home from school that afternoon, with my mother driving, I innocently said: "Mom, I learned the word for what men and women do when they make babies. It's 'f*ck.'" My mother was so shocked she almost lost control of the car, swerving and nearly running into a lamppost. "I *never, ever* want to hear you use that word again!" she sputtered.

The awakening of arousal came a few years later. I was fourteen. My parents, returning from a summer cottage we had rented in Roscoe, New York, brought with them a farm girl they had hired as a live-in housekeeper. The girl was nineteen and new to the big city. That might have been one of the few things to which she was new. When my parents were not at home, she and I would wrestle on the bed, she in a paper-thin cotton summer dress that left little to the imagination. I began to get the idea—but it was only a beginning, not a completion. One day I returned and found my playmate was no longer in our employ and had moved out of the house. I never knew whether this was a result of my parents becoming suspicious, though I surmised that was probably the case.

I would like to think that my early interest in another passion, newspapers, was genetic, though I recognize that as improbable. I was proud that my father, before his military service, had worked for the *Sun,* one of New York's leading and more serious evening newspapers. He worked in the business office in the *Sun* building, then at 150 Nassau Street, probably as a clerk. I still prize a letter of reference on the *Sun*'s letterhead from the legendary Keats Speed, managing editor, that reads, "To Whom It May Concern: The bearer, Abe Phillips, was employed for many years in the business office of the *Sun.* I know him to be a thoroughly conscientious and intelligent young man." The letter is dated March 8, 1918. My father was leaving to join the army in wartime.

As the war clouds again swept over Europe twenty years later and I moved through Leo Dressler's Latin class and others at Franklin K. Lane High School, I began to keep a daily diary of the news. And I filed nearly every week's issue of *Life* magazine, with its dramatic pictorial coverage of the war. *Life*'s December 23, 1940, issue led with a photo whose caption read: "Union Jack still flies through the red glare of bombed Coventry. It hangs on Martin's Bank of High Street which was hit through the roof." Elsewhere in that issue was a story headline: "*Life* Looks Back on a Year of Disaster." Photographs illustrating that year-end report included one of a long line of British troops wading out from Dunkirk, with a caption that began, "The evacuation of Dunkirk saved the disaster from becoming black rout and annihilation, for it showed that at least for one moment in one place the British Army could do one thing that it wanted to do." A later photo showed ranks of German troops marching up Paris's Champs Elysées toward the Arc de Triomphe. The April 13, 1942, edition showed Generals MacArthur and Sutherland, on Corregidor, above this headline: "General MacArthur and His Men Make a Thermopylae of Bataan."

The propaganda I picked up at the German Information Office in lower Manhattan, before America's entry into the war closed it down, included a bound White Paper detailing some of what the Germans cited as their justification for invading Poland in 1939. The title was "Atrocities Committed Against the German

Minority in Poland." A slicker piece of propaganda they were happy to hand out to me and others was a rotogravure magazine titled *Signal*, an English-language translation of the June 1, 1940, *Berliner Illustrirte Zeitung*. Its front cover showed a salvo of bombs in midair, captioned, "Heading for the goal. Bombs drop on a French aerodrome."

A souvenir magazine picked up earlier from the French consulate in New York was by far the prettiest, and the saddest. It was dated January 1940, had a red, white, and blue French tricolor cover, with a protective transparent cover over that, and was called *Memorial de la Guerre*. Its photographs depicted French soldiers and their generals, relaxed and confident amid their artillery and tanks and the bunkers of the Maginot Line, once regarded as an impregnable defense.

About that time, I found a pen pal of approximately my own age in Cardiff, Wales. We corresponded and exchanged snapshots for several years. Eventually, with Britain at war, he enlisted in the Royal Air Force. Then came a day when his mother responded to one of my letters to him. He had been killed.

When war finally came to the United States, I was on the second floor of our house on Harrow Street. I heard the radio news bulletin that the Japanese were bombing Pearl Harbor. I raced down the staircase, my mother later recalled, a skinny kid excitedly shouting, "This means war."

I was home for the weekend that Sunday, December 7, 1941. When I had graduated from high school the previous June, I was still several weeks shy of my fifteenth birthday. My parents decided I was too young for college, and they enrolled me in the Horace Mann School for Boys, as it was then called, in Riverdale, a northern section of the Bronx, for a year of "postgraduate" study, in effect repeating my senior year. I lived in the dormitory near the main campus and commuted home on weekends via a long subway ride. The subway had been extended eastward to Forest Hills by then, and the stop closest to the school was the northernmost stop of the subway system.

I reflected years later on the possible consequences of graduating from high school at fourteen, always the youngest among my classmates, always the mascot and "midget." Perhaps this forced me to develop resilience and tenacity, two qualities often attributed to me in later years and that contributed to my future advancement in the ranks.

At Horace Mann I ran the 220-yard low hurdles on the varsity track team, worked on the school newspaper, and had as a roommate Selim Zilkha, who helped open my eyes to the broader world. He was the youngest son of a wealthy Iraqi-Jewish banking family that had emigrated to New York by way of Egypt. He and his family graciously invited me to lunch at their opulent Central Park West apartment, and it was then that I learned apples were to be peeled and sliced in polite society, not eaten off the core at the dinner table as I had done all my life.

I did not do well enough at Horace Mann on the College Entrance Examination Board tests to assure myself a place at the college of my choice. I applied to about fifteen colleges, including Columbia, Cornell, Hamilton, Middlebury, Williams, and Amherst, but was accepted at only one, tiny Oberlin College in Oberlin, Ohio. So it was to Oberlin that I prepared to go after I graduated from Horace Mann in June 1942.

But on the evening of July 22, 1942, soon after my mother and I had finished dinner at a Catskills resort where we were vacationing and were watching a movie with other guests in the social hall, my mother was suddenly called away to the manager's office. She was told that my Uncle Eli was on the phone from New York. My father had died.

My mother insisted on driving back to the city immediately, but the resort manager persuaded her that she was in no condition to do so and he had a staff member drive our car, with the two of us huddled in the backseat, through the night until we reached home. It was a long night. My father was forty-seven. After working at his office in Manhattan that day, he went for a medical checkup, was pronounced fit, then had a heart attack on the street afterward. He was taken to Kew Gardens Hospital, near where we lived, and died there. The years of my innocence died with him.

CHAPTER 4

College and Army

"YOU ARE THE MAN OF THE FAMILY NOW," my uncles said to me following my father's death, as our relatives all gathered at our Harrow Street house to mourn, console my mother and me, and then attend my father's funeral. Many sons, especially young ones, must have heard these same words through the ages upon their fathers' deaths.

We remained at Harrow Street for a time, but my mother gave up the house two years later and moved into a fifth-floor apartment at 141–72 Eighty-Fifth Road in the Briarwood section of Jamaica, Queens. I had canceled my plans to attend Oberlin College in the fall of 1942 and instead enrolled as a freshman at Queens College, part of New York City's then-tuition-free municipal college system, now known as City University. Queens College, founded only five years earlier, occupied Spanish-style, red-tile-roofed, two-story buildings formerly used by a boys' reform school. They were grouped around a grassy campus quadrangle that looked westward toward an apple orchard and beyond that, in the distance, the skyscrapers of Manhattan. The campus was a twenty-minute drive from home, and I commuted by bus each day.

I attended classes there and worked on the school's weekly newspaper, the *Crown*, for a year. It was wartime. Battles were raging in the South Pacific, North Africa, and Europe. Classmates were going off to war. I was still one of the youngest, skinniest kids on campus, and I continued to be regarded sometimes by older classmates, including the girls, almost as a mascot.

On September 23, 1943, three months after my seventeenth birthday, I enlisted in the Army Specialized Training Reserve Program. The army initially shipped me to Alfred University in the tiny town of Alfred, New York, in the southwestern corner of the state, and later to the Virginia Military Institute, in historic Lexington, Virginia, to be trained in engineering. It wasn't until the following year, November 25, 1944, that I was called to active duty, having volunteered for air crew training.

Though the winter weather at Alfred was icy, the friendships formed were warm. One friend was George "Hammerhead" Lewett. We marched and studied together weekdays, then often on Saturday nights went into the nearby railroad-junction city of Hornell to try to meet girls. Another friend was a farm girl who lived outside of Alfred. It was with her that I lost my virginity one afternoon in a hillside pasture. My principal memory is fighting gravity, trying to keep from slipping down the slope.

At the Virginia Military Institute (VMI) the next spring, at the foot of the Blue Ridge Mountains in western Virginia, Lewett and I and the others in our unit lived in the old, fortresslike, multitiered stone barracks and marched across the vast parade grounds in formation with the cadet corps battalions, they in their gray cadet uniforms, we in our army-issue khakis.

On July 24, 1944, having reached age eighteen, I received notice that I had been "transferred from the Enlisted Reserve Corps to the Air Corps Enlisted Reserve for Air Combat Crew Training." We were sent off from VMI on home leave to await the call-up to active duty. While waiting, I first worked for a month moving around rolls of copper sheet by hand at a metals company in lower Manhattan. The rolls were heavy, their edges sharp. Then George Lewett and I decided to see a bit of the country as we continued to wait. We went out to Mitchel Field, then in Garden City, Long Island, hung around the Operations center at the air base where army pilots were filing their flight plans, and soon persuaded one of them to let us hitch a ride to St. Louis aboard the B-17 Flying Fortress he was piloting. It was my first time aloft. I rode in the tail-gunner position, marveling at the beauty of the sky and the cottony cumulus clouds we flew through.

We stayed overnight in a tent in a camp that local citizens maintained for servicemen in a park in St. Louis. We then hitch-hiked by car from St. Louis to Chicago and on to Detroit, with drivers always willing to pick up men in uniform. Near Detroit, a leathery-faced old geezer gave us a lift; when we climbed in, he grinned and cackled, "You boys going into town for some tail?" He expanded on that with some shockingly colorful barnyard words I had never heard before, being a sheltered easterner. My education was being broadened: I was hearing crude new slang expressions in use among midwesterners at the low end of the social and economic ladder. From Detroit, we hitchhiked to Cha-nute Field, outside Champaign, Illinois, and hitched a ride back to New York with army fliers aboard another military plane.

On November 25, 1944, I was shipped to Fort Dix, New Jersey, to begin my active service. I had volunteered for training as a pilot, navigator, or bombardier in the aviation cadet program. After a few days, I was shipped by train with other soldiers to Kes-sler Field, outside Biloxi, Mississippi, for basic training. Three months later, we were told that we would not become aviation cadets. The Allied armies were by now sweeping across Europe toward victory, and there were more pilots on hand, in training and in the pipeline, than were likely to be needed. The army, in its infinite wisdom, weighing its needs and what it considered my aptitudes, assigned me a new military vocation: military police-man. I was transferred to Sheppard Field in north Texas, outside the city of Wichita Falls.

There I guarded American prisoners, sometimes from a watch-tower overlooking the fence surrounding the camp prison, called the stockade, and at other times out on work details at the sew-age plant and garbage facilities. The prisoners had been con-victed by courts-martial of a variety of crimes and misdemeanors. I also stood duty at the guardhouses at the camp's several gates, screening those seeking to enter or leave the camp, and I did duty patrolling the camp by jeep.

And then there came a time when my fellow MPs and I were called out to help quell race riots—both in sections of a nearby town and within the camp itself, where barriers were hastily thrown up to block off the white soldiers' barracks from those of the black troops. The South, including the Texas-Oklahoma border area where Sheppard Field was situated, was not welcoming to black people in those years, even black servicemen. Driving across the Red River bridge into Oklahoma one day, I came across a highway sign on the outskirts of a small Oklahoma town: "Nigger, Don't Let the Sun Set On You in Our Town."

I made a lasting friendship or two at Sheppard Field, notably red-haired, freckle-faced Bill Neal from Pasadena, California. He and I, after years apart, resumed our friendship when we were in our sixties. I also encountered a bullying bigot or two. "Are you one of them New York Indians?" one would ask, in in-your-face fashion, gesturing to my hooked nose.

President Franklin Roosevelt had died while I was in the service in the South. Now, in May 1945, the Germans surrendered in Europe, and in August the Japanese followed suit. A few months later, I found myself on a troop train headed for the port of embarkation at Camp Stoneman, outside Pittsburg, California, on the northern part of San Francisco Bay. We were to board a ship for Japan, to help police the occupation.

Then, in untypical army fashion, I was given the option to take an honorable discharge. An officer called me into his office and presented me with a letter dated October 4, 1945, from Lieutenant General B. K. Yount, commanding the Headquarters of the Army Air Forces Training Command at Fort Worth, Texas. Though individually addressed, it was one of hundreds of the same form letter being sent "to all men who, like yourself, voluntarily enlisted in the Army Air Forces . . . for the specific purpose of undergoing air crew training, and who, owing to circumstances beyond your control and beyond ours, have not completed training and have not been commissioned as Second Lieutenants or appointed as Flight Officers." It said he and the War Department "are keenly aware of the difficulties you have faced, the long months of waiting you have undergone, and of the successive disappointments you have unavoidably experienced." I thought our "difficulties" were nothing compared to those faced by men who had actually been fighting the war. In any case, the general said that among the choices he was authorized to offer me, and others in the same situation, was an honorable discharge.

I opted to take it. At the time I was discharged, on December 1, 1945, my separation documents show I weighed 134 pounds and was 5 feet 11½ inches tall. I was nineteen.

Back in New York, intent on returning to college, I reapplied to about fifteen colleges, hoping to take advantage of the tuition payments due me and other veterans under the GI Bill. I applied again at Columbia, Cornell, Hamilton, Middlebury, and the other colleges I had aspired to attend. I was rejected by all, no doubt partly because they were then being swamped by returning veterans. So I returned to Queens College, living at home in my mother's Jamaica apartment, and commuting by bus. But for several months before I went back to the Queens campus I spent my time in other ways.

CHAPTER 5

Newsroom Apprentice

HOME FROM THE army and awaiting my return to college, I went looking for any kind of work at a newspaper. At the *New York Herald Tribune,* then at 230 West Forty-First Street between Seventh and Eighth Avenues, I was interviewed in a reception area adjacent to the elevators by Florence Pyewell, then secretary to the city editor. She was in charge of the copyboys, and it was as a copyboy that she hired me. The salary was sixteen dollars a week.

The *Herald Tribune* fifth-floor city room was, to me, an intoxicating place, some of the reporters and editors like characters out of central casting. As I carried copy, take by take, or page by page, from reporters' typewriters to the city desk, fetched coffee and sandwiches, and replenished office supplies, I drank in the drama around me that was part of every day's news cycle.

The city editor was a lanky, giant of a man named L. L. Engelking. His first name was Lessing, but no one on the staff called him anything but Mr. Engelking. When he folded his frame into his chair at the city desk, in the center of the cavernous, open city room, he would speak softly, barely above a whisper. But when he was riled, his roar could be heard from one end of the newsroom to the other, as if his vocal chords had suddenly developed their own built-in amplifier system. Late one afternoon, while reading the story a woman reporter had turned in, he asked Miss Pyewell to summon the reporter. After scouring the newsroom, Miss Pyewell reported back that the reporter was in the ladies' room. "Well, go in there and drag her off the pot," Mr. Engelking bellowed, his voice booming across the room.

The film and food critic was Lucius Beebe. He was an elegant writer and elegant in his attire, definitely a dandy. He would come in late and sit down at his typewriter to peck out his reviews without removing his jacket or scarf or homburg, only his gloves. We copyboys and copygirls called Lucius Beebe, behind his back, Luscious Baby. We heard a story, doubtless apocryphal, about his arrival late, and showing the signs of drinking, at a dinner of the Chevaliers du Tastevin, a renowned wine connoisseurs society. He received disapproving looks, for marring one's palate with strong drink before tasting the wine just was not done. Toward the end of the meal, before dessert, he turned green and left the table hurriedly, obviously to flee to the men's room to throw up. Returning shortly, again to disapproving looks from the other diners, he announced: "Gentlemen, you will be gratified to know that the white wine came up with the fish." Or so the story went.

The *Herald Tribune* newsroom also was inhabited by Red Smith, the paper's famous sports editor, and by returning veterans such as reporter Ken Bilby, who had fought in Italy and onward, had been awarded the Silver Star, and had risen to lieutenant colonel by war's end. In an office in the southeast corner sat the managing editor, George Cornish, remote to us copyboys and girls. Equally remote were the paper's owners, Helen Reid and her sons Whitelaw "Whitie" Reid and Ogden "Brownie" Reid, whom I occasionally glimpsed strolling along the perimeter of the room en route to a meeting with the managing editor. In the late afternoons and evenings, quite a few staff members would adjourn for a drink or dinner at a favorite establishment adjacent to the building's back door on West Fortieth Street, Artists and Writers restaurant and bar, known as Jack Bleeck's, after the owner. There they would await the first papers off the press. The presses were next door in the *Trib* building basement.

It had only been a few years earlier, in 1939, that Stanley Walker, city editor of the *Herald Tribune* from 1928 to 1935, had written *City Editor*, a book I prized for its stories of New York newspapering. The one I remember best was of Charles Chapin, the legendary city editor from 1898 to 1918 of Joseph Pulitzer's old

New York Evening World. Chapin sent a reporter one day to interview an heiress who had eloped with a stevedore. The reporter found them at the dockworker's fourth-floor, walk-up flat; after climbing the stairs, he knocked on the door and, when the new groom opened it, he announced he was from the *World.* The stevedore threw him down the stairs. Picking himself up and dusting himself off, the intrepid reporter climbed the stairs and again knocked on the door—with the same result. Going downstairs to a pay phone, the reporter called Chapin and told him what had happened. "You go back up there," Chapin instructed, "and tell that son of a bitch he can't intimidate *me.*" Years afterward, in 1918, we should note, as did Stanley Walker, Chapin murdered his wife and died in 1930 in Sing Sing prison.

When I resumed classes at Queens College, I continued to work at the *Herald Tribune* every Saturday and Sunday. My duties changed: With a string and a yardstick, I would measure the inches of space given in the *Tribune* each day to world news, national news, city news, sports, culture, and other categories, and compare it to the amount of space the competing *New York Times* was allotting to the same news and feature categories. The *Times* was two blocks north on West Forty-Third Street. My duties also included tabulating the exclusives each of the two papers had in that day's paper in each news category.

At college, I was given credits for the courses studied under army auspices. I chose economics as my major. I worked as an editor on the weekly *Crown*, the campus newspaper. I also was employed by the college's public relations office, writing news releases. And I called on Charlie Bennett, suburban editor of the *New York Times*, at his Manhattan office and won an appointment as the campus correspondent, or stringer, responsible for reporting and writing Queens College news for the *Times*. I also served as the *Tribune*'s college stringer at Queens. While working weekends at the *Tribune*, I submitted and saw published in the *Trib* occasional short, light feature stories. One was about the shortage of candy canes at Christmastime, due to the sugar shortage that lingered even after the war's end. Another revealed the origin of the red-and-white-striped poles that identified barbershops.

On campus, and on weekend evenings, I palled around with Al Levin, his girlfriend Lee Hayes, Lloyd Rausch, and Judith Greenwald. Al was a well-built, good-looking doctor's son from Kew Gardens, who had recently returned from action in Germany as an infantryman. He was more sophisticated than the rest of us, charming in an earthy way, and a ladies' man. I admired him and was pleased to be in his social circle. Judy Greenwald was feisty, lived with her parents in a Flushing apartment house, and eventually became my girlfriend—and later, in 1948, my wife, in a marriage lasting less than a year.

In the summer of 1946 and on some weekday evenings that fall, we friends journeyed into Manhattan to take university extension courses at Columbia University. After classes that summer, Al Levin, on his way home, would often stop off for a drink at the Baby Grand, a piano bar on the north side of Harlem's 125th Street. In the evenings, we sometimes took dates farther north in Harlem, to Small's Paradise, a smoke-filled, tightly packed dining and dancing jazz club at 135th Street and Seventh Avenue. We may have stood out among the mostly black patrons, but it was before the days when we might have been greeted by unfriendly stares and worrisome hostility.

That fall, in an evening course at Columbia, I studied writing in a class conducted by George Britt, a former magazine writer who commuted from Nyack, New York. I remember him fondly as the first to offer me serious encouragement as an aspiring newspaperman. (That was the most honorable sobriquet I could imagine; "journalist" sounded somewhat fancy and pretentious and was not a job description in as common use as today, most practitioners preferring "reporter" or "newspaperman.") I admired Professor Britt, who was gracious and congenial and critiqued my copy professionally and, often, approvingly. Our text was a revised Houghton Mifflin edition of *Newspaper Writing and Editing* by Willard Grosvenor Bleyer, first published in 1933. We also used *Breaking Into Print: Modern Newspaper Technique for Writers* by F. Fraser Bond, a professor of journalism at Columbia. It was also published in 1933, by the McGraw-Hill Book Company. Together, they seemed to me to hold all the secret keys to the world I aspired to enter, and I consumed each chapter voraciously.

Britt would give us weekly reporting assignments. For example: "Do a news story from a store about the Christmas trade at that store—at least three hundred words. Comparison with last year or prewar, price differences, characteristics of the Christmas season." Or: "To practice being concise in a short feature story, condense a long article from a newspaper about some unique person, someone with a job or hobby off the beaten path. Sentences, anecdotes boiled down to a few lines. Boil down verbiage yet maintain a smooth flow." His instructions—to avoid generalizing, avoid editorializing or making assumptions, avoid bromides, write in simple, short declarative sentences, get accurate spelling of names and initials, get accurate addresses—are as valid today as they were then.

As my June 1947 graduation approached, I applied for admission to the Columbia University Graduate School of Journalism. I was rejected. (Many, many years later, in 1980, when I was elected a trustee of Columbia University and served there for thirteen years, and also served on Dean Joan Konner's Advisory Board at the Journalism School, I joked that that was the only way I could get into Columbia.)

When I graduated with a B.A. from Queens College in June 1947, I set about, with my modest clippings, trying to find a full-time newspaper reporting job. There were eleven daily newspapers in New York then, even without counting Harlem's *Amsterdam News* or *Women's Wear Daily*. One by one, I applied to each of them. I started with the *Herald Tribune* and the *Times*, now fully staffed with returning veterans, where I was advised to start on some smaller, out-of-town newspaper to gain experience. The story was the same as I interviewed—or sometimes failed to get interviews—at the *Sun*, the *World-Telegram*, the *Journal-American*, the *Post*, the *Daily Mirror*, the *Daily News*, the *Brooklyn Eagle*, and the *Long Island Star-Journal* in Queens.

The *New York Daily News*, like the other papers, had tight security on the floor where its editorial offices were housed—guards and a tough receptionist at a desk between the elevators and the doors to the newsroom. I was turned away here and told no one was available to see me when I showed up seeking to apply for a job. I got back on the elevator and rode it to the floor above. That turned out to house the advertising department, which apparently felt no need for security. I strolled unchallenged across the advertising floor to the fire stairs, climbed down one flight, opened the door, and found myself in the back of the newsroom. I strode purposefully to the city desk, which I had someone point out to me in the center of the floor. There I presented myself, announced that I was looking for a job, and asked for an interview. I thought my enterprise in gaining access to forbidden precincts, a skill always useful in a reporter, would impress the city desk. Instead, I was summarily shown the door.

Last on my list of the New York newspapers—as I was preparing myself, with considerable disappointment, to turn to smaller towns and cities west of the Hudson—was *The Wall Street Journal*. It was then a thin, one-hundred-thousand-circulation financial paper downtown at 44 Broad Street, a nine-story building wedged close to the stock exchange, just south of Wall Street. There my luck changed.

I was interviewed by Bill Kerby, the executive editor, and Buren McCormack, the managing editor, at the eastern end of the *Journal*'s long, narrow third-floor newsroom, on a couch beneath a huge oil portrait of Kenneth C. "Casey" Hogate, the late publisher of the *Journal* and CEO of Dow Jones & Company, its parent company. Kerby and McCormack hired me, at forty dollars a week.

For the first two months, presumably to familiarize myself with the paper, I read proofs for the front-page department. My guide and supervisor was Betty Donnelly, a former nun, good-humored and generous to me with helpful pointers. Then I was assigned to the copydesk, on a 3 P.M. to 10 P.M. shift. We copyreaders, or rim men, sat outside the rim of the traditional massive horseshoe-shaped desk, editing all copy destined for the paper except the long front-page features. In the slot of the horseshoe sat the "slot man," who distributed stories to us to edit and later checked our work before sending the stories in pneumatic tubes to the composing room one floor below, to be set into hot, lead type. The pressroom was on the floor below that.

As soon as the presses began rolling out the first edition, the one-star, at 7:30 P.M., a copyboy would bring the early copies upstairs to the copydesk. We would read the paper for errors, make corrections that had come in after the first-edition deadline, and prepare updated stories for inclusion in the two-star edition that went to press at 10:30 P.M. On some summer evenings, particularly when his family was at their Twin Lakes, Pennsylvania, vacation home and he was sleeping overnight upstairs in his ninth-floor office suite, the *Journal*'s publisher and Dow Jones CEO, Bernard "Barney" Kilgore, would drop by the copydesk at press time and, when the first copies arrived, would pull a chair up to the rim and scan the pages, before going out to dinner.

The copydesk was near the western end of the long, narrow newsroom, the end that overlooked one-car-wide New Street. Behind the desk was the wire room, alive with clattering Teletype machines bringing in news from the *Journal*'s out-of-town bureaus, the Associated Press, and United Press. To the west of us, flush against the grimy New Street windows, was the so-called ticker desk. There the Dow Jones News Service's managing editor, Eddie Costenbader, his deputy Eddie O'Keefe, and their fellow ticker editors edited and dispatched stories throughout the day to brokers and other customers of Dow Jones's telegraphic news service, nationwide.

Adjacent to the copydesk on the east was the desk at which Sam Lesch, national news editor, worked when he wasn't on his feet, circling the desk and the newsroom, which was most of the time. He had been hired away from a night editor's job at the *New York Post*. Sam was the editor who gave the reporters their assignments, made the second-by-second decisions on which stories would or would not go into the paper (except for the page-one features), and was in charge of the copydesk and the New York reporting staff. He was our immediate boss. He seemed always to have a cigarette sticking out of his mouth—not drooping out of the corner of his mouth but sticking straight out from the middle of his lips like a projectile.

He was short, tough, combative, a bantam rooster. He was very, very quick in scanning copy, making his news judgments, and marking up the copy in a preliminary way before handing it over to the copydesk. He was as good as he was fast.

Though tough, he was capable of displaying a warm and generous spirit. I liked him. He always had time to advise and assist us younger, beginning members of his crew. He took pride in his boys who had moved on to greater responsibilities: Alan Otten, for example, who the year before had been promoted from rim man to reporter in Washington, later to be bureau chief. At Christmas, gift cartons of whiskey would be delivered to the beat reporters, and Sam, as a directing editor, would get cartons sent to him, too. This was before the days when anyone would see the now-obvious ethical issues in gifts from public-relations firms and corporations the paper covered. Whiskey, hams, and travel junkets were considered at the *Journal* and at newspapers nationwide, from the top officers and editors down, as traditional perks of the profession. No gifts, however, came to the copyreaders, faceless and unknown to outsiders. But Sam would always break open his Christmas cartons and distribute the loot to his deskmen.

The paper's top officers and editors, along with their peers at other news organizations, were guests each year of the Chesapeake & Ohio Railroad on a private party train from Cleveland to the C&O-owned Homestead Hotel in the mountains of West Virginia, where they spent the weekend golfing and partying some more. It has been more than fifty years since such junkets would have been condoned.

Even the paper's brass, however, never received as much whiskey at Christmastime as reporter Tom Wise. He covered the liquor industry. One day, when Tom was out, his pals in the newsroom gingerly opened a couple of the cartons that had been delivered to his desk, replaced the liquor bottles with rolls of Teletype paper, and then carefully resealed the cartons. Tom lugged the cartons home that night, and the staff speculated for weeks on his reactions and language on finding that he had expended so much energy only to discover he had been the butt of a practical joke.

Sam was Jewish, the only other Jew of whom I was aware in the *Journal*'s New York office at the time. Alan Otten, who had left for Washington before I arrived, was Jewish also. I recall no prejudice, no discussions of religious affiliation at that time.

One night, sitting on the rim reading the early edition of the *Daily News* after the *Journal* had gone to press, I read a story on page two about the *Journal* correspondent in Berlin, Joseph E. Evans, being thrown down a flight of stairs at the Berlin city hall, then located in the Russian sector of East Berlin, by the "Vopos," the East German Volks Polizei, or People's Police, working for the Russians. The West Berliners, proxies for the Americans, British, and French, were fighting with the East Berliners, in the Soviet sector, for control of the city government. (Later they split in two, with the city divided, eventually by the Berlin Wall.) Ernie Leiser, a correspondent then for the Overseas News Agency, was being beaten up by the Vopos, and Joe, short but wiry, rushed to his aid, only to be thrown down the stairs. I was far removed from this action and did not know Joe Evans, but it was a little over a year later that fate would see us begin an enduring friendship and he would become my boss.

Every night when I would finish work on the New York copy-desk, I would ride uptown on the Third Avenue Elevated line—long since razed—on the first leg of my commute home to our apartment in Jamaica, Queens. As we rattled and rumbled north, I would gaze out the train window and into the second-floor windows of the apartments over the Third Avenue stores, imagining vignettes of New York life in the fragments one could glimpse as the train flashed by.

In winter, my old Queens College friends and I would sometimes take ski-tour buses on our days off to Bear Mountain or Old Forge, New York, or to Manchester or Stowe, in Vermont. At Bear Mountain State Park, I sometimes skied, crouched and without poles, down the approach slope and launched myself momentarily into space off a small ski jump, a miniature version of the big championship jump alongside.

In mid-1948 I was assigned to write the World-Wide column, part of the daily What's News summary that had been invented by Casey Hogate and improved by Barney Kilgore. It was unique then to the *Journal*'s front page. The job was to take the principal nonbusiness stories of the day from the wire services and our own reporters and condense them into capsule items that, in a few concise sentences, gave the essential elements of each major news development and its background and meaning. At the desk facing me sat Dick Edmondson, a newsroom veteran of clear writing, similarly condensing news into the Business & Finance column, the other half of the What's News. We worked directly opposite from Sam Lesch and the copydesk, across the east-west aisle that divided the long, narrow newsroom. At deadline, I would go down the fire stairs to the composing room below, alive with clattering Linotype machines setting the night's stories in type. There, as the galleys of type were being locked into the page forms, I would stand opposite a printer on "the stone," or countertop, reading the type of my World-Wide column upside down and telling the printer the order in which I wanted the items aligned in the column. I could direct him, but I was not allowed to touch the type or move items myself. To infringe on that union prerogative would bring a blast on the union shop steward's whistle and all work would stop, delaying the paper going to press.

One quiet Sunday evening, with the day's news apparently in and the Teletypes having grown silent, I decided to leave after the first edition, and I asked a colleague on the copydesk to cover me in the unlikely event there would be some development that needed to be included for the later edition. After I had departed, stories moved over the wires reporting that after the *Washington Post* music critic, Paul Hume, had panned a Margaret Truman vocal concert, her father, President Harry Truman, had written him a letter saying that if he ever met Hume he would give Hume a black eye, a bloody nose, and Hume "would need a supporter down below." My copydesk colleague failed to see the story as significant and did not cover it in my news-summary column. Next day, when I came to work about 3 P.M., I found the managing editor, Buren McCormack, at my desk. He was bent over, his head buried in the waist-high trash basket beside my desk, searching

for the wire service story so he could check the time stamp showing the hour at which it had been available. I survived that lapse,
but with a reprimand.

It made me think of a story then current in the office of what
William H. Grimes, the older, gnarled editor-in-chief, had said
to another miscreant. Calling him into his office one day, Mr.
Grimes told the offending reporter soothingly: "I believe every-
one is entitled to make a mistake." Then he thundered: "You've
HAD YOURS."

In mid-July 1948, I took the train to Philadelphia on my day off.
The Democratic Party was holding its national nominating convention there in the city's Convention Hall, and the accommodating staffers in the *Journal*'s Washington Bureau had agreed,
at my request, to get me into the proceedings with one of their
press passes. I sat with them in the press gallery near the ros-
trum, watching the floor fight over the party platform and the
nomination of Harry Truman. The heat in the convention center
reached 104 degrees—still no air-conditioning in those days. It
was memorably stifling and we were all drenched in sweat, but
it was my first national political convention, my first experience
being a bystander at a historic event, and I was thrilled. My long-
standing addiction to journalism was reinforced. I was present at
and observing the real thing. On election night that November,
I wheedled my way into the noisy, jam-packed Dewey campaign
headquarters at a New York hotel, to watch the election results
come in. For all the expectant Dewey supporters crowding the
ballroom, the results brought surprise and disappointment. For
them, the real thing was not to be.

By late 1948 I had proposed to my Queens College girlfriend,
Judy Greenwald, and we were married in December of that year
at a New York hotel. We honeymooned in Florida, then took an
apartment in my mother's building that she had, perhaps too
conveniently, scoped out. I shortly decided that it would be both
wise and fun to see Europe while still young and not tied down
by the responsibilities of children. I applied for a job as a civilian
copyreader at the army newspaper *Stars and Stripes*, in Germany,
and was offered the job.

In early 1949 I told the *Journal* editors I was making that move, to experience Europe while still young. Bill Kerby, the executive editor, was nice enough to try hard to dissuade me, but my mind was made up. Henry Gemmill, a former *Washington Star* reporter who had then worked in the *Journal*'s Washington Bureau, was page one editor in New York at the time, responsible for the signature front-page features. He was very sympathetic and wished me well on the move, encouraging me to submit freelance pieces to him from Germany if I found time. That encouragement meant much to me. It also turned out to be a major influence on the course of my journalistic career.

PART TWO

REPORTER

CHAPTER **6**

Germany

IN EARLY 1949, Judy and I set sail on the French liner *De Grasse*, the fare paid by *Stars and Stripes*. We landed in Le Havre, visited Paris briefly, then took a night train to Frankfurt. As the distinctive European water towers, unlike any I had ever seen in the States, rushed by our sleeping compartment window, and I saw and sensed the narrow-gauge European rail tracks and the bombed-out ruins pass in the darkness, I felt I was entering a new mysterious world, a world of shadows and intrigue, one only recently under Nazi occupation and bitterly fought over by the mightiest armies in history.

Our train arrived at the Frankfurt railroad station, the Bahnhof, its roof half open to the sky from Allied air-raid damage that had not yet been repaired. We were driven an hour south to the tiny town of Pfungstadt, a short distance east of the autobahn. Pfungstadt had contained a printing plant, which the army had requisitioned for *Stars and Stripes*, along with other properties in the town. We were billeted in a small house of our own, furnished with heavy wooden Germanic furniture. Pfungstadt had sustained negligible war damage. Outside of town, horse-drawn "honey wagons," with large barrel-like wooden cylinders filled with human sewage, moved to and fro, fertilizing the fields. Only in the woods beyond the fields were the humps of earth and indentations in the ground that remained of old foxholes.

Our house was within walking distance of the *Stars and Stripes* offices, presided over by an army-major publisher and Ken Zumwalt, the managing editor, who later became a longtime editor of the *San Diego Union-Tribune* and one of the confidantes of Helen Copley, its owner. I worked 3 P.M. to 10 P.M., standard hours for a morning newspaper copydesk crew. After work, we all would assemble, with spouses, for food and drink at a *Stars and Stripes* two-story social center building called the Chateau Meaux, a name whose origins eluded me. There we would drink into the wee hours, a company of expatriate newspaper people reminiscing and telling life's tales. The Chateau Meaux was the Pfungstadt equivalent of the *Tribune*'s Fortieth Street watering hole, Jack Bleeck's Artists and Writers.

We were an isolated, insulated community. We did not socialize with our small town's local German population. Among the copydesk coworkers who found their way to the second floor of the Chateau Meaux nightly was Vince Halloran, the slot man. He was prematurely white-haired and wore large, thick spectacles. One night, after many drinks, he stumbled down the stairs, crashing into the floor-to-ceiling mirror at the midway landing. His glasses shattered, the glass embedding itself in circles around the rims of his eyes. Miraculously, the eyes themselves were not damaged.

Others who gravitated to the Chateau Meaux each night included Howard and Shirley Katzander, both of whom worked on the copydesk rim. They were sophisticated, a tad superior to the others, having lived in Paris and worked as copy editors on the *Paris Herald Tribune*. Once, when Howard was away on assignment, another man tried his luck with a pass at Shirley. "What do you do for sex when Howard is away?" he asked. Shirley responded, "I sit on it." Another colleague to be found at the Chateau Meaux every night was J. Alvin "Joe" Kugelmass, bright and burly, warm and cheerful in his friendship, who claimed mysteriously on many occasions that he had lived under a totalitarian regime even more rigorous than Hitler's. We were curious and speculated for a long time, since he always refused to elaborate and would change the subject. Eventually we learned from a mutual friend that he had been in prison.

Nan Robertson, the only other young woman besides Shirley Katzander on the rim, later spent more than three decades reporting for the *New York Times*, winning a 1983 Pulitzer Prize for a *New York Times Magazine* feature on her own horrific experience, at age fifty-five, with toxic shock syndrome. A 1992 book of hers, *The Girls in the Balcony*, chronicled the fight for workplace parity by female employees of the *Times*; the title referred to the place where the National Press Club relegated women. In an earlier book, *Getting Better*, in 1988, she wrote candidly of her battle with alcoholism. I thought back to our nights at the Chateau Meaux as I read these words in her book: "I began drinking seriously when I was twenty-two, just out of college and beginning my career as a newspaperwoman. My generation of newspaper people consisted of two-fisted drinkers. In the circles I moved in, drinking was not just socially acceptable, it was an emblem of maturity."

On many mornings, I would leave early for Frankfurt and spend the hours before the start of my 3 P.M. shift reporting feature stories that I would submit to Henry Gemmill, *The Wall Street Journal*'s page one editor in New York, as a freelance. Frankfurt was gray and threadbare, a city under American military occupation. Large parts of this ancient trading metropolis, such as the Old City, contained barren, rubble-filled blocks where houses and stores had stood. On many streets bombed-out buildings were half standing, slabs of concrete dangling precariously, walls sheared off and the ruined interior floors open to the air. In contrast, the sprawling I.G. Farben building, once headquarters of a German industrial empire, had been spared and now was the humming headquarters of American High Commissioner John J. McCloy and his military government that now ruled the American occupation zone of Germany.

On May 12, 1949, my first front-page "leader" feature appeared in the *Journal*, and on May 16 the second. The first, with the flashline "Reluctant Hans" above the headline, began: "A buyers' market has appeared in about the last place you'd expect—the war-shattered, scarcity-ridden slice of Europe that's now perhaps on its way to becoming the West German Republic." The reasons for this sudden consumer resistance, according to a military government price analyst and German businessmen: "The tighter money supply and credit situation [following the previous year's currency reform that wiped out 90 percent of West German savings], rising unemployment, improved supply of some consumer goods, partially satisfied demand, and public reaction against poor-quality standardized wares." Supporting the story's conclusions were interview quotes from the general manager of the city's largest department store, the Kaufhof; a clothing store salesman; the sales manager of a large Wiesbaden clothing factory; a businessman who had just bought a leather briefcase at a marked-down price; the sales manager of a Lubeck company making kitchen utensils; a U.S. official whose job was to monitor the black market for cigarettes, butter, and other once-scarce goods; a British official who helped supervise the shoe and other leather products industry; and others.

Other front-page leader stories of mine were published in June—one on Allied plans to lift travel restrictions and lure tourists (and dollars) to Germany, another on how Berlin was struggling, with minor success, to revive immediately after the May 12 lifting of the eleven-month Russian blockade of the city. I had taken several days off and had flown into Berlin's Templehof Airport aboard an American C-47 military transport plane filled with coal. It was one of the C-47s taking off from the Rhein-Main air base outside Frankfurt every thirty seconds in a continuing airlift bringing seven thousand to eight thousand tons of supplies each day into the former German capital.

Berlin was bleak, battered, and bedraggled, ruins and rubble everywhere. I visited the seat of Hitler's power, his Reich Chancellery, a neglected tangle of shattered, fallen marble columns and floors covered with puddles of rain water. Outside was the entrance to the bunker where Hitler had died and the blackened earth where his body had been burned. Everywhere, the desolation seemed like the surface of the moon.

Working the 3 P.M. to 10 P.M. shift at the *Stars and Stripes*, traveling most mornings to do reporting for *Journal* stories, and then using what free time I had at home in Pfungstadt to compose and type up my stories—all this left little time for domestic life. I was still too immature, unthinking, and just plain dumb to reflect on what this neglect might do to a new bride, left alone in a countryside town in a foreign country. It had the predictable effect. Soon Judy found a confidante in an army photographer attached to *Stars and Stripes*, and then they vanished for a weekend in Copenhagen. On their return, he was reassigned to another, distant unit, and I put Judy on a plane back to New York. Later, by mutual agreement, since grounds for divorce were few and difficult to prove in New York in those years, and I was an ocean away, she filed court papers applying for an annulment, on grounds of fraud. The agreed-upon alleged fraud was that I had promised children and then refused to have any. On February 27, 1950, her application, uncontested by me, was granted in the Referee's Part of the Supreme Court of the State of New York, at the General Court House, Jamaica, New York.

Back in Pfungstadt, shaken up but surviving, and uncomfortable as the object of pity by my colleagues, I immersed myself even further in my work. My next *Journal* page-one leader, in July, was about smuggling. "Large-scale smuggling of industrial goods is draining a lot of West Germany's production out the back door to the Communist nations of Eastern Europe," it began. Also in July, I took a week of vacation time from *Stars and Stripes* to travel to the French Riviera to report a story from there for the *Journal*. The front-page feature, which didn't run until August 31, began:

> NICE—The whir of roulette wheels and the pop of champagne corks are playing a medley of booming business along the French Riviera this summer. But the tune is not without its discordant notes.
>
> "I never thought I would see a year like 1927 or 1928 again," declares Louis Detraz, manager of Monte Carlo's swank Hotel de Paris. "But this is better."
>
> In smart Cannes, a spokesman for the seafront Carlton Hotel laments that he has only 400 rooms. "If we had 2,000 we could fill every one, and people would still be clamoring for accommodations."

The story reported that hotel owners and transportation company officials were estimating there were 50 percent more tourists than the previous summer, but that the average person was spending less, along the length of the Riviera—"perhaps the most glamorous barometer of luxury spending in the world." The story also mentioned the introduction of *les craps* at the famed Monte Carlo Casino to help attract more American tourists.

In between reporting, I went to an afternoon tea dance at a seaside restaurant in Nice. I spent most of the time dancing and talking with a sweet and attractive young lady, confident a beautiful friendship was ripening. When we stepped outside for fresh air and continued the conversation overlooking the sea, she said in a low voice, "I am a business girl, you know." I had never heard that expression before, but I figured out she wasn't talking about a career as a restaurateur or fashion designer. I tipped her generously for her time and departed, sadder but wiser, having lost yet another layer of naïveté.

On my way out of Nice a few days later, aboard a bus to Genoa across the Italian border, I struck up a conversation with a fellow passenger, Jeanne Sakol, a vacationing New York publicist who also was traveling alone. We enjoyed each other's company on the journey and ended up dining and spending the night together at a Genoa hotel. Next morning, she continued on into Italy and I traveled north back to Germany, after exchanging addresses so we could write. I said I would look her up when I returned to New York, perhaps on home leave the following year.

This turned out to be a more fateful encounter than I ever could have imagined at the time. I had no way of knowing that it would be through a woman friend of Jeanne's that I would meet Barbara Anne Thomas, who would become my second wife, mother of our children, and my lifetime love and companion.

Stars and Stripes moved its offices north about this time to a printing plant in Darmstadt, a medium-sized city about halfway between Pfungstadt and Frankfurt. I made the move, but a few weeks later I made a larger move—away from the *Stars and Stripes* and onto a full-time staff position with *The Wall Street Journal* as its Germany correspondent.

I had demonstrated the ability to write the front-page news stories and features the New York editors wanted. Because I was prolific, they probably figured they were paying me as much or more as a freelance than a salaried staffer would earn. And Joseph Evans, who had been the paper's Berlin correspondent, had left some time earlier to take up the foreign editor post in New York, leaving the *Journal* without a staff correspondent in Germany.

Joe had taken home with him a new wife, the former Marie Petrachkova, whom he had met and courted while she was a Czech diplomatic officer, in Czech Army uniform, working in the Soviet sector of East Berlin. They fell in love, she defected to West Berlin—and twice Communist plainclothes police, in their signature black leather coats, had broken into her West Berlin apartment to try to kidnap her back to the East, something that was common in Berlin in those years. Fortunately, she was out both times they showed up. Joe brought her to live with him, began carrying a gun to protect her, married her, and brought her to safety in the United States as soon as he could.

By late August I was living in the Park Hotel in Frankfurt, near the Bahnhof. That was where almost all American correspondents lived and worked. I would see lounging around the bar Wes Gallagher, Associated Press bureau chief, later to become general manager and CEO of the AP, and Drew Middleton, the *New York Times*'s Germany Bureau chief. I was young and junior, and in my eyes they inhabited a rarefied world of seasoned foreign correspondents to which I could only aspire.

I had covered, as a freelance, the run-up to West Germany's first postwar democratic election August 14, 1949, in which Konrad Adenauer's Christian Democratic Union, advocating free enterprise, edged out the socialist Social Democrats. Adenauer formed the first postwar government as chancellor. I did not realize at the time that some of the Germans I was seeking out and interviewing would rise to prominent positions of leadership in the new Germany that was emerging from the ashes.

In a fourth-floor walk-up office on Frankfurt's Taunus Alle, also near the Bahnhof, I had been talking to Hermann Abs, an Adenauer financial adviser who in later years became president of Deutsche Bank. In Dusseldorf, in the Ruhr, another source was Hans Gunther Sohl, then director of Vereinigte Stahlwerke (United Steel Works), whose nearby August Thyssen mill I toured as it was dismantled and stripped to the ground, its equipment going to Germany's victim nations as war reparations. Herr Sohl years later served many years as the influential head of the Federation of German Industries.

In Dusseldorf, there was a stark contrast between the flattened, bombed-out desolation surrounding the city's scarred but still-standing cathedral and the luxuries of the Breidenbacher Hof hotel where Herr Sohl invited me to join a private dinner party. Each guest was offered a whole fish, including the head, which a waiter brought out on a platter to show the diner before serving it. I always thought one fish head looked like every other—and still do. But one woman, with furs that were incongruous at that time, sent several fish back until the waiter brought her one whose facial expression suited her. At the same dinner, I saw for the first time champagne served with a whole peach in each glass. Holes had been punched into the peaches so that the bubbly wine, entering the peach, would make it spin slowly in the glass. Little did I realize that this might be a symbolic precursor of West Germany's impending rapid recovery, its future "economic miracle."

By fall, the new government had established itself at Bonn, a previously sleepy university town on the Rhine River. I moved from Frankfurt and worked out of a room in a small hotel on Bonn's Beethoven Platz. I was able to get appointments to interview Ludwig Erhard, the free-market economics minister credited since as the chief architect of West Germany's "economic miracle." The interview was conducted through his interpreter. I also interviewed, with his own interpreter, the saturnine-faced Chancellor Adenauer, seated behind his large wooden desk in his spacious office at the Schaumburg Palace, the equivalent of Washington's White House, on the edge of the new capital city. The new Bundestag, or Parliament, Building was nearby. Adenauer—whom Germans called "Der Alte," the Old One—and Erhard did not tell me anything that made striking news for the *Journal*, but

I was glad to get a chance to size up these men face-to-face and to hear how they expressed themselves on the challenges ahead.

Elsewhere in Europe, the Truman Doctrine was in full swing in Greece and Turkey, as American military advisers poured in to try to bolster these two countries against the Soviet Union's efforts to expand its influence and control on its southern flank. Greece was emerging from a civil war against Communist guerrillas. In December, Buren McCormack, the *Journal*'s managing editor, ordered me to Greece and Turkey to report on these cold war fronts.

CHAPTER 7

Greece and Turkey

ARRIVING IN ATHENS, I checked into the stately but tired-looking Hotel Grande Bretagne, on Syntagma Square across from the Parliament Building. There were few guests in the lobby. Dinner was unavailable until late in the evening, the customary Mediterranean dining hour of the time. The large formal dining room was almost empty. It was winter, Greece had been worn down by German occupation and then civil war, and it clearly was not a time for tourists.

I called on Greek government officials and businessmen and the American ambassador and other embassy diplomats and military officers, toured the Acropolis and Agora, climbed the hills north of the city in the chill December air, and then a few days later took off in a military transport plane to the northeast city of Salonika. We landed on long sheets of corrugated metal, the improvised runways used so often in the wartime South Pacific when airfields had been damaged. A driver with a jeep met me and we took off inland. Fifty miles west, on a road still patrolled by armored cars, we stopped at the village of Georgianoi to talk to the mayor, a grizzled farmer named Elias Piperides, about the Marshall Plan aid helping the village get back on its feet. "Every time we distribute seeds or tools, the farmers say, 'This is from Uncle Truman,'" noted a local agricultural service director.

We continued after dark on a winding mountain road to the Greek army base at Kozani, a sizable city in north central Greece. Several times on the way, as we rounded bends in the road, we would suddenly be halted at checkpoints, our faces bathed in the light of heavy-duty flashlights emerging from the blackness. Greek soldiers kept rifles leveled on us as they approached, then scrutinized us carefully before examining our identity papers and travel documents. When we arrived at Kozani, there was mud everywhere. I was shown a barbed-wire enclosure in which a few hundred captured Communist guerrillas were herded together in the mud, and then I was given dinner in a crowded, damp mess hall. A day later, when I told the Greek officers and their American advisers that I planned to drive the jeep south to Athens, they handed me a revolver. "There still are hungry, desperate armed guerrillas cut off up on Mount Olympus," they said, "and they have to cross the main highway as they try to escape north to Yugoslavia." I thanked them, handed back the revolver, and said I would take their suggestion that I wait for the next military flight bringing mail from Athens to Kozani and taking Kozani's mail back to Athens.

My first front-page feature from Athens carried the headline:

Grecian Revival
It's Retarded by a
Political Crisis and
Economic Confusion

Communists Are Licked But
Not Hunger, Labor Strife
Or Inefficiency

A Shaky Coalition Collapses

The lead sentence read: "Greece has jumped out of the fire into the frying pan."

After meeting with Lieutenant General James F. Van Fleet, head of the American military mission in Athens, I flew on to Ankara and wrote a story about how U.S. military aid was being employed in both Greece and Turkey, under the Truman Doctrine, to counter the perceived Soviet pressure from the north. If Athens, seat of one of the world's earliest great civilizations, looked drab and weary after years of war, Ankara looked equally drab for another reason: this capital city deep inside the country on the Anatolian Plateau, unlike Istanbul, was just beginning to emerge from its primitive past.

There were a couple of broad boulevards, with very few vehicles, but the old part of the city, with its narrow alleys and mud-brick-walled huts, and even other newer neighborhoods, looked a long way from modernity. Large photos of Kemal Ataturk, the father of modern secular Turkey, emerging from the country's rigid Islamic past, adorned every office, store, and restaurant wall. Still, when I checked into my hotel, the registration form had a space to enter religion, and when I wrote "Jewish" I was shown to a cramped windowless room beneath the stairs. Afterward, in the hotel's combination dining room and nightclub, I ate dinner while Turkish men danced with other men. There were no women in evidence, veiled or unveiled.

After reporting three other stories on Marshall Plan and World Bank efforts to modernize the Turkish economy and Turkish agriculture, I flew out on an American military transport plane. I had always had a taste for the Turkish candy halvah, with its sesame, sugar, and mild oiliness. Before leaving Ankara I had bought a chunk the size of a slab of block ice. It was wrapped in wax paper. I spent most of the flight out over the desolate Anatolian Plateau eating chunks of halvah on the metal floor of the C-47, trying to keep the oily wrapping paper from making too much of a mess on government property—and on my hands.

Back in Germany, I hurriedly returned to Berlin. After talking with Major General Maxwell D. Taylor, the U.S. commander in Berlin, and other Allied officials and ordinary German citizens and businessmen, I filed a story on the attempts to shore

up the isolated city with millions in Marshall Plan investment—
even as fur-hatted Russian sentries were slowing truck traffic to a
trickle at the single highway checkpoint on the east-west border
at Helmstedt, in a Soviet effort to raise fears of a new blockade
and undermine business confidence in the city's future. I did
another story from East Berlin on how the Russians and their East
German puppets were trying to build a Communist state in East
Germany noiselessly, having seized 50 percent of industry there
from alleged "war criminals" and "saboteurs" while blandly denying any plans for socialization.

Though I would soon be sending stories to New York by transatlantic cable, up to this point I had been dispatching almost all
of them by airmail. While in Berlin, I received a cable from Buren
McCormack saying a couple of my Greek and Turkish stories had
been misplaced and lost in the New York office. He asked if I had
kept carbon copies and, if so, would I send them immediately. I
replied that the carbons were in my "office" room back in Bonn.
I wondered if the New York editors had any sense of the distances
involved when they ordered me to return and get the copies. It
was like getting on a train from Chicago to New York just to get
copies of a misplaced story, then turning around and going all
the way back to Chicago.

On the morning of December 31, 1949, on the spur of the
moment, two buddies and I decided we didn't want to spend
New Year's Eve in the gloom of occupied Germany. The buddies
were Denny Fodor of United Press and Michel "Mike" James,
son of Edwin L. James, then the *New York Times*'s managing editor. We set out by car for Luxembourg, where Perle Mesta, the
legendary Washington hostess of that era, was the American
ambassador. We thought that if we showed up on her doorstep,
she might invite us to join her party if she was hosting one. Mrs.
Mesta received us graciously and invited us in for afternoon tea
and talk. But she had plans to attend a New Year's Eve ball being
given by the Grand Duchess of Luxembourg and did not have
the power to include us. So on we drove to Brussels, where we
ushered in the new year at that city's bars and night clubs. Next

day, New Year's Day, the three of us, tired and hungover, made the long drive back to Germany.

When I returned to Bonn, orders were waiting from McCormack to get over to London on temporary assignment to help the *Journal*'s three-man London Bureau cover the national election campaign getting under way there. Prime Minister Clement Attlee and his socialist Labor Party were battling to stay in office in the face of efforts by Winston Churchill and his Conservative Party to return to power. The British electorate had installed the Laborites and turned Churchill out of office at war's end.

Chapter 8

England

Arriving in London for the first time in early January 1950, I joined *The Wall Street Journal*'s three-man London Bureau—Englishman George Ormsby, the elderly, kindly, capable bureau chief who had served through the war and early postwar years, and reporters John Leonard, an American, and Frank Linge, another Englishman.

My first London interview was with Sir Eric Vansittart Bowater, chairman of the Bowater Paper Corp., Ltd. He was impressive—lean, ramrod-straight, starched in a high-collared shirt and tight-fitting Savile Row suit, the very image of the English aristocrat he was, right down to his spats, even then an anachronism from an earlier age. He predicted that if Labor won the coming election, the unions would unleash a flood of pent-up pay demands that they had been holding back, so as not to antagonize the public in advance of the voting. "Ugly birds hatched at the time of devaluation are now coming home to roost," he said. "And they are not fledglings anymore."

At the opposite end of the social and economic scale were the coal miners with whom I talked in Rainsworth, in north central England. The men and women I interviewed in this mining town liked the improvement they had seen in their lives since the Labor government nationalized the British coal industry three years earlier. I went down the mine shaft with the workers at the Rufford Colliery. At the top of the pit, the air was raw, bone-chilling. Down below, it was sweltering. "A miner would be crazy to vote Tory," said miner George Sedley. "Things would be just like before the war, when we used to walk down the lane at eight or nine every night and have to show up at six in the morning. We got no overtime pay, either, and if we didn't like it we were told there were three or four idle men at the top of the pit waiting for our jobs."

My story led with another miner declaring, "They say Labor's got the country in a crisis. If this is a bloody crisis, I say let's have some more of them. I'm better off than ever before. All my life I've saved, and even built my own home, but I'm not going to save any more. Why should I? They pay the doctor bills and even buy my coffin for me."

There were enough voters like him to give Labor a narrow victory when they went to the polls at the end of February. With most returns in, we reported Labor had won 314 seats in Parliament to the Conservatives' 295. Late the following year, on October 25, 1951, I would cover the voting returns of another British election. That time the Conservatives would emerge victorious and Winston Churchill would be returned to power as prime minister.

But tragically, as the 1950 election campaign wound to a close, George Ormsby, the *Journal*'s London Bureau chief, died suddenly of a heart attack. I was appointed to succeed him. John Leonard, thinking the job should have been his, quit. Frank Linge stayed on, and a young bachelor New York reporter, Albert E. "Jeff" Jeffcoat, was sent over to replace Leonard.

Why should I, a twenty-three-year-old kid, have been chosen as London Bureau chief over more experienced candidates? One theory might be that I was on the spot and by now familiar with the British political and economic scene and, if the New York editors weren't going to appoint John Leonard, choosing me was cheaper than shipping over a senior stateside reporter with family. But I prefer to think the powers that be in New York had developed a certain confidence in me because I had demonstrated over the past year a grasp of the kind of reporting and writing that Barney Kilgore had been championing. The reporting and writing changes he introduced were part of the innovations he had created over the previous ten years as he revolutionized the *Journal* and laid the foundations for transforming it from a sleepy, thirty-two-thousand-circulation financial sheet, in 1941, into the modern powerhouse it became.

Barney's pioneering concepts were threefold: (1) news was not just what happened yesterday, but included trends that developed over time; (2) business news was national, not local, for the economic, political, labor, tax, and other issues that affected the businessman in Portland, Maine, were of equal significance and interest to the businessman in Portland, Oregon; and (3) business news did not have to be dull: it often contained drama and affected everyone's lives, and it should be written in a lively, jargon-free fashion.

These ideas do not appear particularly revolutionary today. So many newspapers have emulated and adopted them in the years since that they seem obvious and commonplace. But at the mid-twentieth-century mark, they were very new indeed. Editors Bill Kerby, Buren McCormack, Henry Gemmill, and Bob Bottorff were Kilgore's trusted lieutenants who understood his purpose and his genius, and they were working hard to implement his plans and aspirations for the *Journal*.

His third basic principle—that business news didn't have to be dull, but should be told in lively style, highlighting its relevance to the reader—was often conveyed by Barney saying, "Remember, there are more savings-account depositors than bankers, there are more hamburger eaters than meatpacking-plant operators." He invented the two leaders, or trend stories, that long were the showcase pieces to be found in the left and right columns of the *Journal's* front page. They were longer than most news stories, running one to two columns in length; they were distinctive from the spot news stories to be found on other newspapers' front pages. Writing these page-one stories in lively fashion included, in Barney Kilgore's formulation, the use of telling quotes and illustrative anecdotes to support and document a story's theme and hold the reader's interest, and always the avoidance of generalities in favor of specific facts and specific color to tell the story and convey the mood and atmosphere.

I believe what the *Journal*'s editors found promising in my performance of the previous year was my demonstrated ability to identify stories of interest and significance to *Journal* readers—call it news judgment—and then do the reporting and writing that was consistent with the new Kilgore standards. The reporting was always there; rarely did I get queries for more information, questions that often went back to reporters from editors requesting that gaps or inconsistencies be resolved. With the writing, however, the New York page-one desk editors sometimes reorganized or rewrote my copy and put on a flashier lead—as they had to do with the overwhelming majority of stories submitted as leaders, for that was the function of the four or five editors manning that desk. I tried to learn by analyzing what they had changed and why, how it had improved the flow of the story. Gradually, my stories received less editing. I was learning.

Perhaps the *Journal* editors who promoted me detected something in addition to diligence in doing thorough reporting and in being a quick learner. Perhaps they also detected, with approval, another trait: tenacity. Over the years, many professional colleagues and family members, when appraising me, have seen tenacity as a core and defining characteristic.

England in early 1950 was still beset by shortages, as it slowly recovered from the ravages of war and the toll that the war had taken on the nation's economic resources. I had a ration book. There still was rationing of eggs, butter, meat, and other commodities. There was a coal shortage and the winter was cold. The word Sir Stafford Cripps, chancellor of the Exchequer, and the rest of Britain used to officially describe this shortages regime was *austerity*. Our *Journal* office was in the Adelphi building just off the Strand, overlooking the Thames embankment, around the corner to the west of the Savoy Hotel. Al Jeffcoat, Frank Linge, and I kept our overcoats on in the office that winter. We typed our stories with our gloves on.

I was living then in a third-floor room in a rooming house just off Bayswater Road, on the north side of Hyde Park. It was run by two jolly spinster sisters. Every morning I and the other roomers would convene in the ground-floor dining room for breakfast. Sometimes the sisters served us giant sausages, which they invariably called bangers. Later I would move to 11 Pelham Place, in the more fashionable Kensington section of the West End. Jeffcoat had made a friend of the house's owner, Peter Newton, a young *Financial Times* columnist who later would marry a Californian and prosper in the vineyard business there. Jeff and I each rented an upstairs bedroom from Peter. The first time I met Peter at a party he gave at the house, I was greeted at the door by a formal-looking young man who turned out to be an ex-commando. I went into the library adjoining the front vestibule and sat down with him, assuming he was another guest, and we had a nice chat. It soon developed he was Peter's butler. The party was going on one floor above. My sophistication still had a ways to go.

After the February election, we covered the new Attlee government's program, British labor union members' pressure to end their unions' "voluntary wage-freeze" (and the effect that would have on prices, including the prices of British exports to the United States), and the impact of Britain's high taxes on wage demands and export efforts. Sir Stafford Cripps's April budget message also occupied us, as did efforts to cut the dollar trade deficit. We reported on world wheat and wool trade negotiations in London, too.

Besides stories for page one and for the inside pages of the paper, we composed a weekly London Cable column that ran on the *Journal*'s front page every Saturday morning. (The Saturday edition was discontinued a couple of years later for lack of advertising, then revived in the late 1990s.) This was one of the page-one columns Barney Kilgore had introduced for each day of the week. Others included Washington Wire, Labor Letter, Tax Report, Commodity Letter, and Outlook. We filled each week's London Cable with a mix of serious items—"Attlee's cabinet members quarrel, but dare not do it openly"—and lighter fare, such as American tourists being offered insurance against the notorious vagaries of British weather, and consideration of a floating hotel for the Thames.

Beginning in the spring, we were visited by tourists who would need our personal attention—some of "the brass" from the stateside *Journal*. None of the paper's top editors had been abroad before, but now William Henry Grimes, the editor, and his wife, Ida, were coming to Europe for the first time. Other visitors included Jessie Bancroft Cox and her husband, Bill. Mrs. Cox was the granddaughter of C. W. Barron, who bought Dow Jones & Company, owner of the *Journal*, in 1902, and she was the matriarch of the family that still owned the company.

William Henry Grimes had been the United Press's Washington Bureau chief in the 1920s, later the *Journal*'s Washington Bureau chief, before moving to New York as editor, in charge of both the news-gathering and the editorial page operations. The two functions were divided when Kilgore came up from Washington as managing editor, and now Grimes's authority was over the editorial page. He continued, with his eloquent editorial writing, the conservative, free-market editorial policies that the *Journal* had always embraced and was to continue to embrace with passion. Close friends and office intimates called him Bill Grimes. His oldest friends and colleagues, from his Washington days, called him Henry. To the rest of us, he was always Mr. Grimes.

I met him and his wife at the London railroad station where the boat train from Southampton brought them, and checked them into the Savoy Hotel. They invited me to accompany them to their room for a drink. When we arrived upstairs, Mrs. Grimes examined the room, then called to me from the bathroom. "What's that?" she asked, pointing to the bidet. They had never seen one before. "They put ice in that to chill the champagne," I replied. My explanation was accepted.

I arranged meetings for Mr. Grimes with high government and opposition officials, British newspaper executives, and the American ambassador. Driving one day through Grosvenor Square, where the American Embassy was located, Mrs. Grimes pointed to the statue of Franklin D. Roosevelt that the grateful British had erected in the center of the square. *"That man!"* she exclaimed, with unmistakable distaste and disdain. *Journal* executives like Grimes and even Kilgore, who had worked as reporters in Washington during the Roosevelt years, had no love for the former U.S. president. They felt he had been deceitful and lied in his dealings with them and the rest of the press.

My own family had been strong Roosevelt admirers, and through my college years I, too, had considered myself a liberal. When I came of voting age, my first vote in a presidential election, in 1948, went to Norman Thomas, the Socialist Party candidate. What transformed me into a conservative on economic and foreign-policy issues—though not on social issues—were my years in London. There I had a chance to observe a socialist government in action close-up. The Labor Party ministers, some of them former Oxford and Cambridge dons, were for the most part brilliant. But their confidence in their ability to control and manipulate and fine-tune British economic life seemed to me to founder on reality. I became convinced that a few individuals, however wise, pressing the buttons and pulling the levers to try to direct and shape an economy, were no match for the way things worked in a free market, in response to the buying, investing, and saving decisions of millions of individuals.

The socialist approach, in my opinion, even if not necessarily the "road to serfdom" that economist and author Friedrich Hayek foresaw, nevertheless was not the path to prosperity. That, I believed, was more likely to be found by allowing the wishes of millions of consumers to determine the flow of financial and industrial resources, and permitting prices to respond to supply and demand. Though the free market was imperfect, not always conforming to the theoretical when put into practice, it held the best hope for permitting a people to prosper. To paraphrase what Winston Churchill said about democracy, it was the worst system except for any other.

Mr. Grimes, originally from Ohio, was considerably older than Kilgore and the other *Journal* editors and executives, and he was crusty. He once killed a leader about women's foundation garments and the engineering principles that governed their construction, saying, "It sounds like something written behind the barn." Another time he killed a Dick Cooke theater review because he thought the play's subject, homosexuality, was not fit for the *Journal*'s readers. But he always extended warmth and encouragement to me, inviting me to dinner several times with him and Mrs. Grimes, after I returned to New York, at the suite they then lived in during the week at the Towers Hotel, in Brooklyn Heights. (Weekends they spent at their turkey farm upstate.) And there was no question that William Henry Grimes could write. His editorials were concise, forceful, and articulate in defense of all freedoms, including press freedom when the *Journal*, years later, stood up against advertising embargoes and other heavy pressure from General Motors.

When Jessie and Bill Cox visited London, they too were gracious. Mrs. Cox, an avid equestrian, was more interested in British horses than in British politics. They invited me to join them for dinner and the horse show at London's White City arena. Hackney racing was Mrs. Cox's specialty. In later years, the Coxes sometimes invited Barbara and me to join them at the National Horse Show at New York's Madison Square Garden, and occasionally to their home, the Oaks, overlooking the harbor at Cohasset, Massachusetts.

As spring turned into summer in 1950, not only was I busy covering Labor government strategy, the struggling British economy, and U.S. Secretary of State Dean Acheson's London visit in early May to discuss post–Marshall Plan U.S. aid, I also was spending more and more time reporting on European rearmament and the birth of the Schuman Plan for a supranational European Coal and Steel Community, an early predecessor of today's European Union. I returned briefly to Bonn, Berlin, and Dusseldorf, and made trips to Paris, to do news stories and editorial-page features on the budding European common market and other trends. In Paris in June, Charles Hargrove, the *Journal*'s British-born Paris Bureau chief, and I interviewed and profiled Jean Monnet, the father of the common market and the visionary driving force who was working toward a future European federation.

The British government was resisting and rejecting overtures at that time to participate in the beginnings of the infant common market. *The Economist*, writing about these rejections, put its story under a headline I never forgot: "Inverted Micawberism: Always Waiting for Something to Turn Down." How I admired that clever inverted wordplay on Dickens's *David Copperfield*, in which the Mr. Micawber character, confident of his prospects, was always waiting for something to turn up.

Hargrove, at war's end, had reclaimed from the German occupiers the *Journal* news bureau's high-ceilinged, second-floor office at 20 Place Vendome, across the square from the Ritz Hotel. A downsized replica of *La Victoire*, the *Winged Victory* sculpture in the Louvre, sat atop the large marble fireplace's mantel. The sweeping curved staircase to the second floor was marble as well. It was a more chic workplace than anything Hollywood could dream up. Charles, his French wife, Rosette, his assistant Bruno Dankner and Dankner's wife, Kay, all extended hospitality and friendship. It was through Charles's nomination that I was elected to membership in the Reform Club, one of the old, stately clubs on London's Pall Mall.

Jeffcoat, Linge, and I moved the *Journal*'s London office that year into second-floor quarters in the Associated Press's new building at 83–86 Farringdon Street, just off Ludgate Circus and around the corner from Fleet Street, with its array of British newspaper offices and newspaper pubs. One of the oldest pubs was the Cheshire Cheese, a former haunt of Samuel Johnson's, in our day a frequent tourist stop. Jeff and I would lunch there often. Occasionally we would strike up a conversation with an attractive American tourist.

A more enduring friendship was born in London in 1950. When Jeanne Sakol, the young woman I had met on the Riviera the previous year, had sailed for Europe just prior to that, she had shared a cabin with Joan Bell, an American returning to the London home she shared with her husband Maurice "Maury" Bell, who worked at an agency affiliated with the U.S. Embassy. Jeanne had written to Joan, mentioned meeting me, and suggested after I was transferred to London that the Bells look me up. The Bells invited me to a cocktail party at their house. It was there that I met Barbara Anne Thomas, a beautiful Virginian whom I would court and marry the following year.

CHAPTER 9

Barbara—and the London Good Life

DR. MAURICE "MAURY" BELL was a physicist. In years to come he would head the Brookhaven National Laboratory, home of the atomic particle accelerator, on Long Island. In 1950 he was head of the London branch of the United States Office of Naval Research. It occupied a house around the corner from Grosvenor Square, diagonally across the street from the American Embassy. Bell's team of scientists included several others who would later rise to prominence in the scientific community, among them Dr. Fred Singer and Hungarian-born George Szasz. Their job was to roam the universities and other research labs of Western and Eastern Europe, on the lookout for theoretical and practical scientific experimentation that had the potential to be applied to advancing the U.S. Navy's defensive or offensive weaponry, such as sonar. I considered it an intelligence-gathering agency.

Barbara Thomas was Dr. Bell's secretary. She had come over from the Pentagon, where she went to work after graduating from Mary Washington College, then part of the University of Virginia. Barbara and I met at Maury and Joan Bell's London cocktail party. Others at the Bell house that evening included scientists and staff from the Office of Naval Research and the American Embassy. I thought Barbara stood out because of her smarts and good looks. I obtained her phone number and called her shortly for a date.

We went to dinner, the theater, and movies frequently after that, often on double dates with my colleague Jeff Jeffcoat, or

Barbara's close American friend Pamela Smith, or her English friends Angela and Godfrey Cavendish, who bore a family name with deep roots in English history. Though Barbara had been brought up in a small town in Virginia, she was a fast learner and made friends quickly with a group more sophisticated than my friends at that time. Others in her circle included Sally Van Deurs, an American admiral's daughter who went about with a U.S. naval officer, then married Don Shannon of the United Press and later the *Washington Post*; Fiona Campbell-Walter, a British model who later married an heir of the aristocratic German von Thyssen family, whose shattered steel mill I had viewed in the Ruhr; and Jean Campbell-Harris, a young English woman who rented Barbara a room in her house in chic Grosvenor Crescent Mews in Belgravia. Later, Barbara moved to an apartment at 60 Ormonde Terrace, overlooking Primrose Hill. She shared that with an office colleague, Frances Mann, until we were married and I replaced Frances. The flat was near the London Zoo, and in the early morning, at feeding time, we would be awakened by the roar of the lions.

Barbara and I did not date each other exclusively in late 1950. She was courted by a young Englishman and another American, among others. I dated two British sisters, sequentially. At the end of the year, I sailed to New York for home leave. Barbara, far from pining away in loneliness in my absence, went off skiing in Zurs and Saint Anton, in Austria, with friends.

I opted to take ships on most of our Atlantic crossings in those prejet days, as did my colleagues, for several reasons. The trip by airplane, propeller-driven Constellations, took about eighteen hours, with refueling stops in Prestwick, Scotland, and Gander, Newfoundland. We rationalized that, counting a day or two to recuperate from the flight, we would be away from work three days, whereas the five-day crossing by sea would in effect only cost us two extra days. Besides, the company was paying for first-class passage, a more luxurious and fun experience.

As my ship slowly moved up New York harbor toward its West Side pier, I was startled to be greeted by Jeanne Sakol, on board an hour before we had even docked. She had persuaded the harbor pilot to let her go out on the pilot boat and board the ship with him far down near the harbor entrance as he came aboard to guide the big liner in. I could not help but admire her enterprise. While I was in New York we went out a few times and, on her own initiative, she demonstrated her publicist powers of persuasion again by getting me interviewed, about conditions in England, on the *Tex & Jinx Show,* a popular radio talk show in those years, conducted by Tex McCrary and his wife, actress and model Jinx Faulkenburg. I also was interviewed on the *Luncheon at Sardi's* radio show.

During the four weeks I spent in New York and Washington, I bought my first car, a used black Chevrolet convertible. I arranged for it to be shipped, at company expense, aboard the *Liberte,* the French ocean liner I was taking on the return voyage to Europe. After I boarded the ship and it sailed, I was in for another surprise. We had barely left New York harbor when I again was startled by the unexpected appearance of Jeanne. She had given up her job and booked passage on my ship without telling me, thinking to surprise me by returning to Europe with me. I was not happy. I felt I had not encouraged that. I believe her keeping her intention secret was further confirmation that I had not. The seas were rough on that midwinter trip across the Atlantic, and she spent most of the voyage seasick. On landing in France, we drove together back to London, after I explained why we had to part company. She found a job there and a place to live, and we did not continue to see each other.

Barbara and I went out with increasing frequency and seriousness through the rest of the winter and the spring. We often ate at a small Maltese restaurant in Soho where, because of the time difference, I would check in with the New York editors during dinner when necessary from a phone beneath the staircase while it was still only 2 P.M. in New York. We also frequented more chic West End dining spots such as Quaglino's, Bagatelle, and occasionally, the Café de Paris. We also drank and dined often at the Savoy Hotel Grill and the hotel's main dining room overlooking the Thames. The nearby Simpson's on the Strand appealed

to us for roast beef and Yorkshire pudding—and never failed
to remind us of Jeff Jeffcoat's story about his service aboard a
navy ship in the Pacific in World War II when his duties included
those of mess officer. He unknowingly served Yorkshire pudding as a dessert. He said no one aboard realized that it wasn't a
dessert, just that it wasn't a very good dessert. Another favorite
restaurant of ours was Rule's, a few blocks from our office and
from the Savoy. On Curzon Street we enjoyed Cunningham's for
Whitstable oysters, and across the street, at 20 Curzon Street, we
were introduced to the pleasures of high tea, with tiny cucumber
sandwiches, Scottish smoked salmon sandwiches, tiny éclairs, and
other treats rolled up to our table on carts. My mouth waters just
at the memory.

On weekends we often drove up alongside the Thames to
Maidenhead for lunch at the Bell & Dragon, a classy pub. The
pound sterling had been devalued and the dollar exchange rate
was so favorable to Americans that our salaries, in dollars, translated into a lot of pounds and went a long way. We were able to
lead more of a high life—or at least more of an expensive life—
than I ever had experienced before. It was in sharp contrast not
only to my earlier life but also to the life of austerity, of rationed
hardships, that the average Briton was living in those economically stressful postwar years.

In late April, I mentioned to Barbara that the New York office
had proposed that I do some reporting from Franco's Spain at the
beginning of the summer. "We could have a good time," I said.
"Why don't you take some vacation and come along with me?"

"*As what?*" she asked pointedly, looking me square in the eye.

I was quick to propose, we became engaged, and on June
16, 1951, we obtained our marriage certificate at London's St.
Marylebone registration district and, Barbara being Methodist,
were married at the Hinde Street Methodist Church. Pam Smith
was maid of honor, Al Jeffcoat best man. None of our family
members made the trip for the occasion, due to the length of
the voyage that would have been required and possibly because
my mother already had been to one wedding of mine. Maury Bell
gave the bride away. We were surrounded by friends at the recep-

tion at the American Women's Club, after which we took off in a hail of rice toward the Channel coast resort of Brighton, not far from the Channel ferry that would take us to France the following morning. Our Chevy bore a "Just Married" sign scrawled by our friends, and a terrible clattering noise emanated from the car as we drove off into London traffic. Our friends had put handfuls of big copper British pennies, or pence, inside each of the four hubcaps.

We spent our wedding night at a hotel in Brighton. Next day, we boarded the Channel ferry at Dover for Calais, then drove the length of France to St. Jean de Luz, where we stayed for a couple of days at the Golf Hotel, overlooking the Bay of Biscay, and visiting nearby Biarritz, before crossing the frontier and visiting the town of San Sebastian, on Spain's north coast. And then it was on south to Burgos and Madrid, with billboards along the roadside proclaiming "Viva Franco, Arribe Espagne"—Long Live Franco, Up with Spain.

CHAPTER **10**

Spain, Churchill, and Married Life

"LOOK," I HAD SAID TO BARBARA before our trip to Spain, "I have this great idea: by adding two weeks of reporting on company time to our allotted two weeks of vacation, we can stretch our two-week honeymoon trip into four." I thought that was clever—but, in retrospect, it was too clever, but not smart. Working on one's honeymoon, leaving one's bride to wander the Prado museum alone, could hardly be held up as a model of sensitivity.

We journeyed in our Chevy convertible from San Sebastian (vacation) through Burgos to Madrid (work), then westward through Salamanca to Barcelona (work) and south of there to the coastal resort at Sitges (vacation), where we watched local fishermen pull an octopus from beneath a pier next to where we were swimming. I reported five front-page leader stories and editorial-page pieces on the durability of the Franco dictatorship and on American efforts to use military and economic aid to recruit his regime into our anti-Soviet alliance.

The New York editors changed the lead on one of my stories on economic aid into what I considered to be a parody of the ultimate reach for reader relevance. The lead they put on the story read: "The land of Spain is a long way from Dallas. And Des Moines. And Los Angeles. But taxpayers in those towns may take a bigger interest in it soon." I could recognize the hand of Oklahoman John O'Riley, who had taken over as page one editor. He succeeded Henry Gemmill, now managing editor, Buren McCormack having been moved from that post to executive editor when Bill Kerby was promoted to vice president. John was a fine, fast writer, and I generally respected his news judgment and his skill as a wordsmith. But occasionally the quest for reader relevance and timeliness would go over the top. There was another example that we quoted with mirth for years to come. Another reporter's lead, to make it timely, was rewritten so that it began: "Now that Labor Day has come and gone—" We joked that that was the ultimate all-purpose lead. It could be put on any story by just changing the holidays as the seasons progressed.

I learned another lesson from a different parody on the Spanish trip, this one a parody of the interpreter's art. Working with a local interpreter we had hired, we interviewed Eladio Uceda, a farmer twenty miles north of Toledo. In the course of asking about his work, we slipped in a question about how he liked certain Franco policies. He grew more and more agitated, gesticulating all the while, as he delivered a long, impassioned, obviously angry reply. The interpreter, straight-faced, summed it all up in one sentence: "He says he thinks everything is fine." After that, we took more care about the credentials of the interpreters we hired, sometimes even bringing along our own Russian speakers or Chinese speakers when we could on future trips.

From Sitges, we drove up the east coast of Spain north of Barcelona, the Costa Brava, eventually climbing high into the Pyrenees, snow-capped even in July, to the tiny, isolated and backward, mountain-ringed independent principality of Andorra, between Spain and France. In the capital Andorra La Vella, we stayed in a hotel where we were awakened in the morning by the bleating of sheep being herded down the main street in front of our window. I reported a feature that ran under the flashline "Happy Feudalism." Smuggling was Andorra's main business. As a result, its five thousand citizens could buy Philco radios, Mickey Mouse clocks, Westinghouse refrigerators, Electrolux vacuum cleaners, cans of Libby's sliced pineapple, and other goods not readily available elsewhere in economically strapped, dollar-short Europe.

On our return to London, with Iranian Prime Minister Mohammed Mossadegh preparing to nationalize the Anglo-Iranian Oil

Co. and the Middle East heating up, the editors ordered me to Saudi Arabia on temporary assignment. They said they had already been in touch with the Saudi Embassy in Washington and had been assured that if the *Journal* wanted to dispatch a reporter, a visa would be granted. They cabled me the questions that appeared on the visa application. Under the question about religion, I entered "Jewish." The visa was denied. I did not get to go to Saudi Arabia until about thirty-three years later.

At our London Bureau in the months that followed were *Journal* reporters Mitchell Gordon and Edward Hughes. Mitch subsequently became Los Angeles Bureau chief and married a Miss Finland, a marriage that foundered when her mother came to live with them and together they put the bride's Hollywood ambitions ahead of domestic duties. Ed Hughes went off to cover Mossadegh in Iran and later to Rhodesia, now Zimbabwe, to cover the Mau Mau uprising and massacres. Many years later, after he had left the *Journal*, he became the Middle East correspondent of the *Reader's Digest*, a job Barbara and I were convinced was cover for work as a Central Intelligence Agency operative. He married a British MI6 intelligence agent, and eventually they retired to London.

In the second half of 1951, there was a mixture of frivolity and gravitas for us. We—and countless others—attended a Queen's Garden Party at Buckingham Palace. Nearby on the lawn we saw the young Princess Margaret and her slightly older sister, Princess Elizabeth, the future queen. And then there was the annual convention of the Trades Union Congress at Blackpool at the start of September, followed by Prime Minister Clement Attlee's September 19 broadcast calling a British general election October 25. Opinion polls were showing a trend toward Winston Churchill's Conservative Party. We immediately plunged into coverage of the election campaigning.

We reported on Churchill's economic and foreign-policy promises, as he warned that the coming election "may well be the turning point in the fortunes and even the life of Britain. . . . There must be no illusions about our difficulties and dangers.

It's better to face them squarely as we did in 1940." We reported on how the Laborites—in the wake of coal shortages, electricity shortages, and reduced train schedules in those industries already taken over by the government—were avoiding talk of further nationalization of industry. Instead, they were stressing central planning and controlling prices, profits, and consumption to assure "fair shares" for all. We reported on the voters' mood from Reading and other "barometer" constituencies as candidates of each party vied to convince the electorate that their party would offer the best hope of future peace and prosperity.

Television sets were just beginning to come onto the scene and were still rare. Al Jeffcoat and I rented a room in a modest hotel near the British Museum, one of the few hotels to offer television. I figured that would be a good way for us to monitor the election results as they came in on the night of October 25. Barbara had a date to play bridge that evening with some women friends, but when their game ended late that evening I drove over, picked her up, and returned with her to the hotel so that she could join us as we watched the election's outcome on the TV set in the room.

"Oh no you don't," said the desk clerk, stopping us in the lobby. I said, "It's OK. We're married." He said he had heard that before. Not being in the habit of carrying around our wedding license, I took Barbara home and she missed seeing Churchill and his Tories returned to power, with a small majority, on one of the nation's earliest TV sets. She said that if I hadn't been so cheap and had registered for a double room, as Mr. and Mrs., instead of a single room, there would have been no problem.

After reporting on reaction to the Tory victory and, in early November, the Conservatives' specific plans for ruling with new policies, I turned with Barbara to packing up our worldly possessions and preparing to move back to New York. I had been appointed foreign editor, succeeding Joe Evans, who became Washington Bureau chief and later a *Journal* editorial writer.

I left Europe a twenty-five-year-old with infinitely more poise and assurance than the wet-behind-the-ears deskman and reporter who had arrived just a little under three years earlier.

There were several reasons. One undoubtedly was meeting and marrying Barbara; she may have started life as shy as I, but she hid it well, and her good looks and quick mind were what impressed me and others; I felt fortunate—and still do—to have won such a wife, and that instilled self-confidence that was not there before. A second reason was that I had learned to force myself to affect more aggressiveness in pressing home a reporter's questions, more of an extroverted manner than I actually felt. Several *Journal* reporters that I met in the years to come—Jack Cooper in Chicago, David Rogers in Washington—were inherently shy individuals, but you would never suspect that when they were onto a story. A third influence was having had the opportunity to mingle professionally and socially with a wide spectrum of British society and expatriate Americans, including diplomats—and gradually growing at ease in their midst.

Our circle was far from as rarefied as those that the dapper Clifton Daniel, the *New York Times*'s London Bureau chief, moved in. We would see him, white-haired, immaculately tailored, and carrying himself elegantly, glide by at the American Embassy. He socialized with Sharman Douglas, daughter of the American Ambassador Lewis Douglas, and her pals, Princess Margaret and other royals. The son of a druggist in the crossroads town of Zebulon, North Carolina, he had come a long way and would go farther, later becoming the *Times*'s managing editor and marrying Margaret Truman. We were not in his circle, but we were more comfortable in ours than I would have been in earlier years.

Without question, another element that certainly bestowed confidence was one that might have applied in Clif Daniel's case, too: we represented respected newspapers. The bureau chief of *The Wall Street Journal* had more access and was indisputably more warmly received and regarded than just plain young Warren Phillips from Queens would have been. And finally, I was getting stories into the paper and onto page one not only regularly but frequently, and they were winning praise. Professionally and competitively, I realized I could hold my own and was doing so.

This gradual accumulation of self-confidence marked a metamorphosis. Yet, as I was periodically reminded in the years ahead, the transformation was far from complete. At a small private lunch years later with Malcolm Forbes, for example, at his *Forbes* magazine headquarters, he proudly showed me an exhibit case that held part of his extensive collection of Fabergé eggs, eggs made of precious metals or hard stones by czarist jewelers and decorated with enamel and gems. I had never heard of Fabergé and, like the boy first learning to peel the apple, I was conscious of my ignorance and not a little ashamed of it. Years after that, I felt the same while staying at German publisher Axel Springer's estate north of Hamburg. Axel showed me and three other guests a wall-high display of his faience collection—earthenware decorated with opaque colored glazes. He later gave each of us as gifts a beautifully printed, full-color hardbound catalog of the collection. I had never heard of faience, and I felt my ignorance was also on display.

But if the chrysalis's metamorphosis was not complete, do we really want it ever to be? Traces and reminders of our origins, and all those who were part of our past, are infinitely greater treasures than Fabergé and faience.

CHAPTER 11

Foreign Editor

WHEN I RETURNED to the *Journal*'s New York office at the end of 1951 as foreign editor, I was invited to join the midmorning "kaffee(coffee)klatsch." This was the informal daily gathering of Barney Kilgore and the paper's senior editors. It was held around a large conference table, in the open, at the northeast end of the newsroom at 44 Broad Street, between editorial-page desks near the elevators and the executive editor's desk by the Broad Street window. Barney would arrive with a copy of the morning's paper he had marked up on his train commute from Princeton, New Jersey. He would have circled typos and more substantive story failings. Over coffee, Danish, and doughnuts, he and Bill Kerby, long his newsroom lieutenant and now his deputy on upstairs executive-suite business matters as well, would join executive editor Buren McCormack, managing editor Henry Gemmill, page one editor John O'Riley, and associate editor Vermont Royster in swapping stories of dinner-party conversations the previous evening that they thought held the seeds of possible news stories that could be followed up. There was no formal agenda, no formality.

These longtime colleagues, at ease with each other, would also swap stories of their weekend golf accomplishments, and in winter, McCormack would discourse on the curling at his Sleepy Hollow Country Club, near where he lived in Westchester County, north of the city. Kerby, Royster, and Kilgore, all veterans of the *Journal*'s Washington Bureau in the days before Gemmill worked

there, would occasionally reminisce about the antics of Gene
Duffield and other reporters in the bureau, including an afternoon or two they spent at the movies when news was slow. These
oft-repeated stories seemed to me as ancient as World War I. It is
hard to believe now that they had taken place only ten or twelve
years earlier and were as fresh in the tellers' minds as yesterday
was to me.

The morning kaffeeklatsches, to which only editors were
invited, reflected in expanded form the exclusiveness Barney
imposed on the *Journal*'s masthead during his tenure. It carried
his name as publisher and the names of the editor and the executive editor, and no others. Only after Barney's time were the
masthead and the kaffeeklatsches enlarged to include the paper's
non-news executives, changing the flavor and the purpose of the
morning gatherings. For decades after, though, generations of
business-side executives continued to chafe under the feeling
that, at this paper and company run by newsmen, they would
always be second-class citizens.

As foreign editor, I assigned and edited stories from the handful of bureaus the *Journal* had then in Europe, Japan, and Canada. Jeffcoat had succeeded Charles Hargrove as Paris Bureau
chief; Hughes was shuttling between London, Africa, and the
Middle East. I also worked with our network of stringers, or part-
time, freelance correspondents. They included Ed Hartrich in
Germany and stringers throughout Latin America, India, and
elsewhere. Trying to plug all the gaps in their stories and get
them suitable for print involved arduous cabling back and forth
and heavy rewrite, like squeezing blood from a stone. But I was
eager to get Buenos Aires and New Delhi datelines into the paper
and did so, endless struggle though it was.

Early in my tenure we printed a mammoth blooper. Ed Hughes,
at the beginning of 1952, obtained an exclusive interview with
General Dwight Eisenhower, then supreme commander of the
North Atlantic Treaty Organization, based outside Paris. Hughes
quoted Eisenhower as saying he had no intention of running
for the U.S. presidency. The *Journal* ran this on page one under
a then-rare two-column headline. Subsequent events made this

story an embarrassment. It has been mostly forgotten over the years—but not by me.

Barbara and I had moved into a new apartment complex at Cadman Plaza, at the eastern end of the Brooklyn Bridge. We later moved to an apartment on Manhattan's West Eighty-Eighth Street, half a block from Riverside Drive and the Hudson River. It was the first of six moves in the next six years. The Eighty-Eighth Street apartment was notable for the dark purple walls we inherited in the dining room, and for its cockroaches.

Barbara went to work for William Melish Harris, head of the Biow advertising agency, and later moved to Grey Advertising, where her boss, Bernard "Bib" Brownold, was a partner and close associate of Larry Valenstein, head of Grey. The agency was modest sized at the time but later grew into a behemoth of the business under Ed Meyer who, with his wife, Sandy, became good friends decades later.

As soon as we had arrived back in the States we had taken the Pennsylvania Railroad train down to Cape Charles, Virginia, at the southern tip of the Delmarva Peninsula, to visit Barbara's parents and for me to meet my new in-laws for the first time. Kathryn "Kitty" Thomas and Herman "Herm" Thomas could not have given me a warmer welcome into their family. I sat on the back porch with Herm as he gamely tried to teach me how to shuck the local clams and oysters. Barbara helped her mother prepare fried chicken, corn pudding, and other Southern dishes. Barbara, like me, was an only child, but also like me, she had many aunts and uncles, in Cape Charles and near Norfolk, across the Chesapeake Bay. We visited most of them, and Barbara's many high school friends as well—Jean Collins, Bobby Rittenhouse, George Savage, and others.

Unlike today, when a twenty-mile-long series of bridges and tunnels crosses the lower Chesapeake Bay, linking the Eastern Shore of Virginia with Norfolk, we took ferries to make the crossing in the days when we first started visiting Cape Charles. The trains that once served Cape Charles and crossed the bay on railroad ferries were discontinued soon after our initial visit. We drove our family to Cape Charles each year for holiday visits and, in summertime, for memorable lazy vacations in a rented cottage on beautiful Smith Beach, on the bay, north of town.

As London Bureau chief and later as foreign editor, I periodically visited the *Journal*'s Washington Bureau. Its State Department reporter, Ray Cromley, invited me to dinner with him and his son at their northern Virginia home. Ray, who had been the *Journal*'s Tokyo correspondent at the time of Pearl Harbor, was married to a Japanese woman, a physician, with a three-year-old son. He was imprisoned as a suspected spy. Four months later, he, with his son, were returned to America aboard the *Gripsholm,* the ship repatriating all Americans in exchange for Japanese diplomats and others being repatriated from the States. His wife was not permitted to leave. Ray returned as soon as the war ended, only to have his wife die of tuberculosis shortly after they were reunited. As the wife of an American, she had not been treated well during the war years.

During World War II Ray, because of his language skills and knowledge of the Japanese, was assigned to an army intelligence unit as a major and sent to Yenan, in north China, as a liaison officer to Mao Tse-tung. Mao was headquartered in Yenan, living with his Communist guerrilla army in the mountainside caves there and waging war against the Japanese. When Mao's Red Army defeated Chiang Kai-shek's Nationalists in the civil war after World War II and assumed power over all of mainland China in 1949, with the United States viewing Mao as a cold war adversary, Ray wrote a rare first-person personal profile of the Chinese leader for page one. The flashline atop the leader headline and the first sentence read: "I knew Mao." I myself never dreamed that twenty years after my dinner with Ray Cromley and his son, when the United States and Mao's China resumed diplomatic relations, I would be in Tiananmen Square for the October 1, 1972, Chinese National Day celebration of the anniversary of that 1949 assumption of power. I would be there as one of the first group of American journalists to tour the People's Republic of China, including the caves at Yenan, once the long rupture in relations between our two countries was mended.

A few years after I met Ray Cromley, my family and I entertained at dinner at our Brooklyn home a postwar Tokyo Bureau chief of the *Journal,* Igor Oganesoff, and his beautiful Japanese wife. They rode the subway to our home, she attired in a stunning, colorful kimono. Alas, this East-West marriage ended tragically as well. Igor took up with the wife of the *Financial Times* bureau chief in Tokyo, they moved to Hong Kong, and his wife and young children were left to be ostracized in their own country. Japanese wives of Westerners in those early postwar years, though tolerated while still wed, were shunned as soiled goods, almost pariahs, when deserted by the gaijin, or foreign, husband. Mrs. Oganesoff, a modern Madam Butterfly, moved to Los Angeles with her children and worked at a motel there, forced to seek sanctuary in an unfamiliar far-off country, foreign to her yet more welcoming than her native land.

When I visited our foreign bureaus, I sometimes made time to follow the consultations there with reporting of my own. I visited our Montreal, Toronto, and Ottawa bureaus in December 1952, then flew to Goose Bay, Labrador, aboard a Royal Canadian Air Force transport plane due to refuel there en route to England. I went to the air base at Goose Bay in search of on-the-spot color to flesh out a story I was reporting on the joint defense the United States and Canada had set up on their northern frontier to guard against a Soviet bomber attack coming across the polar regions, the shortest route between Russia and North America. That was considered a serious threat, as was a land attack in Europe, in those early days of cold war tension, when dangerous confrontations already had occurred in Berlin, Greece, and elsewhere, and the Korean War had broken out. Goose Bay and Thule, in northern Greenland, were fighter bases linked to a network of weather stations and radar posts the two countries ran jointly across the Arctic and subarctic frontier—what later was known as the Dew Line, Dew being the acronym for Distant Early Warning.

The Goose Bay base was isolated, freezing cold, and immersed in packed snow. I flew with an RCAF pilot, flashing over the vast white wilderness of frozen lakes, frozen bogs, and snowy emptiness. U.S. Air Force Colonel Joseph A. Thomas, commander of the American detachment, and RCAF Group Captain R. J. "Spotty" Gray, the Canadian base commander and a Battle of Britain veteran, said temperatures sometimes dropped to twenty or thirty degrees below zero, and it took fifty huge plows and blowers to keep the two-mile-long runways clear of snow—180 inches had fallen the previous winter.

When I was ready to leave I presented my travel orders, issued by the RCAF in Ottawa before I left, authorizing me to fly aboard the weekly England-to-Ottawa transport plane that stopped every Thursday to refuel at Goose Bay. But only then, when I was preparing to leave, was I told that regularly scheduled flight had been suspended two or three months earlier, and none was scheduled until spring. The folks in Ottawa, working from out-of-date schedules, had made a mistake. I was stranded. Fortuitously, a couple of days later I was hastily summoned to the airstrip: a cargo plane was coming in from Fort Chimo, four hundred miles north, with a planeload of sick Eskimos, on an unscheduled mission to take them to Ottawa for medical treatment. I climbed aboard, the crew completed the plane's refueling, and we were off on the long flight southwest to Ottawa. I huddled with the Eskimos on the metal floor of the unfurnished plane. None had ever flown before. Most were airsick throughout the flight.

Back in New York, I interviewed and profiled John Foster Dulles, who would be secretary of state in the incoming Eisenhower administration. In April 1953, I visited our London and Paris bureaus and wrote about Britain's improving economy, the impending Suez conflict, and with Jeffcoat, the Paris meeting of the foreign, defense, and finance ministers of the member nations of NATO, the North Atlantic Treaty Organization, to discuss defense-buildup goals in the face of a new Soviet "peace offensive." In mid-May I returned to Europe with Barbara and we drove south through France to Burgundy, then over the Mount Cenis Pass to north Italy and on to Rome, then up to Trieste and into Tito's Communist Yugoslavia, reporting and writing all the way. I was reporting on a Europe marked at that time, only eight years after World War II, by unstable governments in France and Italy, fragile economies, a divided Germany split between a resurgent western half and a desolate, restive East Germany under Soviet domination—a Europe living under the Damocles sword of an ever-present cold war and the threat of Soviet expansionism and a new hot war.

Driving south to Beaune in our black Chevy convertible, which we had shipped to France on the boat with us, Barbara and I stopped for a leisurely lunch at a two-star country inn. We felt we were a world away from Europe's troubles and traumas. At one point I asked for some more butter. *"Du beurre, s'il vous plaît."* The waiter brought me *"deux bières,"* two beers. My French pronunciation needed more polishing.

A mile off the road connecting Dijon and Beaune, and more than two hundred miles southeast of Paris, was the village of Aloxe-Corton and the vineyards and 150-year-old home of Daniel Senard and his family. We stayed several days with them, trying to probe the French psyche, as others had done before us throughout history. Earlier, as successive French governments had been voted out of office in a revolving door of postwar premiers, I had written an editorial-page piece about the fatalism, the cynicism toward government, the intense individualism that are blended in the French character and were reflected in the political sickness of the time. I began the piece this way:

> Americans living in France are fond of the story of the summer tourist who approached a line of parked taxis in Paris, only to be told by the first driver that the desired destination was too far across town. The second cabbie in line shook his head also—it was time for his lunch. The third driver similarly refused the passenger, for he was almost ready to go off duty and the direction in which the tourist wanted to go was not convenient for him.
>
> Finally, when the fourth driver in the cab line demurred for yet another reason, the visitor exploded in exasperation. "It's because of people like you that the Fourth Republic will fall," he scolded.

"Alors," replied the unruffled cabbie with a shrug. *"Il y'aura une cinquième."* This reply—"There will be a Fifth"—tells a good deal about the people we affectionately call "the philosophical French."

Now, in Aloxe-Corton, I examined the France that was far from the Eiffel Tower, the Folies Bergère and the Champs Elysées, far from the Paris of France's bickering parliament, toppling cabinets on the average of every five months. "What happens in Paris is largely a reflection of the state of mind of the men and women who tend the grapes, till the soil, work in the factories, and run the shops in these towns," I wrote. "Two related mental attitudes—found here and throughout France—are at the root of France's sickness. One is what Daniel Senard and his friends call a fatalism that has turned them into political introverts; harsher observers have diagnosed it as a national hopelessness that has made Frenchmen individually selfish. The other key mental attitude is a deep distrust of strong central government. Both have sprung from France's historical experiences, [including] the demoralizing impact and loss of pride that have accompanied France's last three wars."

For years, Barbara would ask: "How could you write about someone whose hospitality you had accepted?" My answer was that Daniel knew I was a journalist from the start, and that furthermore I didn't write anything bad about him or portray him unsympathetically.

"I work hard, my neighbor Louis Latour works hard, we all work hard," I had quoted Daniel Senard as saying. "But we work for ourselves, for our families, perhaps for our village or town. Paris is far away and the nation and the world are beyond us. People here don't have any influence over what the government or the world do, so they figure there's no use bothering about them." This increasing introversion of the people of France, I postulated, was what was reflected in the conglomeration of small parties that made up the French parliament, each upholding particular regional, economic, or religious interests, and that made formation of a majority to attack France's problems so difficult.

When Barbara and I a few days later drove east for hour after hour, climbing higher and higher into the French Alps, the afternoon light faded and it was dark by the time we arrived at the isolated French and Italian frontier posts at the Mount Cenis Pass. I was summoned inside the Italian customs office and questioned for what I considered an inordinately long time. When I emerged, I saw the reason why: a cluster of border guards had gathered around our car, happy to have the opportunity to engage my attractive wife in conversation for as long as procrastination permitted.

We wound down the mountainside and at long last arrived at our hotel in Turin, memorable because the bathroom toilet paper still consisted of strips of torn-up old newspapers. We drove through the hills of Tuscany in the following days to Florence, through the farm villages south of Florence and the coastal lowlands near Grosseto, and on to Rome, gathering material for stories on the national election campaigns then under way. Premier Alcide de Gasperi's Christian Democrats were struggling to hold onto power. I wrote two preelection front-page leaders—one on the election battle itself and what was at stake, another about the ailing economy the victors would inherit. And when the voting took place at the start of June, I wrote a long spot-news story and two edit-page pieces on the results. Big gains by the Communists, neo-Fascists, and other extremist parties had cut the majority of de Gasperi's democratic coalition to a sliver, threatening Italy with political instability in the French pattern.

While I was consumed by my reporting, Barbara was left to tour the museums and monuments by herself, or to sit in hotel rooms alone awaiting my return. When I did return to the hotel it was to pound away on my typewriter, a boxed portable I carried for years. It was a difficult and lonely time for her.

After we left Italy for Trieste and Yugoslavia, her old friend Joan Bell joined us from London, giving Barbara better company than

I was providing. We drove from Trieste through the Ljubljana Gap, pathway of invading armies for centuries, to Zagreb, capital of Croatia, and then started down the empty highway toward the Yugoslav capital of Belgrade, in Serbia. We had not gone far when our Chevy broke down. A passing farmer on a horse-drawn cart towed us slowly back into Zagreb, to a local mechanic, Ante Ivekic of Auto Mehanicka Radiona. A crowd gathered to stare at us as our horse-drawn Chevy moved through the streets. Yugoslavia was fairly isolated at the time, and foreign visitors a rarity. The country had been behind the Iron Curtain since the war, then Tito broke with the Kremlin in 1948 and pursued his independent Communist course. Out from the milling, curious Zagreb crowd came an elderly woman's voice, calling out in English: "Welcome. I used to live in Niagara Falls."

The mechanic had no foreign auto parts. Nor did anyone else in the country, as far as we could tell. Yugoslavia, short on dollars, did not permit their import. But the mechanic said he could make the parts we needed, machining them by hand. Stranded as we were, we gave the go-ahead. Next morning we returned to find our engine dismantled and laid out, part by part, on his lawn. He said to come back in a week.

After saying a prayer for our car, Barbara and Joan took off by train to tour Dubrovnik and Sarajevo, arranging to rejoin me later in Belgrade. I boarded a train for the capital. In the washroom of our railcar a Serb was giving himself a morning shave, accompanied by sips of slivovitz, the Serbian plum brandy. In the capital and the countryside, those I interviewed ranged from Economics Minister Svetozar Vukmanovic-Tempo, Governor Vojin Guzina of the National Bank, and Edvard Kardelj, vice president and second-in-command to Tito, to factory and collective farm managers, housewives, and foreign diplomats. The story was Yugoslavia's metamorphosis from Soviet-style communism to a brand of communism that blended continued state ownership of factories with a dose of free enterprise, allowing the market forces of supply and demand to function and replacing the commissar's whip with the profit incentive.

Two years earlier, with centralized state planners allocating raw materials to every factory, decreeing what each factory should produce and how much, and directing distribution in minute detail, it only took a few miscalculations to cause even combs, pins, buttons, neckties, and shoelaces to become so scarce they were actually hoarded. "There were only two things in every Belgrade shop window in those days—a picture of Tito and a handful of dead flies," recalled a foreign diplomat. A walk along the Terazije, the Broadway of Belgrade, showed Tito's picture now accompanied by a wide variety of consumer goods. The combs and cutlery, fountain pens and multicolored textiles wouldn't wow any American, French, or German consumers, but the quality and variety were an eye-popping change for Yugoslav shoppers.

Barbara and Joan rejoined me in time to attend Tito's birthday party at his White Palace. We had been invited to the celebration, with many others, to be sure, and it did give us the chance to briefly meet the Yugoslav dictator and his wife. The time was a historic one for him. Russia and Yugoslavia had just agreed to resume full diplomatic relations, after their 1948 rupture. This led to speculation that the Russians would soon lift the economic blockade they had imposed on Yugoslavia, a blockade that had helped strangle Tito's economy. I wrote edit-pagers analyzing the Russian thaw and detailing the seething discontent the men around Tito saw growing in their neighboring Soviet satellite nations of Eastern Europe.

After picking up our successfully repaired Chevy convertible in Zagreb, we headed home by way of Bonn and Dusseldorf, reporting and writing more articles for the editorial page. One was about West Germany now having emerged as "an island of energy in a weak and weary Europe." Another reported the speculation by Germans and others on the course Russia would set in the wake of popular uprisings in East Berlin. The answer came a few years later with the erection of the Berlin Wall, in August 1961, to seal off East Berlin from West Berlin and stanch the steady stream of East Germans fleeing to the west. The Wall did not come down for twenty-eight years, until 1989.

It has been said often that journalism offers a front-row seat on history. As I returned to New York I reflected—and have ever since—on what a marvelous opportunity the journalist is offered in continuing his or her education throughout life. Reporting and researching each new story provided an education in new subject after new subject. I actually was being paid while I reaped such benefits. Surely, I thought, there are few other vocations where one is paid to keep on learning, to keep on broadening one's knowledge.

CHAPTER 12

To Chicago with a Growing Family

IN NEW YORK ON MAY 2, 1954, Barbara gave birth to our first child, Lisa, at Mount Sinai Hospital. Husbands were not welcome in the delivery room as they are today. As I waited with other men in the obstetrics floor's waiting room, Barbara was in labor alone. An attending nurse, looking in after hearing her moaning and crying out in pain, said: "Stop complaining. You brought this on yourself." Hardly a credit to the noble nursing profession.

The first night that we returned to the purple-walled West Eighty-Eighth Street apartment, with newborn Lisa crying with colic and the new parents inexperienced, worried, and tense, my mother chose to drop by for a visit and to bring along her then-boyfriend Max Geiger. Max was a very serious, humorless Communist who, unlike many other American Communists of the thirties and forties, had not turned away from Russia in disillusionment at the time Stalin signed a 1939 friendship pact with Nazi Germany. Max had retained his idealism and devotion to the vision of a halcyon Communist society—but he never used the word *Communists.* He spoke only of "progressives." My mother, doubtless lonely, tolerated Max as an escort for years—and we survived the turmoil of that first shared night at home with baby Lisa—but my mother was not oblivious to his shortcomings.

"The difference between your father and Max," she once remarked, "is that when I was walking along between you and your father, he would always say, 'Aren't we men lucky to be with a woman like your mother?' Max, on the other hand, when the three of us were walking down the street together, would say, 'Isn't she lucky to have the two of us men escorting her?'"

Shortly after Lisa's birth, we packed and sent off our furniture and other belongings in a moving van and then drove to Chicago. I had been appointed managing editor of the *Journal*'s Midwest Edition. The drive to Chicago was a long one for the new baby and the new mother. Stopping for the night at an Ohio hotel en route, we spent the wee hours trying to comfort the crying child. Once in Chicago, we soon were ensconced in a pleasant ground-floor apartment on Hinman Avenue in Evanston, a suburb just north of the city, on Lake Michigan and home to Northwestern University, whose campus was just a few blocks from our new apartment. It was at Evanston Hospital, two years later, that our second daughter, Leslie, would be born. Barbara and I were both angered and amazed at seeing flies in the hospital nursery.

Dow Jones had bought the *Chicago Journal of Commerce* two years before our arrival and had converted it into *The Wall Street Journal*'s third regional edition. The first had been created in San Francisco in the inauspicious year 1929, setting into type stories transmitted by Teletype from New York. A Southwest Edition had been started in Dallas in 1948. The new Chicago edition was put under the direction of Bob Bottorff, a schoolmate of Barney's at DePauw University in Greencastle, Indiana. Bob's previous experience had been running the Pacific Coast Edition. Now the sandy-haired Bottorff, once redheaded and called "Torch" by his wife, Ande, was being transferred to New York as managing editor of the entire paper. I was his successor in charge of the Midwest Edition.

Kilgore and Bottorff had moved the edition from the rundown *Chicago Journal of Commerce* Building to new quarters in a building at 711 West Monroe Street that had been occupied by Brinks, the armored-car company. Its foundations and basement, built sturdily and reinforced to hold the vaults Brinks used to safeguard the cash it transported, were ideal for anchoring the *Journal*'s presses. The building was a short distance west of the Chicago River and the Loop, the city's downtown center, and only one block away from Madison Street, Chicago's Skid Row. Our employees often had to weave their way between cheap saloons and winos on the street as they came to work and went out on assignments. But the *Journal's* new Chicago home was only a few blocks from Chicago's big central post office, a vital consideration for a paper distributed throughout all the states of the Midwest.

Kilgore had sent out his Princeton decorators, Freddy Millholland and Peter Olsen of Millholland & Olsen, to create a luxuriously furnished executive office, with private bathroom, at one end of the newsroom, for his use and that of other visiting executives when they came to town. My desk and that of John McWethy, the *Journal's* longtime Chicago Bureau chief and now my deputy, were just outside that office. We had use of it when it was unoccupied—which was almost always—for conferences, discussions with staff members, and phone conversations that we wanted to be private, and as a quiet refuge when we wanted to write undisturbed.

As managing editor of the Midwest Edition, I was the paper's chief representative in Chicago and also was given day-to-day authority over all departments of the paper when quick, on-the-spot decisions had to be made on matters crossing departmental lines. Al Shuman, a Chicagoan and the paper's production chief, was generous in helping me learn how the composing room and the pressroom operated. Instead of having printers set type manually from copy sent by teleprinter from New York, the paper now had begun to set type automatically and more speedily by Tele-Typesetter. Union printers in New York typed out stories, which were converted into coded perforated tape; the tape was fed into "readers," devices that converted the coded perforations into electrical impulses that were sent by telephone lines to linecasting machines in Chicago and other regional plants that automatically set the stories into type. That way a story had to be "keyboarded" manually only once, in New York, instead of many times at each of what later became multiple regional printing plants.

While Al Shuman introduced me to the workings of the production department, John McWethy was equally generous and gracious in introducing me to the more familiar workings of his

Chicago newsroom. There were about twelve reporters there. They and reporters in the St. Louis and Detroit bureaus, which were also part of our Midwest domain, roamed throughout the Midwest covering its cattle and crops, factories and railroads.

The Chicago reporters were an able, congenial group. John "Jack" Cooper, personally shy but professionally unrelenting, often covered the increasing mechanization of agriculture and other farmland trends. He delighted, as he traveled on his reporting trips, in finding towns with offbeat names that he could use as datelines at the start of his stories. One he used more than once was What Cheer, Iowa. Another was Intercourse, Pennsylvania. Jack took me down to Chicago's South Side to give me, the newcomer, a tour of the stockyards and meatpacking plants we covered, both of which were an integral part of Chicago in those days, but have long since departed for sites closer to the cattle ranges and feedlots. We watched the gory, assembly-line slaughtering of cattle and hogs, and later I took New York visitors there, too, for this glimpse of Chicago local color. Jack Cooper later became page one editor in New York.

Ray Vicker, another reporter, a Chicagoan inherited from the old *Chicago Journal of Commerce*, was a diamond in the rough. He was easily as unrelenting as Cooper in pursuit of news, irreverent in his aggressiveness, and always overflowing with story ideas. He later did distinguished reporting as London Bureau chief and subsequently as Middle East correspondent, dodging bullets in strife-torn Lebanon and other hot spots.

Jim Wallace and Felicia Antonelli were other reporters in the Chicago newsroom. My predecessor there, Bob Bottorff, had noticed that they spent an inordinate amount of time visiting and gossiping at each other's desks. He told them to cut that out and get back to work. Only much later did it dawn on him that after that reprimand, when one was on the phone for a long time, as most reporters are prone to be as they gather facts by phone, the other was on the phone, too. They had resumed their long gossiping and flirting exchanges by dialing each other's intraoffice phone extensions.

John McWethy assigned and edited the bureau's coverage of corporate developments, the commodities markets, and other inside-the-paper spot news. He also toured Midwest college campuses seeking talent he could invite to Chicago for job interviews. He and I approved reporters' ideas for page-one stories about trends on their beats, and originated and assigned some, too. I edited the Midwest Bureau's page-one submissions, sprucing up leads and doing considerable rewrite, something most of the paper's front-page stories needed in those days. I also made time to report and write some editorial-page pieces of my own, including some on Chicago politics.

By the time I arrived in Chicago, the *Journal* had long since modernized the ethics policies that had seen nothing amiss in the Christmas gifts and free trips that reporters, editors, and executives accepted without compunction when I first joined the paper in 1947. Gifts of whiskey still flowed into the Chicago office at Christmastime from businesses we covered, but John McWethy and I sent them back with notes that expressed appreciation but explained the *Journal*'s policy. In the case of turkeys sent to us at Thanksgiving, sides of beef sent by meatpacker Swift & Co. at Christmas, and other perishable gifts, we sent them to local charities serving the poor. We sent notes to the gift givers explaining why we had done this; I am not sure all the donors were happy about it.

Barbara and I found Chicagoans warm and welcoming. Business leaders and bankers there seemed more accessible and talkative than those in New York. We lunched with many of them at two dining clubs that John McWethy, using his numerous contacts, was instrumental in helping me join for that purpose. One was the Chicago Yacht Club, overlooking the yacht basin and Lake Michigan, and the other was the Tavern Club, high in a building near the Loop and also with a view of Lake Michigan and other parts of the city. It was on a terrace at the Tavern Club that we and other reporters and editors met with Adlai Stevenson as he prepared his 1956 run for the Democratic presidential nomination.

Just before Barbara's and my second daughter, Leslie, was born, on September 29, 1956, we moved to a large old house in Evanston, at 1584 Wesley Avenue, to accommodate our growing family. It was a short distance west of the rail station from which I commuted to downtown Chicago each day. The house had a lovely large lawn, dominated by a towering oak tree.

In the summer of 1956 the Democratic Party held its presidential nominating convention at the International Amphitheater, near the stockyards on the South Side of Chicago. The *Journal*'s Washington Bureau sent in a team to handle the coverage, led by Henry Gemmill, who had stepped down as managing editor and had returned to Washington as bureau chief. As the local host, I was responsible for the logistics, from arranging communications to renting furniture for the *Journal* newsroom in the press quarters at the convention center.

The night before the convention opened, I took Henry and a handful of the Washington reporters to dinner at the Silver Frolics, an upscale strip joint on the Near North Side. The choice of such a location was not unusual in those days; in subsequent years it would become unthinkable, as increasing numbers of able women joined the ranks of reporters covering politics and other news and executives were held accountable for setting a more tasteful, gender-blind example. Johnny Grimes, one of the Washington reporters in the group that night and the son of editor William H. Grimes, said, shortly after we took our seats at a stage-side table: "Please don't tell my father I was in a place like this." To which Henry Gemmill replied: "We won't tell your father if you won't tell our editor."

As the convention built to its climax of nominating Adlai Stevenson, with Estes Kefauver as his running mate, I received a frantic phone call from Barbara. The big oak tree behind our house had been hit by lightning and part of it had crashed through the roof over one end of the house. "I can't leave in the middle of the convention," I told Barbara. "You'll have to deal with it." That abdication from domestic crisis was not popular at home in Evanston.

While I was in Chicago, Barney Kilgore asked me to go out to San Francisco to look at a sturdy, former garage building the company was considering buying to relocate the Pacific Coast Edition and its presses. He also asked me to visit the Southwest Edition in Dallas. I was not qualified to appraise potential or existing printing plants, but I went and sent him my impressions as requested. I never found out whether his purpose was to broaden my education, groom me for expanded responsibilities, judge the quality of my observations, or simply gather facts for his own use.

Also during my Chicago years, in 1955, Barney and Bill Kerby hosted and invited me to participate in the first of what would become the annual *Journal* Editors–Bureau Managers Conference. It was held on a weekend on the grounds of the Buck Hill Falls, Pennsylvania, Inn, where the Kerbys had a vacation cottage. The attendees, all male at that first gathering, worked from an agenda in the mornings and evenings and relaxed together at sports or chitchat in the afternoons. These annual gatherings enabled the bureau chiefs to get to know better, in an informal setting, the New York editors and their bureau-manager counterparts across the country and abroad. They were useful in knitting the far-flung staff closer together, conveying the editors' thoughts on the future direction of the paper, and giving the bureau chiefs an opportunity to relay questions or gripes they and their reporters wanted answered. We continued these meetings for many years, moving them after Bill Kerby retired to other locales, ranging from Bermuda to New Jersey, Colorado to Cape Cod.

In March of 1957 our family moved again, when I was promoted to managing editor in New York. The *Journal*'s circulation, 100,000 at the time I was hired in 1947, had risen to 488,156 ten years later. It ranked eleventh in circulation among American newspapers. Barbara, Lisa, Leslie, and I bought a house at 4 Byron Lane, in the Westchester suburb of Larchmont, north of the city. I was thirty years old.

Veteran reporter Tom Wise quit the paper and moved to *Fortune* magazine in reaction to my appointment as managing editor. He thought the job should have gone to him. News editor Sam Lesch, on the other hand, was delighted. One of "his boys," one he had trained on his copydesk, was on the rise. Sam was outwardly gruff, he put fear into many young reporters, but I owed more to his patience and encouragement than I ever found words to express adequately to him while he was alive. That is one of my lifetime regrets.

PART THREE

EDITOR

CHAPTER **13**

Managing Editor

AS SUMMER TURNED INTO FALL in 1957, two stunning, transformational events, a world away from each other, suddenly transfixed the country. In Little Rock, Arkansas, in early September, Governor Orval Faubus, defying a federal court order, called out the National Guard to prevent black children from entering all-white Central High School; in response, President Dwight Eisenhower sent army infantry to clear the way and enforce the court's school desegregation decree. A few weeks later, on October 4, the beep-beep-beep of a radio transmission from an orbiting satellite high above the earth jolted the world with another stunning surprise: Russia had beaten the United States into space with its successful launch of Sputnik I.

Here, in a single month, were two history-making stories, each in its own way clearly signaling the end of one era and the arrival of a new one. Coming barely six months after I became the *Journal's* managing editor, these breaking stories were my first test, my baptism of fire. They would be followed, during the fifteen years I spent as managing editor and then executive editor, by coverage of many other memorable events, including the civil rights revolution, the John F. Kennedy assassination, the Vietnam War, and Watergate.

I sent two of our best reporters to Little Rock—former managing editor Henry Gemmill, who had returned to reporting in 1954, and veteran Joe Guilfoyle. Their assignment was to avoid writing about the troops, the ignorant redneck rhetoric, and the politicians' posturing that filled all the other newspapers' front pages and the television screens, and instead probe behind the headlines into the ramifications of what was happening, what was likely to happen next, what the confrontation boded for the future. Their assignment reflected Barney Kilgore's concept that the *Journal*'s front-page leaders be distinctive, that they not duplicate other newspapers and television by reporting what happened yesterday, but instead try to provide broad-perspective interpretation and insight into trends. This practice is commonplace in journalism today and sounds far from revolutionary—but it was a revolutionary, pioneering approach at the time.

The *Journal,* with its focus on the world of business, had never chosen to cover social change and sociopolitical events before. But I sensed that just as our readers had needed news of politics and foreign affairs, both of which affected their businesses and the larger economy, to say nothing of their families' personal lives, so too would they need the best reporting we could provide on the social changes being wrought in the South and, soon, throughout all American society. Businesspeople's interests were not confined to their businesses. And even if they were, their business's future could not be insulated from societal change.

Gemmill and Guilfoyle reported there was less popular support in Little Rock for Faubus's actions, particularly within the business community, than the nation assumed. Faubus was running for a third term, trying to reverse his declining popularity by stoking race hatred. The *Journal* reporters wrote about how the city's civic and business leaders were trying to defuse the crisis:

> Very quietly—at first entirely behind the scenes, and then more and more openly—many men were organizing to apply the brakes. Their tactic: Do not attack the Governor. Do not force him into a position where he will be suddenly deflated and discredited. Instead, surround him with the evidence that segregationist sentiment will in the long run pack less political punch . . . than devotion to law and order, preservation of the public school system, and restoration of the state's good name.

Newsweek magazine, looking back four years later, said: "While other reporters bored in on obvious, tumultuous events of the school closing, *Journal* hands searched out the economic repercussions. Economics proved to be the key ending the crisis."

On October 4, a Friday, with Gemmill and Guilfoyle still filing their stories from Little Rock, the Soviets successfully sent Sputnik I, the first space satellite, into orbit. The *Journal* had earlier ended its Saturday edition, for lack of readership and advertising on a day most businesses were closed, and had never had a Sunday paper. We mobilized for our next edition, on Monday. We all recognized that the Sputnik launch signaled the beginning of a new era: We had entered the Space Age in earnest. We had crossed a new frontier in science and world history. And we had entered a new, uncharted period of Soviet-American cold war confrontation and competition.

On Sunday morning, October 6, I arrived at my desk at 44 Broad Street—a desk at the southeast corner of the newsroom, a big, open newsroom with no offices—after having already made sure over the weekend that the necessary reporting had been set in motion. The Washington Bureau was starting to send in the fruits of its reporting on the military strategy implications of the space shot, including a missile buildup. It also was reporting on the defense budget outlook and on what the State Department and foreign diplomats were predicting Sputnik's impact would be on the world diplomatic and geopolitical scene. Science reporters in New York were bringing in the scientific community's reactions and predictions, including the implications for future communications. Other reporters had been asked to probe what the Soviet achievement portended for American education, particularly in the sciences and math. Foreign bureaus were cabling reactions from abroad.

I took on the job myself of assembling all those elements into a single page-one leader. While other newspapers normally carried many separate stories on each of such disparate ramifications of a major breaking story, the *Journal*'s thinking at the time was that busy readers were best served by weaving them all together in one, or sometimes two, roundups, or wrap-up stories. We would follow an all-encompassing lead by ticking off the major findings of our reporting, then go on to support each finding with documentation and details. The purpose, again, was not to focus on what had happened, as other papers and TV tended to do, but to interpret its meaning and anticipate what was likely to come next.

It was rare, as managing editor, that I would function as rewrite man and bang out an entire leader on my upright Royal typewriter, as I did that Sunday. But I did stay until deadline each day, reading copies of each leader as it was sent to the printers, often a page at a time. I usually glanced over copies or proofs of the spot news that had been sent to the Linotype machines one floor below, stories that would run on pages inside the paper. If I saw a lead that could be brightened up, significant angles buried too deep in a story, or gaps or inconsistencies that needed attention, I would ask the editors to make the necessary improvements. Occasionally, I would redo the top of a leader myself.

Working late this way as deadlines approached meant I was arriving home in Larchmont late, after taking a subway from Wall Street to Grand Central Station in midtown, then a commuter train to the Larchmont suburb. Our two young daughters at that time, Lisa and Leslie, usually had finished dinner and were preparing for bed by the time I arrived. After two years of that, Barbara and I decided to move the family back into New York City. We rented a small, nineteenth-century carriage house at 12 Middagh Street in Brooklyn Heights, next door to a playground. It was just across the East River from Wall Street, and I often walked to work across the Brooklyn Bridge with neighbors.

Ed Hughes, back in New York on home leave, came to dinner in Brooklyn one night. Also with us that evening were Tom Whitney, home from duty as the Associated Press Moscow Bureau chief, and his wife, Yulya, or Julie, a Russian songwriter and singer. She had just had an album of her recordings published. After dinner, we asked her to play some of her songs and sing. She sat down at the piano and began. Midway through one song, Ed leaned over and whispered something brief to me under his breath. Julie heard him, abruptly stopped playing, turned to him in a fury, and said, in her thick Russian accent, "Ed Hughes, you son of bitch. I no play when people talk." With that, she stormed out the front door into the night, her husband, Tom, apologizing as he retrieved her coat and dashed after her. I have long forgotten whatever innocuous thing Hughes whispered, but Barbara and I have never forgotten how a guest was unintentionally offended in our home.

Among our neighborhood friends were Jim and Janet Hester. Jim was then provost at Long Island University. One evening over drinks at their Willow Street house, he confided that he had been offered a job as dean of the graduate faculty at New York University. He asked our advice, remarking that if he stayed at LIU he could pretty well count on being named president. "Better to be a big fish in a small pond than a small fish in a big pond," I advised him. "Stay where you are." He chose not to take my advice, took the NYU offer, and two years later, to our delight and surprise, he was named president of NYU. So much for my record as career counselor to friends. Jim went on to have a distinguished career and acquitted himself well during the student riots at NYU in the sixties, at a time when students were similarly demonstrating on other U.S. campuses. This was the same period during which Barbara, returning to school, earned her master's degree in education at NYU.

In 1958, when I was thirty-two, the U.S. Junior Chamber of Commerce, or Jaycees, elected me one of the Ten Outstanding Young Men of the Year. Other recipients that year included Henry Kissinger, then thirty-five and a Harvard professor, and singer Pat Boone. I accepted their TOYM Award at a Fort Lauderdale, Florida, ceremony that was broadcast over a local radio station that reached much of South Florida. In the course of my acceptance remarks, I intended to say the award was evidence that to get ahead in America, you didn't have to marry the boss's daughter. In a slip of the tongue that went out over the airwaves, I said it proved you didn't have to marry the boss's wife.

The only other equally embarrassing slip of the tongue that I can recall came about twenty-five years later when, as CEO of Dow Jones, I took our board of directors to visit a Quebec newsprint mill we partially owned at Rivière du Loup, on the St. Lawrence River. En route, we stopped overnight at Quebec City and hosted a dinner for local business and political luminaries at the stately Château Frontenac hotel. Thinking it would be a nice gesture if I welcomed our French-Canadian guests in French, I had a French-speaking member of our staff write out in French a translation of brief remarks I had prepared in English. Standing up at the start of the dinner, I said, "On behalf of Dow Jones, I am delighted to welcome you and your spouses this evening." However, I mispronounced the French word for *spouses*, it came out sounding like another, very similar word in French, and what the audience heard was my delight at welcoming "you and your whores." The silence in the audience turned into the sound of a hundred breaths being sucked in simultaneously in shock.

In the New York office in 1958, we had a celebrity summer intern: the young Winston Churchill, grandson of Britain's wartime prime minister and son of the latter's son Randolph. Oliver Gingold, an Englishman who was actress Hermione Gingold's cousin and who for years had written the *Journal*'s daily stock-market commentary, the Abreast of the Market column, had been approached by a Churchill family friend and had arranged the summer job for young Churchill, then fresh from university. Young Winston was handsome, fair-haired, and charming as he modestly helped out on the copydesk and bustled about doing minor newsroom chores. Fifty years later, after he had prospered as a journalist himself, when he was not serving in Parliament, we met a couple of times at Florida dinner parties and briefly reminisced. His reaction when reminded that I had been managing editor the summer of his *Journal* internship: "My God, you must be old."

As the sixties began, Barbara and I decided to buy a new home, perhaps anticipating enlargement of our family. We made an offer on a roomy apartment in a small co-op apartment building with a striking view overlooking the harbor and downtown Manhattan, on a street, Columbia Heights, not far from our place on Middagh Street. The offer was accepted by the apartment's owner. It then went to the building's board for approval—and the sale was rejected, or rather we as buyers were rejected. The real estate agent said someone on the board had looked me up in Who's Who, saw from my father's first name and my mother's maiden name that I was Jewish, and that ended that. It was personally very hurtful. We soon after bought a house at 257 Hicks Street, also in Brooklyn Heights, opposite historic Grace Church. It was a brownstone but was painted a distinctive robin's-egg blue. It was while living there, in 1962, that our third daughter, Nina, was born. Our girls spent much of their growing-up years in that house.

I was fortunate in not having to confront anti-Semitism at work, with only a couple of minor exceptions. Barney Kilgore, Bill Kerby, and my other bosses and colleagues never exhibited any signs of prejudice. They always were gracious and generous in their relations with me, for which I was grateful. When I first returned to New York as managing editor, and to the morning kaffeeklatsch, Barney invited me to join him and his sidekicks for their almost-daily lunches at a cafeteria a few doors south on New Street, the narrow street that ran behind our building. In the group besides Barney and Bill Kerby, his deputy, were Barney's Indiana college pals, the so-called DePauw University mafia. They included Bob Bottorff, now executive editor; Buren McCormack, Bottorff's predecessor in that post and now a vice president; Bob Feemster, who oversaw all advertising sales, circulation sales, and promotion; and Ted Callis, Feemster's deputy and advertising manager.

Feemster was brilliant in positioning the *Journal* as a national newspaper with a high-demographic readership, and he was responsible for much of its success as he built circulation and advertising ever higher in those years. He ran such successful come-on ads as: "I Was Tired of 'Living on Peanuts' So I Started Reading *The Wall Street Journal*." In twenty years his efforts had helped circulation grow nineteenfold, from 32,000 in 1940 to 635,000 by 1959, making the *Journal* the fastest-growing daily in the United States. But Feemster was not as attractive personally as he was successful professionally. He affected Stetson ten-gallon cowboy hats. To enhance his ego and prestige, Barney had added to his sales titles "chairman of the Executive Committee"—though the Executive Committee never met and existed in name only at that time. Feemster traveled the country introducing himself as Dow Jones's chairman, an implication that he was the top man. Barney just chuckled over that and let it pass.

One day, in the cafeteria line at lunchtime, I overheard Feemster utter an anti-Semitic slur. It was not directed at me, but I nonetheless found it offensive. After that, I found excuses to absent myself from the lunch gatherings.

The only other exception to the bigotry-free atmosphere I found at Dow Jones came in the person of Bob Bottorff's wife, Ande. One night at dinner at their New Jersey home she asked me what business my father had been in, was told he had been a clothing manufacturer, and responded: "That's a good business." It was the exaggerated, mock Jewish accent with which she delivered these words, probably unthinkingly, that delivered, to me, the message about the attitude behind the mimicry.

On March 15, 1958, Barney took me as his guest to my first Gridiron Club dinner, in Washington. It was a club whose members all were Washington-based newspaper correspondents. Leading Washington political figures and CEOs and celebrities from around the country were the invited guests of members at these annual dinners, at which skits satirized the powerful. Three of the latter—one a spokesman for the Democrats, another a spokesman for the Republicans, and the third the president or his representative—traditionally delivered witty commentaries on themselves and their opponents. Gridiron membership and invitations were much sought after then, and they still are. The Gridiron limited its membership, all male and all print media in those days, to the leading Washington correspondents, a fraction of the total Washington press corps. Barney had been elected to membership when he was the *Journal*'s Washington Bureau chief. A later bureau chief, Al Hunt, eventually became president of the club. I attended many annual Gridiron dinners as his guest over the years.

President Eisenhower was not present at the 1958 dinner. Vice President Nixon spoke in his place. John F. Kennedy, then a senator, was the Democratic spokesman that year, while Attorney General William Rogers spoke for the GOP. Kennedy, eyeing the nomination for 1960, held up what purported to be a telegram from his father, Joe Kennedy, and said: "I have just received the following wire from my generous daddy: 'Dear Jack, Don't buy a single vote more than is necessary. I'll be damned if I'm going to pay for a landslide.'" Kennedy went on to say he had a dream that God had anointed him to be president. He said he told this to two of his rivals for the 1960 nomination. He said Senator Stuart Symington responded that he, too, had had a dream that God had anointed him to be president. And then-Senator Lyndon Johnson said: "That's funny. I, too, had a dream, but I don't remember anointing anyone."

My most vivid memory of that evening was Barney later that night, in one of the newspapers' hospitality suites at the hotel, sitting at a piano, happily banging out tunes, his old pal from their Washington days together, Turner Catledge, then executive editor of the *New York Times*, at his side. A crowd, glasses in hand, pressed around the piano, singing along with them. Barney's trademark nervous facial twitch was nowhere in evidence that night.

In the summer months, when his family was away at their vacation cottage at Twin Lakes, Pennsylvania, and he was spending the night at his office suite on the ninth floor of our *Journal* building in Manhattan, Barney would occasionally drop by my desk at deadline time, or after the first edition had gone to press, much as I had seen him do at the copydesk years earlier when I was working there for Sam Lesch. Once, when he suggested going out to dinner together, I took him to Jack Bleeck's Artists and Writers, the *Herald Tribune* hangout I knew on West Fortieth Street. He also graciously invited Barbara and me to dinner with others at the Kilgore family's old home in Princeton and, later, when they moved to grander quarters on Pretty Brook Road, to dinner there, too. I recall him showing us the fruits of the rock-cutting-and-polishing equipment he was using to develop a hobby he could share with his children, Jim, Jack, and Kathryn.

Barney was intrigued by the new popularity of corporate aviation and the possibilities this offered for him and other executives to visit their far-flung offices and printing plants more frequently and with less personal wear and tear. He arranged for Dow Jones to buy a Grumman Gulfstream G-1, a twin turboprop plane, and later added to it a G-2 jet and then a helicopter. In those early days, I sometimes used the G-1 to visit our West Coast offices and other bureaus with Joe Evans or others, if the plane was not in use by Barney or other higher-ranking executives.

In New York, when I dropped out of the executive group lunches at the cafeteria, I began lunching several times a week with Evans, then an editorial writer, at Eberlin's, a restaurant across New Street from our back door. Eberlin's was always jam-packed and noisy, its many longtime waiters reputed to be stockholders in the restaurant, and certainly in their abrupt service acting as if they owned the place. But the food was good, the portions generous, and, unlike some other people at the *Journal,* I liked Eberlin's and enjoyed eating there often.

Joe and I had earlier developed a close friendship, sharing confidences both professional and personal. Our families became close also. We spent some idyllic summer vacation time together on the shore of the Chesapeake Bay in rented cottages at Smith Beach, a few miles north of Barbara's hometown of Cape Charles, Virginia. The bayside beach there on the Eastern Shore was sandy and shallow, sloping gently into the bay and ideal for Marie and Joe Evans's young son and two daughters and Barbara's and my three young daughters. The clamming, crabbing, and boating were beautiful. Our cottages looked west over the Chesapeake Bay—one of the few places in the eastern United States where one could see the sun set into water.

When Joe and Marie later died prematurely—he in December 1971, at age fifty-two, of a heart attack, and she in 1979 of cancer—we felt their loss deeply. With no male friend since have I enjoyed such an open, intimate friendship. I have missed Joe over the years, as I have missed my father, and, subsequently, Bob Potter, Dow Jones's outside counsel and a director. In later years

Bob was both a wise counselor and close confidant, as well as a valued family friend, until he, too, died prematurely.

None of these male friends, however, prized as they were, could ever match the closeness of the friendship forged over the years with Barbara, who brought so much good judgment, good instincts and insights, penetrating appraisals of people, intelligence, and common sense to our conversations. In addition to those qualities, or because of them, she brought the perspectives of the professional editor she is.

CHAPTER **14**

Reporters, Readers, and the Pursuit of Trust

HAROLD EVANS, the respected former editor of the *Sunday Times* and *The Times* of London and then president and publisher of Random House, once said: "Readers trust their bodies to their doctors, their children to their teachers, but they open their morning newspaper like a virgin entering the sergeant's mess."

Polls abound showing widespread distrust of the press. Overcoming that and earning reader trust is a never-ending battle. We took pride in a Harris Poll in August 1969 that found *The Wall Street Journal* was the most trusted newspaper in America. Even so, there always were readers, as well as people we had written about, who complained we had been inaccurate or unfair or biased in our reporting. Sometimes they were right. Other times, their complaints reflected their own prejudices and perspectives, and truth lay in the eye of the beholder.

We began the fight for reader trust by trying to hire, train, and retain reporters of skill and integrity, then having not one but several layers of editors scrutinize their work and that of fellow editors. Some of our reporters were hired regionally by local bureau chiefs, but most job candidates wound up being interviewed by me while I was managing editor. In addition to examining their résumés and clippings, I often asked new college graduates about their grades, thinking it might be one indicator of intelligence— realizing it was only one among many, and imperfect at that. I also asked questions such as: Why do you want to work at the *Journal*? What would you like to be doing in five or ten years? Do you have any questions we can answer for you?

I was taking in the quality of their replies, probing for what that might reflect about the quality of their minds and also the extent to which they had done their homework. The latter, by indicating how much preinterview research they had done about the *Journal*, might shed light on their potential as good reporters.

After Al Hunt had become Washington Bureau chief in 1983 and a frequent panelist on CNN's *Capital Gang* and other TV shows, he recalled on several occasions the time I interviewed him in 1965, fresh out of Wake Forest University in Winston-Salem, North Carolina, for an entry-level reporting job on the New York staff. I had asked him about his college grades, he recalled, and with sinking heart he said he had received a C in economics. He felt that disclosure ended his chances for a job, and he was surprised when I hired him anyway. Al obviously had been impressive in other ways—and he continued later to impress generation after generation of government bigwigs as one of the most knowledgeable and perceptive reporters in Washington, a model also for generations of Washington reporters to aspire to emulate.

Among other impressive young interviewees was R. W. "Johnny" Apple, about to graduate from Princeton and destined years later to be the *New York Times*'s high-profile Vietnam correspondent, Washington Bureau chief, and finally roving reporter on global food, wine, and restaurant discoveries. I have the dubious distinction of having had to fire Johnny from the *Journal* staff—and certainly not because his talents and bright promise went unrecognized. He stood out as an exceptional reporter and writer from the start. Our New York reporters worked nine to five at the time, reflecting the workday of the businesses they covered and the 5:30 copy deadline for the first edition. The deadline was earlier than most papers' because of the need, at our regional printing plants, to accommodate postal-truck schedules for national distribution. Day after day Johnny's colleagues at neighboring desks had to cover for him until he finally drifted in around eleven, at which point he would regale all within earshot with tales of his exploits the previous evening on the New York nightlife circuit and with the details of how he got laid the night before.

I had many heart-to-heart talks with him about how he was imposing on his colleagues, forcing them to take his phone calls and cover stories on his beat until he showed up, and how it was untenable for me to allow the precedent of chronic late arrival for one reporter, no matter how talented, while others on the staff chafed at not being accorded the same privileges. Johnny promised again and again to reform, but he never could, and I issued many more "final warnings" than I would have for anyone else who was less talented and less of an asset we truly wanted to keep. Finally, as Johnny prepared for navy service, I told him: "I'm going to suspend you, not fire you as I had threatened. You go into the navy. Maybe you'll mature and develop more self-discipline there. When you finish your navy service, your job will be waiting for you if you want to return." Two years later, his navy service completed, he did return, avowing he was a new man. But the story soon repeated itself, and after another round of "final warnings," I let him go. He took a job at NBC News, then went to the *Times*—where I presumed their much later deadlines permitted a later start of the working day that meshed more felicitously with Johnny's needs. (I heard in later years that Johnny's version of these events differed from mine. The *Journal* newsroom reminded him of working in an insurance company office and he quit, he allegedly said. But my memory is crystal clear.)

Once, after I had become publisher, years after I had been managing editor, I was strolling through the newsroom and stopped to chat at the desk of Steve Swartz, then a young new reporter. I had not been the one who interviewed and hired him, but I asked him then that question about what he would like to be doing ten years from now. "Your job," he replied without hesitation, looking me in the eye. I admired his guts, answering like that, and thought, "Good for you." Steve later became editor and publisher of *Smart Money*, a magazine Dow Jones and the Hearst Corp. owned jointly. He subsequently rose to be Hearst's chief operating officer, after supervising its newspapers.

We used a variety of techniques to train new reporters in the *Journal*'s methods and standards. At the start, they often were paired, in a buddy system, with more experienced reporters, who were charged with teaching and counseling them. In March 1961 I wrote and distributed a "Guide to *The Wall Street Journal* for New Members of the News Staff." Besides giving background on the paper's history and philosophy, its ethical and accuracy standards, and the demographics of its readers, it most importantly contained instruction on the *Journal*'s reporting and writing techniques from Lindley Clark, the page one editor, Lindley's predecessor Jack Bridge, national news editor Sam Lesch, and others.

In addition, the copydesk editors and the page-one desk editors were charged with trying to teach reporters how to improve their reporting and writing, in the course of correcting flaws in their copy. Most younger reporters were more receptive to this help than some of the old-timers, who tended occasionally to resent copy editors' changing their stories for reasons and in ways they didn't always agree were necessary. Hence the age-old reporters' insult: "Every copy editor should have a pimp as a brother—so he'd have somebody he could look up to."

Norman Isaacs, former editor of the *Louisville Courier-Journal,* who became a good friend and was a credit to his profession, wrote a 1986 book, *Untended Gates,* about journalistic shortcomings. He opens the first chapter with the story of Jim Detjen, who had worked for a midstate New York newspaper, had had an environmental series of his considered as a finalist for a 1978 Pulitzer Prize, but had quit his reporting job at the paper at age twenty-nine to attend the Columbia University Graduate School of Journalism. "Every time there was a protest call [at the paper he had left]," Detjen was quoted as saying when asked why he had quit, "whoever was on the city desk would take it. The call might have something to do with a fouled-up obit, or a wrong date for a meeting, or a totally warped quote. The city editor or his assistant would cup a hand over the mouthpiece of the telephone, turn and shout so everybody could hear, 'I've got a crazy on the line.' No matter what the goof-up, the caller was always 'a crazy.'"

This was not our mind-set at the *Journal*. There was, and doubt-less still is, a reflexive action by some newspaper editors, hope-fully not many, to stand by a story almost automatically, even if a complaint might have merit, to protect and demonstrate loyalty and support for the reporting staff and, not incidentally, pro-tect the editor's own relationship with his reporters. We were not always immune from this failing over the years. But we worked hard at avoiding reflexive defensiveness. We were committed to investigating every complaint seriously, and then to doing the right thing if we were found to be in the wrong.

Despite all the effort that went into training reporters and editors and into trying to maintain the highest standards, the daily flow of complaints and our follow-up investigation of them showed we sometimes slipped. If the truth be told, though, one would think we slipped much more frequently if one took at face value the sheer volume of complaints that poured into the office. Errors of fact, when investigation showed a complaint of inaccu-racy was justified, were dealt with in a daily corrections column to set the record straight, and once in a while in a retraction story if the sin was of sufficient magnitude. Less clear-cut were some of the charges of unfairness, or even bias, that we examined. The complainant's sense of injury was rarely assuaged even when, after careful reexamination, we concluded the story in question had indeed been fair and accurate.

I recall the chairman of Southern Company, a large Atlanta-based electric-utility holding company, coming in to see me, incensed about something we had written about his company. His temper rising when I told him we had gone back over the story and double-checked it after learning of his displeasure, and we stood by the story, he hissed "You lack manhood" as I escorted him to the elevator. In another incident, Andrew Heiskell, then publisher of *Fortune*, phoned to tell me he was "outraged" by our story on *Fortune*'s labor negotiations, which he felt echoed the union position. And Dick Fisher, a friend and neighbor from Brooklyn Heights, later to become chairman and CEO of Mor-gan Stanley, phoned and reached me while I was traveling to say his boss, the Morgan Stanley CEO at that time, had asked him to let me know that a story of ours that day about a trading scandal at Morgan Stanley had carried a headline that he thought impugned the firm's integrity and reputation, and that they were enormously upset and resentful.

One of the most bitter, long-lasting fracases occurred years later, however, after I had left the newsroom and was publisher of the *Journal* and CEO of Dow Jones, its parent company. It involved Mobil, the global oil company, and what we perceived to be conflicts of interest there. The *Journal* published a front-page leader detailing how oil-shipping contracts had been awarded to a tanker company partly owned by the son of William P. Tavoulareas, Mobil's president. Later, we ran another story about Mobil purchasing real estate in Chicago from a real estate company affiliated with the son of Rawleigh Warner, Mobil's chairman and chief executive. Mobil pulled all its advertising out of the *Journal*—it was substantial and lucrative—when we saw no reason to back down. It also embargoed any press releases that normally would have gone to our paper, right down to earnings and dividend reports, and forbade any Mobil officials from talking to *Journal* reporters. We stood our ground and they stood theirs, never resuming their advertising while I was there.

It so happened that Jim Riordan, vice chairman of Mobil, a friend, and at one time in his youth a pitcher for a Brooklyn Dodgers farm team, was a Dow Jones director at that time. I was sure he would feel obliged to resign from our board, because I imagined his Mobil colleagues questioning why he stayed on and perhaps questioning his loyalty as well. But to my surprise and delight, Jim remained on our board as the intercompany warfare dragged on. He and I avoided bringing up the controversy. But early one morning preceding a Dow Jones board meeting, it came up at a meeting of the board's Executive Committee. A front-page profile of Mobil President Tavoulareas was in the *Journal* that morning. It recounted, among other things, that he was a diamond in the rough, a street-smart guy who had worked his way up from a tough Brooklyn neighborhood, and that he was prone to pepper his speech with salty language, including obscenities.

Bill Agee, chairman of appliance maker Bendix Corp. and a Dow Jones director at the time, called to Riordan across the table, as I looked on uncomfortably: "Jim, what did you think about the story on Tav in this morning's *Journal*?" Riordan snapped back: "Any story that implies that foul language is used around Mobil is a f*cking outrage."

Jim's wit complemented a keen intelligence. He was as savvy a director as any on our board. And the reach of his retentive memory was nothing short of phenomenal.

Another battle that erupted, also long after I had left the newsroom and was publisher of the paper, similarly involved charges of bias and our alleged intransigence in refusing to acknowledge that. The government of Malaysia took umbrage at our Asian edition's coverage of the resentment the country's Muslim majority felt toward the Chinese minority's strong economic influence and disparity of wealth, and the political jockeying related to that. Longtime Prime Minister Mahathir bin Mohammed and his ministers charged repeatedly that, by reporting this, we were trying to foment racial unrest in their country. For weeks and months at a time, they would delay our papers at customs for several days, until the news in them was stale, sometimes releasing the paper only after censors had cut out what they regarded as offensive stories or editorials.

At one point, Maurice "Hank" Greenberg, chairman of the American Insurance Group (AIG), with operations and influence in countries throughout Asia and elsewhere, approached me and suggested he thought he could broker a settlement of this long-running confrontation. He suggested that he arrange a meeting between Mahathir and me in the prime minister's Waldorf-Astoria Hotel suite when Mahathir was in New York for a United Nations General Assembly meeting. I was not optimistic but agreed to the meeting, wanting to leave no stone unturned.

In Mahathir's suite, Greenberg proposed, with the prime minister assenting, that we replace our correspondent in Malaysia's capital, Kuala Lumpur, and that we then let bygones be bygones and start with a fresh slate. I said we could not do that. "You didn't like the coverage of our last correspondent and you probably won't like the coverage of our next one," I told Mahathir as respectfully as I could, "since their job is to report on what is going on in your country, not ignore what is troublesome. And besides," I explained, "I could not live with the precedent of replacing a reporter on a beat whenever the leader of a company or a country became displeased with his coverage. I would soon be replacing our Houston Bureau chief every time an oil company was angered, and our Chicago Bureau chief every time a banker there was displeased by our coverage and wanted to see if it would get more sympathetic if we put a new reporter on the beat."

"I can't do business with this man," Mahathir said to Greenberg. He arose and walked out of the room and the meeting was over. Later, demagoguing the issue in a public speech to a rally of members of his Muslim majority base, he charged that those running the *Asian Wall Street Journal*, presumably meaning its editor and publisher but also including me, were "agents of the Mossad," the Israeli intelligence service.

I was confident we were on the side of right and truth in the Mobil and Malaysian disputes. I found more troubling, ironically, questions that arose in my mind but were never raised by readers about certain nuanced elements or implications within other stories, stories that won much public praise. One story was about an American company whose Latin American operations were accused of bribery and the exploitation of local workers. The CEO, a devout man who was schooled as a theologian, leaped to his death from his office high in a New York skyscraper. The clear implication was that inner conflict with his moral upbringing brought pangs of conscience and guilt, and this resulted in his taking his own life. I hoped the reporter and editors had checked whether he had any previous history of clinical depression. That could have led to suicidal thoughts, unconnected to his troubles at work, something that is common among depressives and even more so in those days when antidepressant medications were not in wide use.

Another story examined a company's labor practices, particularly its recent large-scale layoffs. A laid-off worker's suicide was cited as evidence of the human toll. I wondered if anyone had looked into whether the number of suicides per thousand among the company's discharged personnel did or did not exceed the suicide rate in the general population.

If earning readers' trust was a difficult, never-ending goal, satisfying ourselves that we had done our very best to be fair and accurate was often more difficult and equally endless.

CHAPTER **15**

The Early Sixties

OUR FAMILY WAS GROWING at 257 Hicks Street in Brooklyn, and the *Journal* was growing across the East River. Nina was born on September 11, 1962, at Long Island College Hospital, in Brooklyn. Barbara survived a serious blood clot in her calf following the birth; it was called deep-seated phlebitis. Lisa and Leslie were attending Packer Collegiate Institute, then a private all-girls elementary and high school about three blocks east of our brownstone.

Our daughters' birthday parties, if not in the small garden behind our house, were in a restaurant in Chinatown or aboard the ferry to the Statue of Liberty. We shepherded their friends to these places, a cohort of tiny tots. Barbara and I made Brooklyn Heights friends, with children the same ages as ours, and we remained close to several of them and their children all our lives. Among them were GeeGee and Hamish Maxwell, he rising to the chairmanship of Philip Morris; Gloria and Jim Riordan, he with Mobil; Sara and Seth Faison, he an officer of Johnson & Higgins, insurance brokers; Claire and Tom Peacock, who split up but remained friends with each other as well as with us; Nancy and Otis Pearsall; Carol and Ted Reid, he a lawyer, as were Tom and Otis; Connie and Donald Reich, he on his way to becoming chairman of Airco, a supplier of oxygen and industrial gases; and Nina and Jason Bacon, our tenants in an apartment on the ground floor of our house, who subsequently went on to live their working lives in London, he as head of European operations for Kidder Peabody, a once-proud investment firm. Those Brooklyn years were not ones in which two-career families were common.

Neither Barbara nor I observed the rituals of the organized religions in which we had been brought up. But we thought our children should have the opportunity to have a religious identity. We chose the First Unitarian Church of Brooklyn, attracted by its willingness to let congregants find and worship God in their own ways and attracted, too, by our fondness for its minister, Don McKinney, and his Dutch-born wife, Julie. While our daughters attended Sunday school there, Barbara and I would listen to Don's sermons in the high-ceilinged nineteenth-century church. I would squirm in the pew with impatience at some of Don's sermons on the Vietnam War, chafing at the thought that he had a captive audience who could not easily argue back. As the years passed, our church attendance waned to the vanishing point, but our affection and respect for the McKinneys endured for a lifetime, our friendship never waning.

We had a succession of au pair girls from Europe to help with the children, particularly after Barbara enrolled at NYU later in the sixties for her master's degree in education and then began teaching high school English at Packer. The first au pair, Sadie, was a thin wisp of a girl from Ireland; after a couple of years, she fell in love with a doctor who treated her at Long Island College Hospital and, depressed when he did not return her love, she ran away one night in the wee hours; she later married a New York City police officer. Her successor, Elke, was blond, buxom, and German. Barbara picked her up at the pier when she arrived by boat. She immediately informed Barbara, on the drive home, that she had to leave her last job, in England, because the husband kept chasing her around the dining room table—and she hoped she would not encounter that at our house. Elke accompanied us to Smith Beach, in Virginia, in the summertime. She always looked bored, taking care of children. Eventually she left to take a job she described as a hostess for a company that arranged trade shows. We learned long after she left that she introduced the children to cigarettes.

Across the river in Manhattan, Dow Jones in early 1965 moved its headquarters to expanded space at 30 Broad Street. The *Journal* at that time was selling for ten cents a copy, and the paper was averaging twenty-six pages. But circulation was on its way to exceed one million in 1967, second largest in the country behind only the tabloid *New York Daily News*. Barney, Bill Kerby, and their colleagues had opened a new regional printing plant at Chicopee, Massachusetts, and printing for the New York distribution had been transferred there, later to be switched to another new plant at South Brunswick, New Jersey, just outside Princeton. In this way production of the paper was removed from the control of New York City's difficult typographical and pressmen's unions. The *Journal* thus escaped the strife and strikes that paralyzed other New York newspapers at times in the sixties, and which contributed to the deaths of some.

In our expanded quarters, my managing editor's desk and the page-one department were moved from the southeast corner of the newsroom, where I overlooked Broad Street, to the southwest corner, where I overlooked New Street and Eberlin's restaurant. For the first time, I was ensconced in a private office, separated from the rest of the still-open newsroom by head-high glass partitions that offered privacy for conversations combined with clear visibility in both directions. Bottorff moved his executive editor desk upstairs to a ninth-story executive floor. And the morning kaffeeklatsch, with Barney in attendance, moved to a new, elegant conference room in a corner of the news floor, a room that could double as a dining room and permitted us to entertain guests at editorial lunches.

In 1960, a member of the *Journal* staff, Ed Cony, won the *Journal*'s first Pulitzer Prize for news reporting, the first of three to be won in the next five years. It was awarded "for revealing questionable intercompany dealings which forced Carrol Shanks's resignation as Prudential Insurance Co. of America's president and, further, set off a general public reappraisal of business ethics."

I continued to visit the European bureaus periodically, traveling more swiftly by commercial jet airliners now, forgoing the slower but more enjoyable and luxurious ship crossings of earlier years. Barbara and I were en route to London on one such trip in November 1963 when, over the mid-Atlantic, the pilot announced to his stunned passengers that President Kennedy had been assassinated in Dallas. When we landed, our old Chicago colleague Ray Vicker, now London Bureau chief, was waiting at the disembarkation gate with return tickets on the next flight to New York. He had anticipated our desire to get back home as quickly as possible. We turned around and, without leaving the airport, boarded another plane and flew back across the ocean, eager to help as the Washington Bureau and others filed postassassination stories for the paper.

It was the end of another era, an era of hope to be followed by a time of violence, widespread disillusionment, and cynicism. It was a psychological and cultural watershed in the nation's history. It was the end of many of my generation's convictions that our country could do no wrong, a notion nurtured in our elementary and high school civics classes and carried into adult life. This era was to be followed by a reexamination of our society and its history. This encouraged the rise of investigative journalism and increased emphasis on laying bare the sins of our society and its business and political components.

After President Kennedy's assassination came those of Martin Luther King and Bobby Kennedy, civil rights riots, escalation of the war in Vietnam, and then Watergate. These events, as we shall see, were reflected not only in the pages of the nation's newspapers but also in protests—on campuses, in city streets, and even in our newsroom.

While I was managing editor, officials of the Central Intelligence Agency called on me several times, seeking cooperation and participation in their cold war combat against the Soviets.

They asked, for example, that they be allowed to use the *Journal* as a "cover" for one of their agents, to place a covert agent on our foreign news staff. He would be professionally competent, they assured me, writing publishable stories and functioning outwardly like any other correspondent—but he would perform certain other CIA functions on the side. At other times, they asked to interview our correspondents returning from trips through Eastern Europe. Or to give correspondents embarking on trips there certain questions to insert into their interviews with government officials, or a list of certain things they were interested in a reporter observing should these things be visible from train windows or in travels to various cities. In return, they promised to feed us story tips or information that we might find helpful in our story coverage.

I declined this type of involvement, and not without a touch of regret. The cold war was a serious, dangerous conflict between our country and the Soviets. They had obtained the secrets for making atom bombs from American and British spies. They were extending their influence, through subversion and other tactics, in Africa, the Middle East, Cuba, and elsewhere. I respected what the CIA was doing on the front line of this battle and the necessity for countering the enemy's subversion and intelligence-gathering methods with similar undercover methods, meeting fire with fire. In those days, subsequent failings of the CIA at the Bay of Pigs, at assessing the so-called missile gap or Soviet armed strength, or at preventing the World Trade Center attacks had not provoked the condemnation of the agency so prevalent today. I certainly had no reason to condemn the CIA when its officials sought help and cooperation.

I rejected their overtures for completely different reasons of conscience and practicality. I told them that I believed the CIA and all other intelligence agencies probably had been penetrated by KGB agents, or moles. If the Soviets learned, as I felt they would, that even a single CIA agent operated under *Wall Street Journal* cover, and that not all *Journal* correspondents traveling in their orbit were reporters and nothing more than reporters, as we represented them to be, then I would be placing any and all *Journal* correspondents traveling in Eastern Europe in jeopardy. This I was not prepared to do.

The *Journal*'s editorial page was being run from 1958 to 1971 by Vermont Royster, a World War II navy lieutenant commander and former *Journal* Washington Bureau chief. He had been brought up from Washington by Grimes in 1948 as an associate editor, to write editorials. When Grimes retired in 1958, Royster succeeded him as editor. He was known as Roy. His full name was Vermont Connecticut Royster. He came from a Raleigh, North Carolina, family that was partial to naming its children after states. His relatives included Arkansas Delaware Royster (a great-uncle), Georgia Indiana Royster (a great-aunt), Iowa Michigan Royster (a great-uncle), Virginia Carolina Royster (a great-aunt), Wisconsin Illinois Royster (a great-uncle), and another Vermont Connecticut Royster (a grandfather for whom Roy was named).

Roy had had a fine classical education, including both Latin and Greek. He was smart. And, oh, how he could write. His writing was classy—beautiful, eloquent, concise, precise. He was a star, and deservedly so. He won a Pulitzer Prize in 1953 for editorial writing, and another in 1984 for commentary after he retired but continued his column, Thinking Things Over. Roy and I were good friends. He was five feet six inches tall. He could be prickly, combative, some thought arrogant at times, certainly irreverent. But I liked and admired him. He sometimes didn't try to dissuade outsiders from thinking his editor title conveyed authority over the *Journal*'s news operations as well as its editorial page, but the fact is that the latter was where his authority began and ended. His influence, though, was nationwide in scope, by virtue of the power of his pen.

Barney recognized Roy's talents, virtues, and value—and also his quirks and ambition. Roy remembered Barney saying, when he promoted him to chief of the Washington Bureau in 1946, "Now maybe the britches will be big enough for you." Soon after we moved into 30 Broad Street, we were sitting around the table in the new dining room one day, having the ritual morning coffee, when Barney made an observation about some political development. Roy strongly disagreed, then Barney persisted and pressed his opinion. "I can't argue with ignorance," said Roy as he stood up and stalked out of the room. The rest of us sat there dumbfounded. "Aren't you mad?" someone finally asked Barney. "I'm the only one around here who can't afford to get mad at anyone," Barney replied, smiling. (I subsequently heard that Roy had come around later that day and apologized.)

Many years later, I recalled Barney's willingness to turn the other cheek to retain star talent. After I became CEO, we had a younger executive, Bill Dunn, who was instrumental in advancing Dow Jones's technology and bringing the company into the electronic age. His irreverence sometimes bordered on the insubordinate. One day I asked him why he never took his annual bonus in cash but always banked it into a deferred-compensation fund. "That's my f*ck-you money," he responded. Eventually he did quit, after he was not chosen as my successor.

Royster's sharp, sardonic tongue was usually unleashed more as biting wit than was the case the morning he left the coffee table in a huff after failing to bring Barney around to his viewpoint. In the 1970s, after we had bought Richard D. Irwin Inc., a book publisher located just outside Chicago, we scheduled a board meeting there. As we toured the directors through the plant, Roy spotted galley proofs of Bill Kerby's memoirs, which the Irwin company was publishing. Roy picked up a galley, glanced at it, then said to Kerby, in front of the assembled directors: "Bill, I didn't know you wrote fiction." Another time, I had just returned from a vacation in London, where our family had exchanged homes for a few weeks with our friends and former tenants, Nina and Jason Bacon, then living in the British capital. I had grown a moustache on vacation as a lark, intending to shave it off soon after our return to New York. Roy took me to lunch at the Recess Club, a lunch club a few doors south of our office on Broad Street. I had not yet shaved off the moustache, and I was puzzled that Roy never mentioned it throughout the meal. After dessert, I asked him, "How come you haven't mentioned my moustache?" His reply: "If a man wants to make a fool of himself, that's his business." So I kept the moustache, to this day.

CHAPTER **16**

Storms and Other Not-So-Carefree Days at Sea

"The family that sails together drifts apart."
—BARBARA PHILLIPS, proposed bumper sticker

VERMONT ROYSTER AND I shared a love of boats. He had commanded navy ships. I helped him bring *Covenant,* a Hatteras motor yacht he had bought, from Providence, Rhode Island, where its previous owners turned it over to him, to an anchorage near New York City. It was a rough voyage: We came down Narragansett Bay in pea-soup fog, then through turbulent water and steep following seas in The Race, the famously tricky passage off Fishers Island, before entering the more protected waters of Long Island Sound. I preferred sailboats. Like skiing or flying, they offered the relative quiet, solitude, peace, and immersion in nature's beauty and wonders while alone, or almost so, and the soul-satisfying experience of harnessing natural forces and testing one's skills on one's own.

I bought a sailing dinghy from Paul Lancaster, one of the page one editors, and he gave me a couple of sessions of rudimentary sailing instruction while sailing it within the breakwater of the Stamford, Connecticut, harbor, near where he lived. I read a couple of books on the basics, then sailed the dinghy with one hand on the tiller, the other holding a small instruction manual. When our sailing ambitions outgrew the dinghy's potential, I purchased a secondhand Nomad, a twenty-one-foot fiberglass sloop with twin bilge boards, similar to centerboards but protruding from the port and starboard undersides of the hull. I named it the *Mitty*, after the fictitious character Walter Mitty, confident that it would similarly enable me to realize flights of imagination, fantasy, and adventure. The boat was docked, when I bought it, on the Sassafras River, near the head of the Chesapeake Bay on Maryland's Eastern Shore. For a couple of summers we would go there on weekends, motor the *Mitty* the two miles down the river into the northern waters of the bay, and sail it short distances in all directions. Though cramped, it had a propane gas stove and bunks to sleep two.

Then, one spring, I embarked on a voyage down the entire length of Chesapeake Bay, from the Sassafras River at its head to the mouth of the bay at Cape Charles, Virginia, Barbara's hometown and close by where the bay emptied into the Atlantic Ocean. I recruited friends and sailors or would-be sailors on the *Journal*'s staff, including Fred Taylor and Dan Cordtz, to join me as crew on different weekends as we did passages from port to port, docking the *Mitty* each Sunday night to get back to work and then returning to the boat on Friday night for the next weekend leg. The first leg of the journey was from the Sassafras River mouth southwest across the width of the bay to Gibson Island on the western shore, near the mouth of Baltimore Harbor. That crossing taught me two things. One was always, always be guided by the compass and the chart, never by eyeball navigation and confidence, ill-placed as it turned out, in one's own sense of direction. The second thing it taught me is that God sometimes protects fools from their own stupidity and inexperience.

As we headed southwest across the bay, I was certain I could make out the Baltimore Harbor entrance on the distant shore, and I steered for it. But as every sailor knows, distant offshore islands, mainland hills, and other aspects of topography can give a dangerously misleading impression of a shoreline, and one should always set the course by the compass. I was too green and dumb to do this, and after hours of sailing we found ourselves in the midst of fish nets fastened to a maze of poles planted in the bay bottom in shallow water. We were hopelessly off course. And we had lost precious daylight hours we could ill afford to. We took hours to sail back out into the bay and belatedly get back on course. By then it was late in the afternoon, the wind was rising, and darkness was fast overtaking us. As darkness fell and the now-large following seas lifted our little twenty-one-foot boat and sent it shooting forward, huge cargo ships and tankers suddenly began passing close by. We were in the Baltimore ship channel. I realized that a collision or a swamping by the big waves chasing us from astern were distinct possibilities. But, again stupidly, I did not ask my crewmate to don his life jacket and I did not put on mine, not wanting him to perceive fear or lack either of confidence or competence in his skipper. Eventually, we pulled into the quiet waters of Gibson Island's harbor and dropped anchor, way past the dinner hour and totally exhausted. Next morning we pushed on to Annapolis.

On subsequent weekends, I and one other companion sailed south to Solomon Island, at the mouth of the Patuxent River, then back across the bay to the Eastern Shore and Crisfield, Maryland, "crab capital of the world," where we tied up alongside Skipjacks and Bugeyes, the last of the bay's fleet of oystering working sailboats. We climbed ashore, walked into town, and feasted on, guess what, the world's most delicious crab dinner. On weekends after that it was on down through Pocomoke Sound and along the shore to Cape Charles, Virginia, where dock space awaited us for the summer.

On the stiflingly hot Fourth of July weekend in 1965, Barbara and I set sail, with little Lisa and Leslie on board, for a leisurely cruise up the bay. Baby Nina stayed in Cape Charles with Barbara's parents. When we were off Occohannock Creek, the wind died completely, the sails flapped lifelessly—and suddenly a jet-black squall line appeared, spreading across the northwest horizon and bearing down on us. The sky grew blacker than I had ever seen it before or since. Other boats passed us, racing for the shore and shelter. We tried and tried to start the *Mitty*'s outboard engine, but it had chosen that moment to die on us. So I lowered and secured the sails and dropped the anchor and let out plenty of line, figuring the boat would ride bow into the wind. And this time I did have everyone don life jackets.

The wind where we were was clocked at seventy-five miles an hour, the Norfolk papers reported next day. When the force of that wind hit us, roaring down on us with the sound of a runaway railroad train, it was too strong to permit me to struggle forward to check the anchor line. I stood in the companionway, my body in the cabin, only my head and shoulders outside the half-open hatch. Suddenly the boat was slammed over onto its side and I was hurled out into the churning water. The conventional wisdom is to stick with the boat in a capsize, but I could not possibly fight my way back upwind to the anchored boat. I saw it right itself, then get slammed down on its side again by the howling wind, then right itself, only to get slammed down again. Barbara, below with the two children and fearful they would be trapped if the cabin filled with water, brought them up on deck, where they were all immediately thrown into the water, too.

All I could see then was churning water and mist, cutting off visibility. "Like in the movies, the storm scenes in the movies," I recalled thinking about the unreality of it all. I could see no trace of Barbara and the girls in this maelstrom. I remember the dread of that moment, seeing no sign of them, as the worst moment of my life. Then I saw orange blobs in the distance, the life jackets, and I knew Barbara had the girls. I somehow got to them as we all were swept downwind. Barbara held onto one daughter; I held onto the other. Fortunately, the wind was blowing us toward the shore, not out farther into the bay. When we washed up ashore, pelted by large hailstones, cornfields were leveled and outdoor advertising signs and power lines were down, as were trees. We dragged ourselves over oyster shells and debris until we found a farmhouse, whose occupants wrapped us in blankets, gave us hot drinks, and called the Thomases in Cape Charles to come pick us up.

Next day we got a fifty-foot commercial fishing boat to return us to the site. The *Mitty*, still anchored in place, was floating bottom up, mast down under the boat. Enough flotation was built into it to keep the water inside its cabin from sinking it. The commercial fishermen dragged the upside-down boat into shallow water alongside the beach, pumped it out, and righted it, then towed it back to Cape Charles. My theory is that, even with sails down and anchor out, the boat swung just enough in the wind and the current to enable the full force of the wind to catch its freeboard, its side, and its rigging and drive it down into the water, where the cabin filled and the *Mitty* capsized. Perhaps if I had closed the companionway hatch tight, in an effort to make the cabin airtight and watertight, it might have stayed upright. We were fearful of being trapped in the closed cabin, and perhaps that was our mistake.

We trailered the *Mitty* back to Long Island and sailed it again, though despite ceaseless efforts we never got all the sand and oyster shell fragments cleaned out of all the boat's nooks and crannies. A year later, we bought a keel boat, a twenty-nine-foot Pearson Triton, the Chesapeake Bay experience having converted us to the increased stability and other virtues of sailing with a keel. The boat had berths for four. We named the new sloop the *Leilani*—its letters taken from the names Lisa, Leslie, and Nina.

It took a lot of spirit for Barbara and the girls to continue sailing after that experience, but they did, for many, many years afterward. Perhaps I owe that more to their love of me than to their love of sailing. Barbara always said sailing was 98 percent boredom and 2 percent sheer terror. Hence her proposed bumper sticker: "The family that sails together drifts apart." But I believe our family was brought closer together, even if not loving every minute of it, as we sailed the *Leilani* from its anchorages in the Mount Sinai and Port Jefferson, Long Island, harbors, near which we had successive summer cottages.

We cruised often to the Thimble Islands, in Long Island Sound off the Connecticut coast; sometimes up the Connecticut River to Essex and Hamburg Cove; other times through foggy, rock-strewn Fishers Island Sound to New London, Fishers Island, and Stonington, Connecticut; often through the turbulent waters of Plum Gut to Shelter Island and Montauk; and periodically to

Block Island and Newport, Cutty Hunk, and Martha's Vineyard; and on to Nantucket. Other times we did bare-boat charters, sailing Pearson 35s and Hinckleys ourselves off the coast of Maine and, in winter, through the British Virgin Islands, including Tortola, Peter Island, and Virgin Gorda.

On the *Leilani*, Barbara and I rode out the fierce tropical storm Doria in 1971 after making it into Newport Harbor from Nantucket, and on a later trip we managed to get through rough seas from Nantucket to Block Island Sound without the help of a crewman we had counted on. He was a Christian Scientist friend from Barbara's school, a fellow teacher at Packer, who was incapacitated by seasickness after saying his religion prohibited him from taking Dramamine, even though I said an exception should be made when it was necessary for "the safety of the vessel." But we never again had the mishaps we experienced on the *Mitty*. It was mostly smooth sailing after those close calls.

CHAPTER **17**

Executive Editor

THE YEAR 1965 ushered in a period of watershed changes at the *Journal* and Dow Jones, changes that were not all apparent at the time. There were changes for our family, too, and certainly for the nation as the Vietnam War heightened in intensity.

Barney Kilgore's restless mind and restless energy began to find new outlets, and in so doing he left the running of the *Journal* more and more to his longtime lieutenant, Bill Kerby. Barney had personally purchased the *Princeton Packet*, his hometown weekly newspaper, in 1955, and became engaged in his off hours in building it up. In 1962, he initiated and orchestrated Dow Jones's start-up of the weekly *National Observer*, in which he applied some of *The Wall Street Journal*'s techniques to giving perspective to "the business of living" and to the week's political, international, cultural, and other general news developments. In 1964, he retained a Princeton pal of his, Brad Mills, of New York Securities, an investment firm, to recommend a diversification strategy for Dow Jones. Mills's report was delivered in late 1965. The company at that time was dependent on the *Journal* for 94 percent of its earnings.

In our family, 1965 was the year my widowed mother remarried. Her new husband, Al Heller, was a widower himself, and a good-hearted, sweet man. In Virginia, Barbara's parents continued in good health, but on our visits there we would see them grow progressively more frail over the next ten years, with Barbara's mother, Kitty, losing her sight. Barbara's father, Herman Thomas, died October 10, 1975, and her mother soon after.

In May 1965 I was appointed executive editor of the *Journal* and of all other Dow Jones publications. These included *Barron's* magazine, the *National Observer*, the Dow Jones News Service, or ticker, and other publications we might start or acquire in the future. My pay for that year rose to $45,127. Bob Bottorff, one of Kilgore's close friends from DePauw days, was elected a vice president in early 1965 and, in January 1966, general manager. I succeeded him in the executive editor job and moved upstairs to an office on the executive floor. It was a natural transition at the *Journal* for a managing editor to move up into the executive editor's job when the latter came open, so my advancement by Kilgore and Kerby was part custom, part vote of confidence.

No one ever accused Bottorff of being soft and cuddly. He could be brusque and he was tough. But he always extended encouragement to me. He was available whenever, as managing editor, I sought advice, but he mostly left me alone, not burdening me with direction and instruction. Ed Cony, who was managing editor of the Pacific Coast Edition, was appointed, on my recommendation, to take my place as managing editor, and he moved from San Francisco into my old glassed-in office in the New York newsroom.

What we did not know at the time was that 1965 was the year Barney Kilgore was diagnosed, during the summer, with cancer. He was fifty-seven. He did not at first confide this news to anyone at work other than Bill Kerby. In the spring of 1966 Barney retired and Kerby, Barney's choice, was elected to succeed him as president and chief executive officer. Barney died at home on November 14, 1967.

Through other deaths and retirements, Barney's longtime colleagues in the DePauw crowd and from his Washington days also were gradually disappearing. Grimes had retired by 1958, Feemster in 1962, only to die less than a year later in a plane crash. Then Ted Callis, vice president for advertising, and Bob Bottorff both retired in 1970, Royster in 1971. Royster continued writing his column from Chapel Hill, North Carolina, however. Buren McCormack died of cancer in 1972. Except for Kerby, the Old Guard was soon almost gone. The torch was being passed.

I visited Barney at his Princeton home a few months before he died. I went alone. He was weak, obviously in the grip of a terminal illness. But his interest was still strong in knowing what was going on at the office, in the *Journal*'s News Department. That's what we talked about.

I had written an article about the *Journal*'s brand of journalism for the *ASNE Bulletin*, the publication of the American Society of Newspaper Editors. The piece, under the headline "How the *Journal*'s Fully Textured News Stories Get That Way," appeared in the October 1967 issue. It mentioned Kilgore's role in developing the reporting and writing approach that went into the paper's distinctive front-page leaders. He saw a copy of it. He dictated and sent a memo, with copies to Kerby, McCormack, Bottorff, Royster, and me, that said: "My chances these days of writing things for the paper, even for the file, are pretty limited, so I thought I'd send you a copy of this." He mentioned having seen a copy of the article I had written for the *ASNE Bulletin*, and then said:

> It was not an especially startling statement in any way, but it pleased me greatly to read something that I myself might have written twenty-five years or even longer ago. Insofar as my participation in making news policy is concerned, my role apparently is still meaningful, although it has been inactive in the sense of holding the highest news executive job at the paper, as Warren Phillips does today. It means to me that the staff must still understand quite clearly what we are trying to do even though we do not always succeed.
>
> What is *The Wall Street Journal* anyhow? The most significant thing to me about it is that it is a newspaper and not a trade paper. It has more to do with the *Pittsburgh Post-Gazette* than it does with *Iron Age*. It serves a community which is not

geographic, except in a national sense, but includes so many different fields and interests and shapes and sizes that its community behaves more like a city than it does any occupation or interest. . . .

A good many *Wall Street Journal* readers, even today, do not fully understand the basic nature of the publication. . . . In any event, it doesn't make any difference to them as long as it serves their purposes adequately, but the basic definition of any publication is of utmost importance to its editors. And, while it doesn't make a great deal of difference to anyone else, it makes a great deal of difference to me as to what Warren H. Phillips, executive editor, says even in what appears to be a rather casual or routine discussion of his purpose.

Bill Kerby, the new publisher and Dow Jones CEO, was not the visionary that Barney Kilgore was. None of us were. But he was good—a good executive, with all the right values and instincts, and a crackerjack newsman. He had been responsible, twenty-five years earlier, for getting out a memorably superb issue on the day of Pearl Harbor, looking forward to the industrial mobilization that would follow swiftly on the heels of the attack, transforming the national economy. And I had seen him in action in more recent years, and had watched admiringly as he hunched over his typewriter, banging out clear, clean, well-organized copy under deadline pressure. I respected his abilities and held affection for him as a person. He was a warm, generous guide, always fatherly with me.

Bill and Fanny Kerby and their two daughters lived in a stately old house only two doors from us in Brooklyn Heights, on the corner of Hicks Street and Grace Court Alley. We were friends as well as neighbors.

At that time, in the mid-1960s, Lisa and Leslie attended elementary school at the Packer Collegiate Institute in Brooklyn Heights. They shared their home, and other homes over the years, with a procession of their pets—dogs with names like Gyp and Beau (for Beauregard), cats with names like Dill, Inky, Daisy, and Augie, and hamsters whose names have faded from memory. My family, reflecting on that period in the 1960s and later, remembers me coming home to dinner dog-tired, often complaining of headaches, and sitting with them at the dinner table with a distracted look. I don't recall that, but I do know I brought a lot of office reading home—drafts of page-one leaders and various memos and other documents. And I was often on the phone to the office, including on weekends.

Even during the idyllic summer vacation days at our beachfront rented cottage at Smith Beach, near Cape Charles, I spent considerable time on the phone to the New York editors, discussing what was going onto the front page of the paper while I was away. The frequency of the phone calls, from there and elsewhere over the years, upset Barbara. They were symptomatic, she complained, with justification, of my mind being in the office twenty-four hours a day, even on vacation. Was I putting Dow Jones ahead of family? This struggle to balance work responsibilities and home life caused compromises and sacrifices that put long-lasting strains on our marriage. At one time we sought help from a marriage counselor to avoid irreparable damage to our relationship.

During one of the summer vacations when I often was on the phone to the office, in 1965, we were doing a story on local residents' opposition to New York's Verrazano Narrows Bridge, then under construction by a mostly Italian workforce. Jack Cooper was running the page-one desk while Lindley Clark, the page-one editor, was on vacation. When the paper containing that page-one leader arrived at Smith Beach by mail, I was appalled to read a paragraph that said local residents were calling the bridge "the guinea gangplank." Several layers of editors apparently had thought that an ethnic slur inside a quote was all right, as long as it was reported accurately, even if bigoted and hurtful. I told those editors that was not the case and left no doubt about how appalled and angry I was.

Slanderous comments or certain obscenities within a quote are not acceptable either. A friend of mine, Charlie Alexander, was fired from the editorship of the *Dayton* (Ohio) *Journal Herald* by its publisher, Dan Mahoney, in March 1975 after Alexander approved use of the f-word in a front-page story—because, he argued, it was inside a quote and was important, in his view, to conveying the essence of the story. Newspapers cannot abdicate their responsibility for harmful words that appear in their pages just because someone else said them.

The challenges in whipping the *Journal*'s front-page show-piece stories into shape, however, were not so much challenges of taste as challenges of reporting and writing, the challenges of getting their presentation, no matter how sound and thorough the reporting, to meet the standards of clarity and liveliness set for those features. Many accomplished reporters continued to have trouble presenting their material in a form that was up to the page-one standards. Other newspapers continued to have trouble trying to imitate those in-depth, magazine-quality pieces, until they hired away some of our staff members who had mastered the art. We could lay down the essential ingredients in our staff guide; we could encourage reporters to analyze how their stories were changed and why; our editors could point the way to improvement in conversation after conversation. But even so, many front-page stories still needed heavy editing or rewrite to bring them up to the standards we had set for those leaders.

Sterling E. "Jim" Soderlind, who as assistant managing editor oversaw the front page from 1966 to 1970, once said: "There is no such thing as bad writing. Only bad thinking." His point, of course, was that the reporter had to know, before sitting down to write, what the focus of the story would be, how he or she was going to document and illustrate his or her main points, and how the material was going to be organized.

The times were turbulent. Lyndon Johnson, having moved into the presidency after Kennedy's assassination, was expanding

American involvement in the Vietnam War. Protests were growing, too, and soon would reach a flash point with the riots in Chicago during the 1968 Democratic Party nominating convention there.

Ed Cony sent Peter Kann to cover the war in 1967. Peter was a young reporter who had worked in our Pittsburgh and Los Angeles bureaus since 1964. He would win a Pulitzer Prize in 1972 for his coverage of the Indo-Pakistan war and the birth of Bangladesh. Years later, he would succeed me as the *Journal*'s publisher and Dow Jones's CEO.

Peter was based in Vietnam until 1968, when he moved to Hong Kong but kept commuting to Vietnam to report from the capital and the countryside—the Mekong Delta, beleaguered Khe Sanh, the Laotian and Cambodian border areas, and other scenes of action, big and small. Bob Keatley, Fred Taylor, and other reporters would arrive from time to time to help. In keeping with the *Journal*'s determination not to duplicate every other newspaper's coverage of the daily military briefings, the ebb and flow of every battle and the political wrangling in Saigon, Kann focused on analysis and on stories that, through revealing details of everyday life and death, provided more perspective on the war's progress than any recital of body counts and troop deployments.

In 1968, for example, Kann wrote from Mo Cay, a town sixty miles south of Saigon:

> The chief nurse at the local hospital, the only person in town with formal medical training, was taken away by the government's recent call-up of reserves. He hasn't been replaced. . . . Capt. Nguyen Huyen Hiep, the fifth district chief in seven months (one of his predecessor was killed, another fired, and two transferred), is the best local leader within memory. He even mounts pre-dawn raids against the Vietcong. Former chiefs tended to keep bankers' hours.

In late 1969, Kann wrote from Saigon:

The war drags on. President Nixon has ruled out any quick withdrawal, and the enemy attacks seem to be increasing once again. No progress is reported in Paris. But if there is no progress at the peace table, is there at least progress on the battlefield? . . . There isn't a clear answer. Progress is measured here in many ways. The Air Force computes the tonnage of bomb loads dropped. The Army tots up bodies. Pacification planners neatly categorize hamlets on computerized evaluation charts. Psychological warriors conduct mini-Gallup Polls among taxi drivers. Embassy officers sip tea with Saigon legislators and seek to divine their Delphic utterances.

Outside our offices in downtown Manhattan, on May 8, 1970, an antiwar rally drew about a thousand high school and college students and others to demonstrate at the intersection of Broad Street and Wall Street, in front of the New York Stock Exchange building. At noon, about two hundred construction workers, wearing hard hats, marched down Broadway and attacked them. During the riot, a group of hard hats entered our offices to demand that the American flag be displayed from the flagstaff on the front of the building.

In the fall of 1969, a delegation of reporters on our staff requested that the Dow Jones News Service teleprinters, known as the ticker, be suspended for a minute of silence as a form of war protest. We refused, saying the news wires were not to be used for political purposes of any kind. In 1971, the *Journal* editorial page gave space on one day to two pieces by *Journal* reporters debating the proper role of journalists. Washington reporter Fred Zimmerman argued they should stick to reporting the news; New York reporter A. Kent MacDougall argued they should picket in Washington against the war when they felt morally bound to do so.

Later, MacDougall resigned to take another job. In leaving, he ignored our rules against personal messages on our internal intercity news wires by sending out an announcement of his quitting. He memorably ended by summing up his own emotions on the occasion in words paraphrasing Martin Luther King, words King used about his future vision at an August 1963 March on Washington, quoting an old Negro spiritual: "Free at last, free at last, Thank God Almighty, we are free at last!" Kent later pursued his passions for many decades as a professor of journalism at the University of California at Berkeley.

CHAPTER **18**

Asian Beachheads

DOW JONES BEGAN its evolution into a global publishing company in 1966 and 1967. Thus began not only a journalistic and business expansion, but also the introduction of my colleagues and me to cross-cultural adventures more exotic, sometimes bizarre, than those I experienced in the days when I lived and traveled through Europe.

As European and Asian markets grew and began to beckon American exporters and investors as never before and foreign traders and investors became more active in the United States, it became clear that the past's narrow definition of domestic news would no longer suffice. As our economy became more intertwined with the global economy, it didn't take a visionary to realize that we needed to expand our coverage of developments abroad that affected the United States. And we needed to offer other nations more comprehensive coverage of the American economic developments affecting them—before someone else beat us to this opportunity. Our first move was a worldwide economic newswire service first launched in Japan, followed by an Asian edition of *The Wall Street Journal*, and later by a European edition.

We were often asked, why Asia before Europe? First, Asia's economy was growing explosively, far faster than Europe's. Second, Europe presented obstacles of well-entrenched competition that did not exist in Asia. And third, we had partners in Asia whose influential connections and printing presses we could use, whereas it took us longer to link up with such allies in Europe.

The global expansion began with Bill Kerby assigning me to try to extend the Dow Jones News Service into Europe, to serve European investors and businesspeople increasingly interested in American markets. We began talks with Reuters about distributing the service over their networks. Reuters was initially encouraging in these partnership negotiations, then suddenly ended them, having decided to invade the U.S. market on its own to compete with us on our home turf. United Press International then approached us about starting a joint international economic wire service. We were enthusiastic and I tried for many months to move them forward on the project. But for whatever reason—internal weaknesses and lack of will in their organization at the time, lack of resources, or just an inability to make decisions and get approvals—we were no further along after nearly a year than we were at the start. Convinced that UPI was moving too slowly and would make a poor partner if that was an indicator of what working with them would be like, I recommended to Kerby that we end the discussions and approach the Associated Press. He agreed.

We went to Wes Gallagher, the AP general manager. He was enthusiastic about partnering to produce an international economic news wire service that would be distributed worldwide. He assigned Stan Swinton, the hard-charging chief of AP's World Service, to represent the AP in this endeavor. We recruited Ray Shaw, chief of the *Journal*'s Dallas Bureau, to be the first managing editor of the new AP–Dow Jones Economic Report. He was an alumnus of the AP, known and liked by our AP partners. Swinton soon persuaded Kyodo, Japan's national news agency and the AP's distributor in Japan, to be our first wholesale customer, paying a large annual fee for the right to resell the new AP–Dow Jones service to business firms, investors, newspapers, and other clients in its country.

That was enough to launch the new enterprise with a firm economic foundation, preparatory to extending it into other countries in Asia, Europe, and elsewhere. So Stan Swinton and I, both elated, flew off to Tokyo for a ceremonial contract signing with Shintaro Fukushima, president of the Kyodo news agency. This would be the first of many visits to Asia for me. Before leaving, I prepared by reading three or four books about Japan's culture— from anthropologist Ruth Benedict's *The Chrysanthemum and the Sword* (originally commissioned by the Office of War Information to help the American military understand its World War II adversary) to more contemporary studies of Japan's mores, politics, and economy.

Fukushima was a warm host. He took us to a restaurant foreigners would rarely find, a fugu restaurant, which specialized in making all its dishes, from soup and main course through dessert, from a poisonous blowfish. Fugu chefs had to be specially trained and licensed to remove the poison glands and prepare the dishes. We were assured that only once or twice a year would a fugu chef make a mistake, with fatal results for the diner but providing grist for newspaper stories about the occurrence.

Henry Hartzenbusch, the AP's Tokyo Bureau chief, took us on the weekend to a *ryokan,* or country inn, overlooking the sea at Atami, south of Tokyo. I had always thought the Japanese custom of sleeping on the floor sounded overly Spartan and uncomfortable. But when I crawled into my futon bedding, laid over the straw tatami mat that covered the floor, I found it the height of comfort and luxury.

On subsequent visits to Japan, at least once a year, we celebrated the growth of AP–Dow Jones, to twenty-three countries by 1972, five years after its start-up, and to forty by 1979 and more than fifty by 1988. On these visits, we always thanked Kyodo and its executives for the confidence it, as our first client, placed in us when our wire service was just starting out. On those later trips, I visited the Buddhist temple at Nara, a very early capital; the noble palaces at Kyoto, the seat of the emperors in the centuries before the capital was moved to Edo, or Tokyo; both modern and very old *ryokans* at Hakone, with its views across lake waters to Mount Fuji; hot-spring resort *ryokans* and ancient temples several hours north of Tokyo; and of course the many different districts of the capital itself, taking in the emperor's palace (from the outside), the restaurants, geisha houses, temples, and other sights. Barbara accompanied me on several of these trips, as did a few Dow Jones colleagues and their wives, and we took daughter Leslie with us in 1977 when she turned twenty-one.

Though we usually stayed at the luxurious Hotel Okura in Tokyo, I once told Fukushima how fond I was of the *ryokans* and asked if any existed within Tokyo. He used his influence to get me into a very old, traditional one, nestled within sight of sky-scrapers yet surrounded by walled-in gardens, a running brook, and solitude. It had no sign out front, did not advertise, and was not known to tourists, nor did it want to be. I stayed there in the dead of winter one year. My room had a modern toilet, but the seat was covered with a felt sleeve—to keep one's rear end from getting chilled by coming into contact with any cold surface.

In 1976, we started publishing *The Asian Wall Street Journal* in Hong Kong, with Peter Kann its first editor and publisher. And that changed the dynamics of our visits to Japan in telling, yet amusing, ways.

The push to publish the *Journal* in Asia was spearheaded by Don Macdonald and Ed Cony. Cony, my successor as managing editor, by 1976 was Dow Jones's vice president for news. Mac-donald, a blunt, aggressive but good-hearted and immensely lik-able executive, had risen through the ranks of the advertising department. He eventually became vice chairman, in charge of marketing all the company's publications and services. Kilgore had spotted Don's potential in earlier years and had sent Kerby a memo: "Bring him on fast. He's got brass balls."

Aw Sian, known as Sally Aw, who published Chinese-language newspapers in Hong Kong, first suggested a joint venture to pub-lish an Asian edition of the *Journal* on her presses. She was heir-ess to a fortune her forebears had built making and selling Tiger Balm, a cream and an ointment for relieving aches and pains, based on an old Chinese herbal-medicine formula. We might call it a patent medicine, but it was and is immensely popular throughout the Far East and beyond. The talks Don and I held with Sally Aw bogged down—much as had those with UPI on the earlier global newswire venture—and we developed serious doubts about what priority our paper would be granted on her far-from-modern presses.

So Don and Peter approached the British owners of the English-language *South China Morning Post* and soon had a deal for them to house and print *The Asian Wall Street Journal*. We earlier had purchased a 10 percent ownership share in the *Post* and 49 percent of its subsidiary magazine, the *Far Eastern Economic Review*. We now sold them a small stake in our new paper. Sally Aw thought our switch was racially motivated and resented it for years.

Peter Kann had been the *Journal*'s bright and able South Asia correspondent based in Hong Kong, and he was well connected with the British owners of the *Post*. He brought Norman Pearlstine, Tokyo Bureau chief, down from Japan as managing editor. They assembled a staff, and on September 1, 1976, the *Journal* was off and publishing in Asia, its copies distributed in sixteen countries throughout a six-thousand-mile region, at first by air freight. The Asian reporting of this new paper, as with the AP–Dow Jones newswire's overseas reporting and later that of the *Journal*'s European edition, contributed an expanded flow of foreign news back to the U.S. *Journal* and the Dow Jones News Service, strengthening their international coverage in the years when the need of our U.S. readers for global news and insights was growing.

In the years after the *Asian Journal* start-up, my colleagues arranged with the *Singapore Straits-Times*, the *New Straits-Times of Malaysia*, and later, in 1987, *Nihon Keizai Shimbun*, Japan's big economic daily, called *Nikkei* for short, to also print our Asian newspaper on their presses for speedier distribution in South Asia, Japan, and Korea. In return, we sold the *Straits-Times*, the *New Straits-Times*, and *Nikkei* small ownership stakes in the *Asian Journal*. And in May 1987 we began printing *Nikkei*'s U.S. edition on our presses in New Jersey and California.

Although our AP–Dow Jones partner in Japan, Kyodo, was a newswire service and *Nihon Keizai Shimbun* was a newspaper, we soon discovered they harbored competitive feelings and jealousies toward each other. There was no love lost between the two. We found the two competing to be regarded as our "primary partner" in Japan. We had to be careful to see that neither lost face in our dealings with the other one.

On one of our visits, Kyodo's executives took us to dine in a private room at an exclusive, unimaginably expensive restaurant patronized by the upper levels of the Japanese business and political worlds. For entertainment, they proudly produced an aging geisha so accomplished in singing, traditional Japanese dance, playing a traditional Japanese two-stringed instrument, and other geisha arts, such as intricate table tricks, that she had been officially designated a "living national treasure." Our hosts were proud that they had procured someone so famous to enliven our evening. While our Japanese partners thought the geisha's performance beautiful and enthralling, I thought it not just clever but intriguing mostly as a window on traditional Japanese culture and what the Japanese, as represented by our hosts, found moving and beautiful.

The next night, we were taken to dinner by *Nikkei*'s publisher, Junzo Ohnoki, and his colleagues at an equally elite restaurant in another part of the city. And lo and behold, who should they trot out but the same "living national treasure." They were beside themselves with pride at the treat they had been able to bestow on us. As the geisha displayed her artistic accomplishments and poured sake for us at the table, neither she nor we gave any hint that we had ever seen each other before.

On a visit in September 1987, Kyodo's executives told us with obvious pleasure and pride that they had arranged for me and my associates to have a private interview with Prime Minister Yasuhiro Nakasone the following day, the 30th. We did meet and have an exchange of views with the prime minister. When we later met with our partners at *Nikkei*, they had seen the write-up in the newspapers and they were not happy at being one-upped by Kyodo. "If you had only told us that you would be interested in meeting with the prime minister," they said in a tone of pique, "we could easily have arranged that for you and would have been glad to do so."

The prime minister, when pressed about Japan's international role in the next three to five years, would say only that Japan is like a "freshman in a world university" and that it should carry out its international responsibility step-by-step, taking lessons from Britain and the United States. This was a common Japanese posture in the postwar years; our *Nikkei* partners kept saying, almost obsequiously, how much they had to learn from us—until Japan gained so much economic strength that the tone changed and became patronizing. Touring our South Brunswick, New Jersey, printing plant one evening, they could scarcely conceal their disdain for our older presses there, indicating that we had much to learn from them, at least in the realm of modern, more efficient equipment.

Macdonald journeyed to Japan often to play golf with our *Nikkei* partners, and he entertained them on the golf course whenever they visited New York. On one such New York visit, we thrilled them with an aerial tour of Manhattan on the Dow Jones helicopter before flying them to our South Brunswick, New Jersey, printing plant, where they saw their American edition coming off our presses. It was published in Japanese for their many fellow countrymen living and working in the States.

The Japanese, whether visiting us in New York or hosting us in Tokyo, always were interested in our perspective on American politics, particularly during election campaigns. They would ask, "Please tell us about your American elections." We had trouble keeping a straight face when their interpreter translated this, with his imperfect pronunciation, as: "Please tell us about your American erections."

Once in Tokyo, at a dinner hosted by *Nikkei* executives who included Ko Morita, who succeeded Junzo Ohnoki as *Nikkei*'s publisher, the hour grew late, the sake cups were drained and refilled again and again, and Macdonald kept regaling our hosts with joke after joke, each producing great bursts of laughter. At one point I whispered to Mr. Ohara, the interpreter, that I was more than a little surprised that Macdonald's jokes were so well understood and appreciated, since I had imagined the sense and standards of humor in our two countries would be quite different. Mr. Ohara, a little tipsy, confided: "What I do is translate everything Mr. Macdonald says, then I say, 'Now everybody laugh.'"

CHAPTER 19

Journalistic Pals and Working Lunches

SOME OF THE LIVELIEST and at the same time most thoughtful individuals I met were editors at other newspapers. As executive editor of the *Journal* and later as publisher, when I retained the title editorial director, there were several ways I came in contact with other editors, many of whom became good friends.

One way was through my participation in the work of the American Society of Newspaper Editors; I served on several of its committees, chaired its Journalism Education Committee, was elected to its board, and then served as the ASNE's president in 1975 and 1976. I also met many other editors when I served with them for several years on Pulitzer Prize nominating panels and then was elected to the Pulitzer Prize Board from 1977 through 1987. The board makes the final choices for Pulitzer Prizes after examining the recommendations of the nominating panels. I met other editors when I was president of the American Council on Education for Journalism from 1971 to 1973 and when I was asked one year to help interview and select candidates for Harvard's Nieman Fellowships.

One year, on the Pulitzer Prize Board, the *Chicago Sun-Times* was recommended for the public service award for a series of stories that exposed corruption in Chicago and led to reforms. To conduct a sting operation, the paper had purchased the Mirage Bar, where many city building inspectors hung out. Reporters

posing as the Mirage Bar owners persuaded inspectors to over-
look numerous building code violations in return for bribes. I
was impressed when a fellow member of the Pulitzer board, Clay-
ton Kirkpatrick, editor of the *Chicago Tribune,* argued eloquently
and selflessly that his chief competitor, the *Sun-Times,* deserved
the award for the public good that he testified this series had
achieved in his city.

I was equally impressed by the strength of the opposition
argument put forth by another board member, Ben Bradlee,
executive editor of the *Washington Post.* He said awarding the
prize to the *Sun-Times* would send the wrong message to young
reporters everywhere: that it was all right to lie to get a story, to
pretend to be not a reporter but someone you were not. He said
he could not vote for such a precedent that would encourage
the kind of subterfuge and lying, even if it was the means to a
good end, that we in the press were the first to condemn when
we found it in government or business. The prize did not go to
the *Sun-Times* that year. And the *Journal,* among others, reexam-
ined and ended about that time reporting practices that previously included, in the *Journal's* case, condoning reporters posing
as job candidates and getting hired by Ford Motor Company, to
expose quality-control flaws on the auto assembly lines, and by
Texas Instruments Company, to illustrate labor practices from
inside the factory walls.

Not all Pulitzer Prize Board discussions illuminated ethical
issues and disagreements within our profession. For the non-
journalism prizes, we broke into subcommittees for fiction, nonfiction, biography, poetry, music, and drama to be sure each
nominated work was carefully examined. I was on the fiction sub-
committee along with John Hughes, editor of the *Christian Science
Monitor,* and Eugene "Gene" Patterson, managing editor of the
Washington Post, who was elected to the board when Ben Bradlee's
term expired. Gene delivered a passionate recommendation of
one novel to the full board for the fiction prize. I opposed him,
asking the board to choose a novel I thought better. Gene then
said, before the full board, "I'm sorry Barbara didn't like that
other book, the one I favored." He, and many of my friends on

the board, knew that my wife was the more literary member of our marriage, and they knew how highly I valued her judgment. Gene always knew how to draw a laugh.

Other Pulitzer board members included James "Scotty" Reston, a *New York Times* columnist, who was there during my first year, and Joe Pulitzer, grandson of Joseph Pulitzer; the elder Joseph owned the old *New York World* and founded the Columbia Graduate School of Journalism as well as the prizes that bore his name.

Gene Patterson and I had known and teased each other long before we crossed swords that day at the Pulitzer meeting. We were colleagues for years on the American Society of Newspaper Editors board. A highlight after dinner at each fall's ASNE board meeting would be Gene being persuaded, without much difficulty, to break into song with his sentimental rendition of that Irish classic "Danny Boy." The year Norman Isaacs was ASNE president, he took the board to London for its fall meeting to examine operation of Britain's Press Council, which investigated grievances against newspapers. Gene at one time had been stationed in London as a United Press correspondent. About midnight one night, after many drinks with our fellow ASNE board members, Gene insisted I accompany him in a taxi so he could show me the apartment house where he and his wife, Sue, had lived. He wanted to point out their top-floor apartment and tell me that's where their daughter Mary was conceived. In his mind and in his heart, it was a shrine.

I encountered many other lively minds at "news lunches" at our offices, at which our invited guests were political, business, or cultural figures with whom we anticipated an exchange of views that would be useful to our editors and the reporter covering the guest's organization. One of our most memorable guests was Margaret Thatcher, when she was Britain's prime minister and on a visit to the States. It was memorable at least to me—because she lectured me sternly, all the while wagging a finger toward my face. Most of my colleagues and I admired her and we had had what I regarded as a love feast, exploring all the views we shared on foreign and economic policy. Then she brought up what was really on her mind: The *Journal* had been editorially criticizing Britain's moves to deport the Vietnamese refugees, the so-called boat people, who had sought sanctuary on the British-controlled islands that were part of Hong Kong. After she had defended Britain's decision, I made what I thought was a conciliatory response. "We have been consistent in advocating an open-immigration policy, not being any more harsh on Britain than on our own government," I said. "We have been just as outspoken in favor of open borders with Mexico as we have with Hong Kong." (That was the paper's editorial position, at least at that particular moment in history.)

At that point, Mrs. Thatcher pointed her index finger at my face from across the table and said emphatically, "You are wrong, Mr. Phillips. You are wrong." After another moment of discussion, she said again, even sterner this time: "You are just wrong!!"

One of our executives, a former Atlanta newspaper editor, was Don Carter. When his cousin Jimmy, then governor of Georgia, was preparing to run for the Democratic presidential nomination, Don asked if his cousin could come to lunch so that we could meet him. "Sure," I said, and soon after, Jimmy Carter visited with us at our office. We asked him questions relating to the economy. We asked his views on foreign hot spots. So many of his replies struck me as superficial, unknowledgeable, or otherwise off base that I thought, "This guy isn't going to go anywhere." So much for the clarity of my crystal ball.

Among the many other lunch guests over the years were Bobby Kennedy, Tom Watson of IBM, Gloria Steinem, South Africa's Zulu Chief Mangosuthu Buthelezi, and Al Gore, when he was a senator. Bobby Kennedy came when he was running for his party's presidential nomination, after his brother's death. It was no secret that the *Journal* editorial page had been critical of the Kennedys. Bobby set the cool tone of our meeting when lunch was served. He studied the chicken dish on his plate with a look of distaste, then asked, "Can I have an egg?" Afterward, Vermont Royster and I accompanied him down in the elevator and to his waiting car. "Well, did you get what you wanted?" he asked curtly before stepping into the car.

The luncheon fare also figured in the conversation when we met with IBM's chairman Tom Watson. He was known as a tee-totaler and I was surprised when he accepted the offer of a sherry. Among the things we talked about were his devotion to ocean sailing and his imminent departure to skipper his yacht on a transatlantic race. At the elevator, as we saw him out, I remarked that I was surprised to see him have a sherry. "I'm so excited about going to sea on our race tomorrow that I thought I would cut loose," he said.

I invited Gloria Steinem to come and give us her views of the women's movement she was helping to lead. She did so, eloquently. At one point she said, "I get so sick and tired of all the stereotypes and stories about women in business sleeping their way to the top. What about all the men who marry the boss's daughter? Don't you call that sleeping their way to the top?" She was right, about that and many other things.

As often as we had newsmakers in to lunch, businessmen and others would invite me and some of our editors and reporters out to their corporate dining rooms for lunch or dinner. We under-stood, of course, that their purpose usually was to convey a sympa-thetic picture of their company and their public-policy views and to establish goodwill with a newspaper whose coverage and editori-als they thought were important to them. They were sensitive as to whether our future reporting of their affairs would be "positive" or "negative," though we never viewed it that way, but tried to report both the good and the bad of what was going on. We accepted most of their invitations, when we could, because we were eager to appraise up close the people we were covering and hear what was on their minds. We always asked, at these meetings and those in our own offices, how the guests viewed *Journal* coverage and if they had any thoughts on how we might improve the paper.

David Rockefeller, then chairman of Chase Bank, on Wall Street at the time, was one of the early ones to invite me and a couple of colleagues to lunch after I became managing editor. George Champion, then Chase's president, would invite me to lunch at other times. David's private dining room at the bank was decorated with paintings by some of the best-known contemporary artists of the time. Modern art was famously one of his life-time interests and the object of his generous patronage. George Champion's tastes ran in a different direction. His separate private dining room was decorated with Remington sculptures and paintings of the Old West. He told me once that he had been a member of the bank's Art Committee, which chose works to be displayed throughout the bank. "But I quit after a while," he said. "I got tired of being outvoted by David."

Another banker, Gabriel Hauge, invited me often to dinners at a private dining room at his bank, Manufacturers Hanover. He wore a black patch over one blind eye and was smart and gracious. He invited me to serve on his bank's board of directors. I declined, since our ethics rules forbade us from serving on the boards of companies we covered. I felt complimented, though—and possibly that was part of his intention.

Jimmy Robinson, later to be president of American Express Company from 1977 until his retirement in 1993, was a less smooth banker when I was managing editor and he invited me to lunch at White Weld & Company, the investment firm where he was then a general partner. He sent out for sandwiches and we ate them in his office, he lobbying hard and unceasingly the entire time about what he did and did not expect in the way of *Journal* coverage. One such lunch was enough for me. I wondered how he, known as a courtly Georgian, could be so ham-handed as to not save his hard pitch for sometime around dessert, and to not know enough to precede it with small talk or smooth talk to first warm up his prospect. Maybe he didn't realize that whatever he learned in the Deep South about master-servant relations in those days wouldn't travel well to Wall Street, particularly if he couldn't discriminate between who were his servants and who weren't. I assume he figured that out before he got to American Express, but I never had occasion to find out.

Government officials, foreign diplomats, and others also regularly extended lunch or dinner invitations to me and other editors, both from the *Journal* and from other publications. Some were one-on-one meetings, others large group gatherings. We went to dinners at, among others, China's United Nations

Embassy in New York, at the Canadian ambassador's residence in Washington, at the White House a couple of times, and once or twice at luncheons given at the State Department, such as one Secretary of State George Shultz gave for Philippine President Ferdinand Marcos and his wife. When the ASNE would hold its conventions in Washington, whoever was president at the time would usually invite the visiting editors from around the nation to a White House reception.

President and Mrs. Johnson hosted such a reception April 21, 1967. Bobby Kennedy, hoping for his party's presidential nomination, hosted the editors, with Ethel and their children, at their McLean, Virginia, estate the same day, two hours before the Johnsons. Five years later, Barbara and I were standing in the White House receiving line April 20, 1972, waiting to see President and Mrs. Nixon and chatting next to us with Al Romm and his wife, Ethel. Al was editor of the Middletown, New York, *Times Herald-Record*, then owned by Dow Jones. Ethel remarked that she planned to tell Nixon what she thought of the Vietnam War. Apparently her remark was overheard and reported to the Secret Service. Within a minute or two, the Romms were escorted out of the receiving line and out of the White House.

I appreciated most of the dinner and lunch invitations from businesspeople and government officials, and I enjoyed the chance to size up those individuals and hear them expound their views firsthand. But I knew full well that these invitations came to us because I represented the *Journal* and it was viewed as an influential institution. I harbored no illusions that these invitations came to me because anyone perceived me as a fount of charm or good looks. I remember well a story that Punch Sulzberger, publisher of the *New York Times*, told me in the 1980s when we were together at a meeting of the American Newspaper Publishers Association in Washington. He had been invited to lunch with President Reagan at the White House, and upon arriving found Secretary of State George Shultz and Secretary of Defense Caspar Weinberger there at the lunch table, too.

When he returned to his hotel, Sulzberger said, he phoned his mother to tell her about the lunch. His mother, Iphigene Ochs

Sulzberger, was the daughter of Adolph Ochs, who had bought the *Times* in the late nineteenth century. She was the wise family matriarch. As Sulzberger related the story, "'Mother,' I said. 'I just returned from the White House. The president had me to lunch. And the secretary of state and the secretary of defense were there, too.'

"'That's nice, dear,' she said. 'What did they want?'"

CHAPTER **20**

News and Editorials

Setting the Course

WORKING WITH MY SUCCESSORS as managing editor was satisfying but not always easy. They brought the *Journal* to new journalistic heights. Circulation grew. They were dedicated, good-hearted, congenial men, well liked by the staff. But I always was driven by a conviction the news coverage could be improved. And at times we had serious disagreements about the direction of the paper.

Paradoxically, working with the highly controversial editorial-page editors was easier. Their editorial positions drew sharp attacks, not only from some readers but, at times, from our own Washington Bureau members and from some Dow Jones directors. I spent far more time and energy defending them than disagreeing with them.

When I was promoted to vice president, general manager, and editorial director of Dow Jones in late 1970 and Ed Cony moved into the job I had held as executive editor, my choice to succeed him as managing editor was Jim Soderlind, the brilliant former Rhodes Scholar who was then page-one editor. He shared my visions on how the *Journal* should be improved. As an editor, he already had proven himself superb. However, within a year of his becoming managing editor, he developed a serious problem with alcohol. The risk of having someone with possibly impaired judgment making split-second decisions daily in such a critical job was a risk we could not take. Cony and I named Fred Taylor the new managing editor. I moved Soderlind aside into jobs free of managerial responsibilities and stress and worked with him to seek treatment; several times he recovered, only to have a relapse after a year or two. I conferred with him, his wife, Helen, and his doctors at a New Jersey sanitarium about how we could be of further help at work after one such serious relapse; finally, Jim's efforts and those of his family paid off, his cure became as permanent as an alcoholic's "cure" can ever be, and eventually we were able to recapture his wonderful talents as Dow Jones's vice president for planning. He continued to attend Alcoholics Anonymous meetings, wherever in the world he was, all his life.

The sharpest differences I had with Ed Cony and Fred Taylor were over what I considered their occasional drift away from keeping our reporting staff's primary focus on business news, and their misreading of what they sometimes portrayed as a lack of enthusiasm by me for broader, nonbusiness stories. Symbolic of this rift was my criticism of a page-one leader on life in a Scottish monastery, and another on wife abuse in the United Kingdom. One of my problems with such stories was a lack of relevance to our readers. Another was that they failed to measure up to the standards we applied to all stories: they just were not strong stories, period.

I had long worked to broaden the paper's coverage to include trends in education, medicine, science, social changes, and most definitely, readers' personal and family budgets and finances. The *Journal* had defined its mission, under Kilgore and then Kerby, as covering everything that had to do with earning a living and spending those earnings. Put another way, everything affecting the reader's pocketbook. My oft-proclaimed supplement to that sermon was that our readers' interests were not confined to their businesses, but very much extended to their health, the education of their children, and the social forces shaping our society and its future. In another area of coverage, I was not opposed to the whimsical features that occupied the center column on page one each day, and which we called the A-head, after the three-quarter-boxed headline style that identified them. I loved those stories, provided they were on intriguing subjects and well done. What I did oppose was allowing reporters to concentrate so much time on such stories that it resulted in neglecting our core coverage.

I was concerned with balance—not overfocusing so much staff time and front-page space on light, whimsical features or other nonbusiness subjects that our specialty, being best in the coverage of business, was weakened in the process. I emphasized this over the years to counter a far less nuanced, all-black-or-all-white impression—a wrong one—voiced by some in the newsroom that "Phillips wanted to fill the paper only with dry, dull business stories, a throwback to pre-Kilgore days, and had no tolerance for the A-heads, other offbeat features, and investigative projects that had drawn so many readers—and reporters—to the paper."

This tug-of-war over the direction of the *Journal*'s news coverage waxed and waned over many years. Even when we had a managing editor who was in sympathy with my goals, such as Larry O'Donnell, Taylor's successor, he was not always able to get his staff to execute to my full satisfaction the mission of successfully broadening our coverage while at the same time improving our core business coverage, including the pursuit of investigative exposés. Finally, however, with indispensable help from Peter Kann, we found the ideal managing editor in Norman Pearlstine. He had the judgment, skills, and other strengths to mobilize his staff resources to succeed, far better than I ever could, in achieving all these goals for the paper. His talented successor, Paul Steiger, did a distinguished job of continuing and building on these successes.

If Norm Pearlstine was the ideal editor to lead the *Journal*'s news department, Bob Bartley was the ideal editor, to me, to take over the paper's editorial pages after Vermont Royster retired and Joe Evans died suddenly soon after.

Barbara and I were returning from a Caribbean vacation in December 1971, a year after I had been promoted to general manager, when I was surprised to see a colleague meet us at the Kennedy Airport disembarkation gate. He had come to tell us Joe had just had a heart attack and was dead. Joe was only fifty-two. That evening and the days that followed were sad ones for our family as we tried to comfort Joe's wife, Marie, and their children, and then attended his funeral in Pelham. We and the Evans family were the closest of friends.

Later, in deciding who should replace Roy and Joe and take over the *Journal*'s editorial pages, I recommended to Bill Kerby, and he agreed, that we skip over a couple of more senior editorial writers and tap young Bob Bartley for the job. Bob, an Iowan, had worked as a *Journal* reporter in Chicago and Philadelphia, then was recruited by Roy and Joe for the editorial-page crew on the basis of thoughtful, well-written book reviews that Bob had submitted, on his own initiative, while in Philadelphia. Bob stood out because he wrote with a distinctive flair and his thinking was clear and incisive. He exhibited these promising qualities more than those around him, more than any others since Grimes and Royster.

In his memoir, *My Own, My Country's Time,* Vermont Royster recalled the decision to promote Bartley, not yet thirty-five, this way:

> Warren's role in this shows how rapidly he was rising within the company. It also shows how he would step into any power vacuum when the need arose and was willing to make decisions he thought best while knowing they would not be everywhere well received. It was that way with this Bartley appointment; Bob was years younger than his colleagues, and naturally there was some disgruntlement. Theoretically the decision wasn't Warren's to make; the selection of anyone to fill that important a post on the paper should have been Bill Kerby's. Warren, of course, cleared it with Bill, though there was no real consultation. He just did it. The fact that he "consulted" with me was more a courtesy than anything else, just as when later in 1979 he telephoned to ask if I would "object" to his giving Bartley the editor's title. I had by now acquired a sort of unofficial status as "elder statesman" or whatever. But had I objected on either occasion I'm sure Warren would have made his decision anyway.

Alan Otten, the Washington Bureau chief, lobbied hard against the Bartley appointment on the grounds that "he's an ideologue." Some members of his bureau, and others on the staff, echoed that description in the years to come, sometimes calling Bob a zealot and adding that he was brash to boot, the latter a characterization that surprised no one. But Bob could think and Bob could write, and he surrounded himself with similarly talented editorial writers, including the brilliant and warmhearted Paul Gigot. Years later, my successor as publisher, Peter Kann, selected Gigot, with Bob concurring, to be the new editorial-page editor when Bob retired. Bob for many years increased mightily the influence of the *Journal*'s voice in foreign-policy councils, in the business world, in fiscal and monetary policy debates, and in the rise of "supply-side economics" during the Reagan years.

I was asked often whether I agreed with everything Bartley wrote and how I could support so enthusiastically an editor many regarded as "a right-winger." I frequently would recall and quote, approvingly, the copy of a letter Barney Kilgore had sent me that he had sent to Laurence Lombard, a Dow Jones director representing the controlling Bancroft family. Laurie had questioned Barney's tolerance for the "right-wing" views editor Bob Bleiberg was voicing in *Barron's* magazine. Barney had replied, and here I must paraphrase:

> The country has many newspapers and magazines expounding the liberal point of view. What it doesn't need is a publication that hews to the middle of the road, writing "on the one hand" this and "on the other hand" that. It needs a publication that can articulate, with force and eloquence and in well-reasoned fashion, the conservative position and philosophy on issues before the country. Then the reader can examine the best-presented arguments mustered by both sides, and form his own conclusions.

That is the role we were playing and contributing to the national debates: giving the best voice we could to the conservative side of the argument, so the reader could pick and choose what he or she wanted to believe from the many points of view available to him or her. In fact, Bob and his staff made room on the op-ed pages for many writers who offered opposing viewpoints. Among them were a liberal such as Washingtonian Al Hunt and an infinitely more extreme spokesperson for everything leftist, Alexander Cockburn. Alex, born in Scotland, grew up in County Cork, Ireland, and emigrated to the United States when he was thirty-one. He might have started his op-ed pieces from a flawed premise, but one could not help but admire the beauty of his writing and the skill with which he wove argument and logic into essays that made the most unreasonable advocacy appear oh so reasonable.

After selecting Bob Bartley with confidence that he was philosophically in sync with the *Journal*'s longtime editorial policies advocating free markets and the supremacy of individual freedoms, and would express them vigorously, I gave him great day-to-day independence, following with him the same procedure Barney Kilgore had followed with Grimes and Royster. Royster often recalled one day in early 1959 when he offered an editorial critical of President Eisenhower to Kilgore for comment.

"I laid it on his desk," Royster related. "He picked up the typewritten sheets, handed them back to me, and said, 'I'll read it in the paper tomorrow.'"

I did not want, any more than Kilgore, to review and participate in formulating editorial positions day to day. Down that road would lie weak editors who would rely on the boss to make the tough editorial decisions, and I soon would find myself doing the editor's job.

Bob and I did discuss the general thrust of his staff's editorials from time to time, not in a way intended to command compliance but rather to advise him of my thinking, which, if persuasive, might be considered in his future decision making. Occasionally, for example, an editorial would appear that I thought lessened its impact by being too shrill. We would talk then about how much more effective the stiletto could be than the meat axe. Once, as Watergate moved toward its climax, I phoned him from Washington to say that now that President Nixon had been revealed as having lied to the American people, perhaps the time had finally come to call for his resignation, based on this egregious breach of the public trust. Bob replied that if Nixon were forced from office by the public clamor for his resignation, the nation would be split for years over whether or not he was driven from the presidency unjustly by his enemies. On the other hand, Bob argued, impeachment proceedings were in the works, that was the constitutional means a president could be removed from office, and if that resulted after due process, the country would be placed on the road to healing much faster. I thought his argument made much sense.

When we recruited new directors to Dow Jones's board of directors, we invariably made sure they understood beforehand that debating or influencing news coverage or editorial policy was not part of the board's function. We wanted to avail ourselves of their wisdom on corporate business issues; there would be no advise-and-consent role affecting news or editorial policy. Even so, a strong-willed director would occasionally speak his mind on these off-limits issues. Not often, but every once in a long while.

This happened one evening, after I was publisher and CEO of Dow Jones, at a dinner meeting of the board's Executive Committee in a private dining room at New York's St. Regis Hotel. A veteran director suggested something be done about what he considered badly misguided editorials Bob was publishing on some controversy, now long forgotten, that the director thought was affecting business adversely, and unfairly and unnecessarily so. I replied that Bob was not right 100 percent of the time—who was?—but that I thought he was right about 98 percent of the time, and that struck me as a pretty good batting average, better than the batting average of any other editor I might find. I said, "Your quarrel isn't with Bartley; it's with me. I appointed him, I'm responsible for his performance, and if I thought he wasn't doing a good enough job it would be my responsibility to replace him. But I think we're lucky to have such an able editor and I don't intend to replace him. So I'm the one you should replace if you want a different editor."

PART FOUR

PUBLISHER

CHAPTER 21

China

IN 1972, I WAS ELECTED president, chief operating officer, and a director of Dow Jones, remaining editorial director as well. That year was the best of times and the worst of times for me, or so it seemed then—and neither had anything to do with my promotion.

Taking the worst first: In that year I fell under a dark cloud of clinical depression. It was characterized by the usual accompaniments of depression—feelings of despair, worthlessness, and hopelessness. I visited a psychiatrist several times a week. He was a Freudian who mostly listened, but I became disillusioned with him. I theorized that I had nothing to be depressed about and that depression was likely caused by a chemical imbalance, perhaps inherited. I switched to my cousin, Larry Kaplan, a former neurosurgeon who had built a psychiatric practice. He took more of a pharmacological approach and prescribed Tofranil, an antidepressant. He hinted at the possibility of electroshock therapy if that did not bring improvement.

I was scheduled to visit China in the fall and was growing increasingly dubious that I would be in condition to make the trip. President Nixon had visited China in February 1972, opening relations with the Communist government there after many decades of hostility and estrangement. The American Society of Newspaper Editors had received permission from the Chinese to send the first delegation of American journalists to tour their country since the rapprochement. As a member of the ASNE board, I was part of the delegation preparing to go.

In August, I felt too despondent to be able to make the long plane flight, let alone travel throughout China, and I was on the verge of dropping out. That loomed as what would be a disappointment beyond words. But at the last minute the Tofranil, after several dosage adjustments, began to take effect. My outlook grew brighter day by day, and I decided, happily, to go forward on the China trip. It was a trip I had very much wanted to make and for which I had earlier prepared with voracious background reading, from *The Chinese Looking Glass*, by London *Observer* correspondent Dennis Bloodworth, and Edgar Snow's *Red Star Over China*, to the works of Harvard China scholar John K. Fairbank and background papers available from the CIA.

That China trip, the first of three for me, left me feeling it was one of the best times of my life. For nearly four weeks in September and October I traveled more than four thousand miles in China with twenty-one other American editors; we interviewed Premier Chou En-lai; and I wrote ten articles from China—*Journal* leaders, *Journal* editorial-page analytical pieces, and one *National Observer* piece. I felt exhilarated, like I was on a roll, and delighted to discover that I had "kept my hand in," so to speak, as the reporter I once was. My articles subsequently were republished in book form, along with several pieces by coauthor Bob Keatley, under the title *China: Behind the Mask*. In reviewing the book for *The American Scholar* magazine, Supreme Court Justice William O. Douglas called it "faithful to fact [and including] one of the best accounts of the commune I have seen. It is a stirring story." Another review, in a publication of the National Council of Churches' East Asian Office, called it "among the most perceptive journalistic reporting of this period."

I never confided to any of my colleagues the crisis that preceded the trip, nor did I apply for company medical insurance reimbursement of my doctor bills. I wanted to avoid the stigma and the gossip that attached to any mental illness such as depression in those days, and even today. Because the crisis peaked in midsummer, in the midst of vacation time, I was able to be out of the office at the time I felt I was barely functioning. And fortunately, as it turned out, my illness was relatively short-lived. I

The author's parents, Abraham and Juliette Philips.

In the Army Air Corps, 1945.

Reporting from Turkey, 1949, with the help of some local sources.

At a Paris café with fellow correspondents Denny Fodor, left in beret, and Mike James, 1949. Author on right.

Sam Lesch, national news editor and author's first boss at the Journal, 1955.
(Photo courtesy of Bernard Kilgore)

Bill Kerby, right, and William Henry Grimes, third from right, at first *Journal* Editors–Bureau Managers Conference, Buck Hill Falls, Pennsylvania, 1955.
(Photo courtesy of Bernard Kilgore)

With Barbara on our
wedding day, London.

As managing editor, with
Dow Jones CEO Barney Kilgore,
New York newsroom, 1958.

With Barbara and our daughters, from left to right, Lisa, Nina, Leslie, at Smith Beach, Virginia, 1964.

Cavorting with the *Journal*'s London Bureau in the sixties, with cardboard moustache party favors at a nightclub called Churchill's. From front right, Frank Linge, Barbara, Ray Vicker. From front left, Jody Melloan, George Melloan, Margaret Vicker, the author.

Chinese villagers troop behind the author, a curious oddity in their midst, 1972.

With Chinese Premier Chou En-lai in the Great Hall of the People, Peking (now Beijing), 1972.

Author working between flights at Tokyo's Narita Airport en route home from China, 1972.

Visiting German publisher Axel Springer at his estate north of Hamburg, 1973. From left, Ernst Cramer, Bill Kerby, the author, Springer, Springer's wife, Friede, Ray Shaw, and Don Macdonald.

With the inaugural edition of *The Wall Street Journal Europe* on opening night in Heerlen, The Netherlands, 1983. From left, Norm Pearlstine, Don Macdonald, the author, and the manager of the Dutch printing plant.

With Peter Kann in the author's office.

In the Oval Office with President Reagan and *Journal*
colleagues. From far right, Peter Kann, the author, Bob Bartley.
Counterclockwise on the left, backs to camera, Al Hunt
(with white hair), White House reporter Rich Jaroslovsky,
and Norm Pearlstine.

With Japan's prime
minister, Yasuhiro
Nakasone, in
Tokyo, 1987.
(Photo courtesy of the
Office of the Prime
Minister, Tokyo)

With President George H. W.
Bush at the *Journal*'s 1989
centennial celebration in the
Winter Garden of New York's
World Financial Center.

As houseguests of *Washington Post* publisher Kay Graham at her Martha's Vineyard summer home. On the far left, beside Barbara, is Felix Rohaytn. The author and Graham are to the right of Barbara.

Copublishers of Bridge Works Publishing Co., surrounded by their books—and those of others, 1999.
(Photo courtesy of Morton Hamburg)

realize that I had treated myself differently from the way I reacted when I removed Jim Soderlind from the sensitive managing editor's job, fearing impaired judgment. I felt—perhaps selfishly, perhaps deluding myself—that I would be able to judge when and if I reached a point that would endanger Dow Jones. To my relief, that point never came.

My first glancing brush with China occurred slightly more than a year before the trip, in an apartment on Manhattan's East End Avenue. It belonged to John Diebold, who had built a pioneering international computer consultancy firm in the early days of computers and who was credited with popularizing the word *automation*. He periodically drew business and media executives to salonlike evenings he hosted. Henry Kissinger, then Nixon's national security adviser, in the spring of 1971 had accepted an invitation to be the guest of honor at one of these gatherings. That acceptance came before anyone, perhaps even Kissinger, knew that in early July 1971 he would be making a secret trip to Beijing, called Peking at that time, to negotiate with Chou En-lai the conditions and groundw.ork for the Nixon visit. Kissinger's date at Diebold's apartment fell only a few days after his return from China and the July 15 public disclosure of his journey and the planned Nixon visit. Kissinger kept his commitment to Diebold, nevertheless, and I was among the dozen or two at the dinner table that evening who heard him talk about the trip.

The first thing I saw on entering the apartment was the federal plainclothes security agent sitting just inside the door, with something like an attaché case on his lap. Our host said it held an automatic weapon. At dinner, Kissinger surprised me with his candor discussing the logistics of his secret trip and his impressions of Chou and the other Chinese with whom he had met. He thought the Chinese enormously sophisticated and intelligent and said the contrast with the Russians had been striking. He discussed the differences between negotiating with the Chinese and the Russians, in terms most unflattering to the latter, whom he described as humorless, stolidly stubborn, and not nearly as knowledgeable about the world outside their country as he had found the Chinese to be.

Diebold's dinners were among several Manhattan "salons" whose hosts or hostesses were kind enough to invite Barbara and me to be their guests from time to time. Lally Weymouth, journalist daughter of the *Washington Post*'s publisher, Katharine Graham, had Israel's Ariel Sharon, actor Warren Beatty, and entertainment-industry entrepreneur Barry Diller among her guests on different evenings when I was there.

Similar salonlike parties, but focused less on the worlds of politics and business than on the literary world, were hosted across town on the West Side by Jean Stein, editor and publisher of the literary magazine *Grand Street*, author of a biography of Andy Warhol acolyte Edie Sedgewick, and daughter of onetime Hollywood mogul and MCA Chairman Jules Stein. Among those we encountered sharing her hospitality were Norman Mailer and wife Norris Church.

Though Manhattan had more than its share of such intriguing, worldly people, few were as fresh and exotic in my eyes—or as proletarian—as the men and women whom I and my fellow editors encountered after we traveled north out of Hong Kong in September, past the border crossing at the covered railway bridge at Shumchun, and into the once-forbidden People's Republic of China. On the two-hour train trip from the border to Canton, now called Kwangchow, where we were to board a flight to Peking, the villages, bamboo groves, water buffalo, and green rice fields of the eternal China glided by outside the train windows. Once in Peking, from a room on the sixth floor of the Peking Hotel, I could look through another window and see the contrast of the old and the relatively new, and the contrast between power and ordinary people.

In the distance were the high walls behind which the Ming and Manchu emperors had lived, the orange-tiled roofs of the Forbidden City's ancient palaces, Tiananmen Square and the Mao government's Great Hall of the People in front of them, massed red flags flying from the Great Hall's roof to mark some state occasion. There was all the panoply of authoritarian power, both past and present. In the foreground, beneath the hotel window, were tightly packed one-story dwellings. One courtyard nearby was used by several families living in what might once have been a single L-shaped house. It now was divided into several apartments, whose back doors opened into the court. A mother brushed and braided a little girl's hair in the courtyard the morning after our arrival. A man swept the courtyard clean after a breakfast cooked outdoors on a primitive charcoal stove. Three little boys pranced around the courtyard, waving their arms. A younger one followed them at a gallop. The mother, her work on her daughter's hair completed, began to wash her own in a bowl on the floor of the yard.

All seemed in high spirits. None were aware they were being observed. Here, in the shadow of the seats of power, the universality of family life was unfolding, much as it was doing in a hundred other lands. Tempted to know more about this particular family, I knocked on their door a few days later and asked, through an interpreter, if an overseas traveler might visit for a short while. Inside was the Chang family. The mother, Wang Hsu-chen, was a pretty, animated woman of thirty-one who worked in a hospital admissions office. Her husband, Chang Nai-hua, thirty-three, was a construction worker. They, their two children, her sister's three children, her mother, and her father lived packed into two small rooms. The sister and brother-in-law lived in a single room in another house nearby. Outside in the courtyard was the stove on which the family did its cooking. A homemade wooden canopy protected it from rain. The stove was brought into one of the bedrooms in winter to provide heat. Water came from a tap in the courtyard.

It was hard to visualize four adults and five children squeezing into the two double beds and two singles that occupied most of the space in the two rooms. Or how eating, schoolwork, and general family life could be conducted in such sardine-can quarters. But Wang Hsu-chen wasn't complaining. "We earn enough to keep our life at a very good level," she said. "It's been improving gradually. The prices of food and the things we buy for everyday use have been stable. And where we work, there are medical services that are free for workers. We have everything we want—a radio, a sewing machine, watches for everyone."

Like others we were to meet on our journey, her family members measured their lives against what they had known in the past and what others around them had, and they felt prosperous. Or so they said. As one wag commented later, the Chinese had graduated from destitution to poverty.

One evening, in sharp contrast, we were among the foreign guests at a magnificent banquet in the Great Hall of the People at which Premier Chou En-lai, Vice Premier Li Hsien-nien, Mao Tse-tung's wife, Chiang Ching, and numerous other dignitaries marked the twenty-third anniversary of their government. Austere and somber Mao-style tunics were the fashion with most of the civilians; the generals wore their uniforms without insignia of rank to distinguish them from the privates, as had been the custom in China since the mid-1960s. But there was nothing egalitarian about the eleven dishes served. They ranged from Peking duck and balls of lobster meat to that local delicacy, sea slugs. And there was nothing egalitarian about the long lines of limousines that carried the officials and guests away.

A private reception room within the Great Hall of the People was the setting later in our visit for a midnight interview with Premier Chou En-lai. We had been summoned from our hotel rooms at 10 P.M. Chou, then seventy-four, was relaxed and in good spirits. He talked with us for three hours and forty minutes. When we broke up at ten minutes past two in the morning, we editors were bleary eyed, while he was bouncy and wide awake. His conversation often sparkled with wit. Some examples:

- While he said he was precluded from visiting the United States as China's premier so long as the Chiang Kai-shek government in Taiwan had representatives in America, "If I resigned, maybe I could go. Maybe I'll go as a member of the table tennis team."
- Noting that the *New York Times,* the *Washington Post,* and certain other newspapers weren't represented in the visiting editors' group, he said: "But *The Wall Street Journal* is represented. . . . So you get special consideration because you are from Wall Street."

- At the conclusion of the meeting, Chou said, "I made more serious replies to your questions than I did to President Nixon, Mr. Rogers [William Rogers, secretary of state], and Dr. Kissinger. Dr. Kissinger can talk to you for half an hour and not give one substantive answer. It would be unfair of me to do that to you. But I understand he has to keep some things confidential."

Chou ranged at length over such diverse topics as the grooming of future leaders, relations with the United States, China's economic priorities, Chairman Mao's philosophy, Russian shortcomings, his own enjoyment of Ping-Pong as a source of relaxation, future pollution problems, and New York traffic. And he discussed in detail the death the year before of Defense Minister Lin Piao, once Mao's designated successor. He elaborated at length and with new details on the official story that Lin, believing his path to the succession was endangered, had unsuccessfully plotted to assassinate Mao and seize power in September 1971, then had been killed in a plane crash while trying to flee to Russian-controlled Mongolia.

"Do you expect the world to believe that?" one editor asked, in the belief that Lin's plane had been shot down over China, if he had not been executed before he could ever take off. Responded Chou, turning the tables: "Do you expect the world to believe that Lee Harvey Oswald acted alone in assassinating President Kennedy? I have told you everything. It is much clearer than your Warren Report on the assassination of J. F. Kennedy." He said he was convinced the identity of the "principal culprit, the man who planned the assassination" of President Kennedy had never been divulged. "It couldn't be" that Lee Harvey Oswald is "the one who really killed him," Chou said firmly. "It is not possible."

As we traveled west and south around China, to Shensi and Honan provinces, to the ancient capital of Sian and to Shanghai, we visited farms and factories, primary schools and universities, newspaper offices and hospitals. Everywhere we went, citizens gawked at us. They had seen far fewer foreigners pre-1972 than we had assumed. They dropped whatever they were doing to stare directly and unblinkingly at our strange faces and even stranger clothes. On one occasion, a woman bicyclist stared so intently that she failed to watch where she was going and fell off her bike. In cities and towns away from the capital, large crowds followed us down the street and clapped in greeting or rushed to the roadside to wave and clap as we drove past.

At nursery schools, we heard tots shrilly singing songs like this one:

> We're called little Red soldiers,
> We listen to Chairman Mao's every word.
> We want to be revolutionaries even when we're young.
> We want to be workers, peasants, soldiers when we're grown up.

In Sian, capital of the Chinese empire from the Chou Dynasty in the eleventh century B.C. to the end of the Tang Dynasty in A.D. 907, we were treated to an evening of music at a local theater. A male soloist sang "We Poor People Follow Chairman Mao." There was a rendition on a two-stringed fiddle of "Up the Mountain Come the Manure Carriers." The glorification of manual labor was everywhere, reinforced by the Cultural Revolution that had convulsed China from 1966 to 1969. That was when Mao turned out the nation's youth, as Red Guards, to attack privileged managerial, academic, and professional elites, and all vestiges of past traditions and privilege, in an attempt to avoid the "revisionist, capitalist-road, careerist" course he thought he had seen Russia follow.

In the Wei River valley, forty miles east of Sian, we met farmer Liu Shu-hsien. He was fifty-six but looked seventy. His face was like the fields he tilled: it was deeply furrowed and sun-strengthened and reflected a people and a land mated in adversity long before the fall of Troy. A few hundred yards from his house on the Shuang-wang Commune, women still picked cotton by hand, others in nearby fields were digging out old corn roots, also by hand, and men were driving oxen pulling wooden plows, as they had through the ages. But there also were some things there that weren't there before: three red tractors and electric pumps bringing water from wells to irrigate the fields. These and other changes were responsible for a new optimism in Liu Shuh-sien—an optimism that China would be able to win its race to keep food production rising faster than its growing population.

Before the Communists came to power, "I was a hired hand and had never been to school," Liu recalled. "Now I've been to literacy classes in the village and can read the newspaper. Before liberation, we only had grain for half a year; after that we ate husks and roots. There were forty-six households here then and seven families died of starvation between 1929 and 1949."

Did government officials and our guides, from China's official Hsinhua news agency, take us to showplace farms, schools, and factories and steer us to individuals there who had been coached on what to say to foreign visitors? Of course. No doubt about it. Yet ours was no Potemkin Village tour. We wandered into residential neighborhoods of our selection, knocking at random on the doors of houses that were a far cry from the model, modern blocks of apartments. We then went inside to look at the residents' accommodations and ask them about their lives. We walked the aisles of cross-country trains, stopping to talk with riders we selected in the coaches. We questioned people at random on the streets of the cities and in farm villages. Members of our group who had visited Russia said there was no comparison; our reporting in China was far less restricted. We saw much of the bad side—the poverty, the pervasive totalitarianism—as well as the good.

Even after making allowance for our dependence on official interpreters, the caution Chinese citizens must have felt compelled to exercise when talking to foreigners, and the impossibility of reading the minds of eight hundred million Chinese, a picture emerged that indicated the vast majority of Chinese were satisfied with their progress to date and widespread distaste for the present system was not to be found. The Chinese people, never having lived in freedom in a democracy, had no basis for comparison with foreign systems, only with what they had known before—which in the 1920s, 1930s, and 1940s had been war and widespread famine. I quoted a Western ambassador with long service in China who put it this way: "The government has removed the fear of want and the terrible uncertainty—not knowing whether you would starve, or lose your home, or freeze in the winter." I summarized my conclusion: "Millions of Chinese," I wrote, "thus appear willing to put their faith in the regime, not because of its Communist ideology but because it has bettered their lives and they look to it as the means to further improvements."

The year after our China trip, in 1973, the Chinese accepted an invitation from the American Society of Newspaper Editors to send a reciprocal delegation to visit the United States. It was the first visit to America by what they called "Chinese journalistic circles" since the Nixon trip had begun the thaw in relations between the two countries. I was chosen to host the Chinese in New York and Washington, and I did so with the logistical help of the State Department.

One evening Barbara and I invited the leader of the delegation, Chu Mu-chih, director of Hsinhua, and several of his colleagues to dinner at our house in Brooklyn Heights. We cooked hamburgers, thinking it would introduce them to a typical American dish. It was not a big hit. We did not realize that almost-raw beef was not a popular part of the Chinese diet. After dinner, we walked them, accompanied by State Department security guards, to the nearby apartment of my Uncle Eli Phillips and Aunt Hilda. He was clerk to a New York state judge, she a teacher. It gave the Chinese a look at the apartment-living conditions of typical American middle-income professionals.

Next day we toured public housing in Harlem. We realized, as did the Chinese, that the apartment that the State Department had chosen, one overlooking the East River, could be considered a showplace, far better than the typical public-housing unit. We said, "Let's push on, deeper into Harlem." As we drove north in our leased bus, the Chinese at one point suddenly shouted "Stop." They pointed to a small park and said they wanted to talk to people there at random, as we had in China. So we all piled out of the bus. As the Chinese struck up conversations with people in the park, the State Department security men suddenly went almost berserk. They had concluded it was what was known as a "needle park," a place where drugs were being traded. Fearful lest the denizens of the park think they were being raided, the security men rapidly herded the Chinese back into the bus. A few blocks later, the Chinese shouted "Stop" again and asked to disembark to interview people at random on the sidewalk. One of the Chinese rushed up to a very heavyset woman pedestrian and asked her, "Do you know anything about the People's Republic of China?" She gave him a friendly smile and replied: "No. Do you have any literature?"

In Washington, our news bureau helped me arrange a White House audience for them with President Nixon. As they filed into the Oval Office and lined up around one side of the circular wall, the president lost track of which was the front of their line and which was the rear. Neither his aides nor we corrected him as he delivered his welcoming remarks to the Hsinhua photographer at the rear of the line, turning his back on the delegation leader, Chu Mu-chih. Later, as a memento of their visit, Nixon gave each of the visitors a cheap ballpoint with a reproduction of his signature printed on it.

In 1979, we achieved one *Journal* goal for which we had lobbied during these reciprocal visits: permission to open a *Journal* news bureau in Peking. We were the third, after the *New York Times* and the Associated Press, to obtain such authorization. In the years that followed my 1972 visit, I had periodic lunches and dinners, sometimes accompanied by Barbara, at the Chinese Embassy in Washington and at their U.N. Embassy in Manhattan. And in early January 1984, Barbara and I were invited by President and Mrs. Reagan to sit at the dinner table with visiting Chinese Premier Zhao Ziyang at the state dinner the Reagans gave at the White House in his honor. Poached turbot was served as a first course that evening; beef farci en croûte, with truffle sauce, was the main course. Isaac Stern played the violin.

I visited China two more times after the 1972 trip. The second trip was in October 1977, the third in 1981. Both were trips on which I was accompanied only by *Journal* colleagues, our wives, guides provided by Hsinhua and the foreign ministry—and, in

1977, by daughter Leslie as well. Leslie had graduated from the Dalton School in Manhattan, was enrolled at Stanford University, and was nearing her twenty-first birthday. Others on the 1977 trip included Ed and Sue Cony and Peter and Francie Kann.

We visited Sinkiang Province in the far west, just north of Tibet and south of Mongolia and Siberia. From its capital at Urumchi we traveled north into the Tien Shan Mountains, close to the tense and contested border with the Soviet Union, and south into the forbidding Takla Makan Desert. The latter's name, in the language of Sinkiang's Muslim minority Uighur people, means "go in and you won't come out." Sinkiang was a frontier province in which new oil refineries rose near nomad sheep herders' conical sheepskin yurts, or tents. Trucks swerved on the highways to pass donkey carts and small camel caravans. Toward the end of our visit, I became terribly ill with dysentery, contracted perhaps from eating unpeeled grapes offered to us at a commune, or from drinking tea from a cup our peasant host there had washed in a nearby canal. After recovering from the worst of the dysentery while in a daze in an Urumchi hotel room, I flew back to Peking with the others in a nearly empty airliner, stretched out prone over three seats. Because of my weakened state, we cancelled the final leg of that trip, to Shanghai, opting to spend more time recuperating in Peking.

Cony and Kann reported a page-one leader about Sinkiang Province and China's Wild West. I wrote one about developments in China's foreign policy, including its evolving stance on Taiwan. Among the government officials we interviewed in Peking was Li Hsien-nien, then vice premier and later to become state president of China from 1983 to 1988. I believe that Leslie's presence at that interview, watching the give-and-take of the questioning, fired her interest in a career in journalism. She later worked for United Press International in Atlanta, covered Congress, politics, and presidential election campaigns for *USA Today*, and eventually became communications director of the Senate Homeland Security and Governmental Affairs Committee and an aide to Senator Joseph Lieberman, chairman of that committee. He also, in those later years, became the Democratic Party vice presidential nominee in 2000, on the Al Gore ticket that lost to Republican George W. Bush after the Supreme Court rejected challenges to crucial Florida ballots.

Our 1977 China trip also was notable in three other respects. Chu Mu-chih, director of Hsinhua and sponsor of our trip, gave a surprise twenty-first birthday party for Leslie at Hsinhua headquarters, complete with an American-style birthday cake and ice cream. In another trip sidelight, Ed Cony brought along a supply of Frisbees, and everywhere we went he introduced Frisbees to China, to the delight of our guides and the children we encountered en route. The third sidelight was our discovery of the limits of trying to translate American idiom in China. Sometimes, when we wanted to ask why something was done, we would ask, "How come?" Our guides invariably would reply, "By train."

On the 1981 return to China, Barbara and I brought Don and Ruth Macdonald, Bill Cox and wife Marty, Bob and Zobby Potter, the Conys, and Frank Ching, a Chinese-speaking *Journal* correspondent. Bill Cox, a member of the Bancroft family, Dow Jones's controlling owners, worked for the company and was a member of its board of directors. We flew from Peking to Chungking, China's wartime capital in Szechuan Province in the southwest, and boarded a riverboat there for a trip down the Yangzte River to near Shanghai. It was before the days of Linblad and other luxury boats in China. Ours was a working boat, carrying passengers and freight from town to town along the river's length. The scenery and the cities en route were beautiful and mind-expanding. The boat itself, however, was a bit on the primitive side. Bob Potter, eventually finding the filth and stench in the men's lavatory more than he could take, began using the facilities in the ladies' bathroom.

As we began and ended these trips, we usually spent time in Hong Kong. There we observed the progress of *The Asian Wall Street Journal* and often met with our fellow owners and board members of the *South China Morning Post*, on whose presses the *Asian Journal* was printed, and the overlapping board members of the *Far Eastern Economic Review*. They included the chairmen of the Hong Kong and Shanghai Bank, of Jardine Mattheson &

Company, the trading company whose roots went back to the nineteenth-century China opium trade, of Cathay Pacific Airways, and others. I also used the trips to Hong Kong to visit A-Man Hing Cheong, a Chinese tailor in the arcade of the Mandarin Hotel, who made suits of fine British woolens for less than good suits cost in New York.

I never imagined on those visits to China that years later Barbara and I would have a wondrous Chinese granddaughter, Lola Mei-ming Phillips. Our daughter Leslie returned to China in 2000 to adopt her from an orphanage in Yiwu, in the eastern coastal province of Zhejiang and south of the provincial capital of Hangzhou, south of Shanghai. Lola is a sparkling gem, treasured by our family. We could not imagine the emperors and mandarins of her native land, down through the centuries in China's long and storied history, treasuring their riches more.

CHAPTER 22

Pioneering the Sky,
Diversifying the Corporation

SIX MEN FROM DOW JONES and the Communications Satellite Corporation stood in a darkened room in the fall of 1973 at Comsat's laboratories in Clarksburg, Maryland. With the push of a button, an image of page one of *The Wall Street Journal* was transmitted to the Intelsat IV satellite twenty-two thousand miles over the Atlantic Ocean, and the satellite retransmitted the image another twenty-two thousand miles back to earth to a receiver in the Clarksburg lab. The round-trip, resulting in identical reproduction of the printed page, took six minutes and twelve seconds.

The experiment, jointly conducted by Comsat and Dow Jones, demonstrated the practicality of using orbiting satellites for the speedy, efficient, and economic transmission of newspaper pages. A year later, in the fall of 1974, Dow Jones and Comsat successfully transmitted *Journal* pages by satellite, under actual production conditions, from our plant in Chicopee, Massachusetts, to our South Brunswick, New Jersey, printing facility. Later that year, a new plant was opened in Orlando, Florida, served by satellite. These breakthroughs opened the way to sending a global newspaper's pages to more far-distant printing plants, closer to readers around our country and around the world. The incredible was turned into the commonplace.

The space pioneers at Dow Jones were George Flynn, vice president for operations; his deputy, Bill Dunn, business manager and later George's successor; and Glenn Jenkins, Bob Vedder, and other technicians working for them in the *Journal*'s Production Department. At the time of the Apollo space program, scientists had developed a computerized shorthand permitting the astronauts to send massive amounts of data back to earth. This data compression enabled the radio circuits to carry much greater quantities of data than had been possible before. Dow Jones's technicians then raised the question, could a similar technique permit all the data necessary for facsimile transmission of the *Journal* to be squeezed onto ordinary telephone circuits? After years of effort, they succeeded in having equipment developed to accomplish this; they also developed the transmitters and receivers that were used that day in 1973 in Clarksburg—all essential to launching the satellite age at the *Journal* and, subsequently, other newspapers.

Bill Kerby and I had no technical expertise and played no part in these breakthroughs other than as rapt admirers and cheerleaders. We were transfixed by their potential, of course. The *Journal*'s national network of printing plants was expanded from nine regional plants in 1970 to twelve by 1979 and then to seventeen a few years later, in the early 1980s, all served by satellite. Our publishing centers in Asia, and later in Europe, were able to bring newspapers to printing presses—and readers—in far-off regions by satellite transmissions, too. *Journal* circulation had risen from 930,879 at the end of 1965 to 1,298,482 at the end of 1972. Now the beanstalk growth would accelerate: to 1,930,400 by year-end 1980, up 32 percent in the previous five years to make the *Journal* the largest newspaper in the nation. By 1980 its circulation was three times that of the *Washington Post*, twice that of the *New York Times*. It had more subscribers in California than in New York.

Dow Jones at the same time was diversifying, by internally initiated ventures and by acquisitions. By 1977 these activities accounted for 30 percent of Dow Jones's earnings and revenues, compared with only 6 percent from non-*Journal* sources in 1965. That was the year Barney Kilgore had commissioned Brad Mills to do a diversification study in a first step to lessen the company's almost total dependence on the *Journal*.

Two of the recommendations in the Mills report were that Dow Jones explore expanding into general community newspapers and the book business, and Bill Kerby soon moved the company into both areas. Jim Ottaway Sr., Bill's golfing partner at Buck Hill Falls, Pennsylvania, where both owned vacation cottages, had built up a group of nine community dailies in the Northeast. He agreed to sell them to Dow Jones in return for stock. Because Jim was a friend, Bill turned the negotiations over to me.

Jim and I met in a suite at the Buck Hill Inn. After we had used standard formulas to arrive at a value—multiples of cash flow, multiples of revenues, multiples of earnings, and the like—I said to Jim, "Your company's debt has to be deducted from the final value and price, of course." He bristled and said, "If you are going to insist on that, there will be no deal." Jim Ottaway was a canny and tough negotiator, but we finally settled on a price both sides thought fair and Dow Jones acquired Ottaway Newspapers on July 11, 1970. We went on to have a warm and happy relationship for more than two decades, first with Jim and then with his successor, his son Jim Ottaway Jr. By 1990 Dow Jones and its Ottaway Newspapers subsidiary had acquired additional newspapers from Medford, Oregon, to Santa Cruz, California, and Traverse City, Michigan, building the community newspapers group from the original nine dailies to twenty-three in twelve states.

In 1975 we acquired Richard D. Irwin Inc., a respected college textbook publisher based in Homewood, Illinois. We had courted its founder, Dick Irwin, for a few years before that, by starting a joint venture to publish business books and then buying a 20 percent interest in his company. Dick, like many founders, didn't find it easy to adjust to the rules that governed life in a publicly owned company. The Irwin company owned a plane and a motor yacht. The boat was useful for entertaining and signing new authors, Dick maintained, but I told him we could not justify owning a yacht and would sell it to him at its depreciated value. He said all right, and we settled on June 30 as the closing date on the transaction and time of transfer. A month after that we discovered that just before the transfer, while the boat still was Dow Jones property, he had had both engines replaced with new ones—at Dow Jones's expense. We had agreed he could keep the plane as a company plane so long as it was used to fly Irwin executives, not just him, around the country on company business. A year or so later we found that he had used the plane to fly a friend and her son to his Ocala, Florida, horse farm. So we got rid of the plane, too—selling it to him at its depreciated value—rather than try to police the Irwin company's founder, who was continuing to serve as its chief executive.

Another profitable acquisition was a 40 percent interest in a newsprint mill that was built in 1974 at Rivière-du-Loup, Quebec, on the south shore of the St. Lawrence River. Our partner in that venture, Peter Brant's Bato Company, was majority owner and operator of the mill. In 1979, with Bato in the same role, we both joined with the *Washington Post* to build a second newsprint mill in Virginia. Newsprint manufacturing was cyclical. In boom times, when newspaper advertising and circulation rose, demand for paper to accommodate this growth rose, resulting in rising newsprint prices and often shortages. In recessions, the opposite usually occurred: a supply glut and falling prices. Dow Jones's ownership stakes in newsprint mills were designed to safeguard our supplies in times of shortage and serve as a hedge against rising prices, with the higher costs to the *Journal* and our other newspapers being offset by rising profits from the mills in those times; in recessions, profits from the mills might decline, but lower paper costs would benefit our newspapers at the same time.

Barney Kilgore always opposed the acquisition of radio or TV broadcast stations. He argued government control of their licenses would give Washington too much potential power over the parent company. Kerby and I followed his lead in this. Dow Jones began to produce and sell business-news programming to the broadcasters, however. By 1988, the weekly "Wall Street Journal Report" was carried by 102 American TV stations, and others in Japan and Europe; 132 radio stations broadcast Dow Jones business-news programs.

A much bigger step was the purchase in 1981 of 24.5 percent of Continental Cablevision, then the country's twelfth largest operator of cable television systems, with 450,000 subscribers in ten states. Continental had been built by Amos "Bud" Hostetter, a youthful, charismatic leader, active in Amherst College alumni affairs. I joined his board and attended his wedding. We all liked him and admired his vision and energy. By 1986, Continental had grown to the nation's third largest cable systems operator.

Of course, not all of our early diversification efforts, or later ones, were successful. In July 1977, two years after Bill Kerby retired and I was elected chief executive officer, I made the difficult decision to close the weekly *National Observer*. It had more than four hundred thousand loyal subscribers and had won wide respect for its high standards. But we had not succeeded, in fifteen years of hard effort by many of us on the news and sales sides of the company, in making enough readers and advertisers feel sufficient need for it to turn it into a profitable venture. Some Dow Jones veterans said the audience, though sizable, was diffuse and thus not clearly enough defined to attract large-scale advertising.

We had other failures, too. We acquired the magazine *Book Digest* in mid-1978, convinced it had much potential. We did not succeed in getting enough advertisers to agree with us. We closed it in 1982. There would be larger stumbles in future years.

But one internal diversification move, in 1973, though modest at the time, marked the planting of the seed that would grow in future years into a major business, the electronic part of Dow Jones, increasingly important as print weakened as a medium throughout the country in the 1990s and 2000s. This precursor of things to come was the introduction, in partnership with Bunker Ramo Corporation, of a computerized news retrieval service. Stock brokerage firms, banks, and other businesses gained the ability to bring up on their employees' existing stock-quote desk terminals information that the *Journal, Barron's,* and the Dow Jones News Service had published on particular companies or particular industries that day or over the previous several months. This entry into electronic publishing, sometimes called computerized information retrieval or database publishing, was pioneered by the same visionary innovators who were harnessing space satellites for the company, George Flynn and Bill Dunn.

The original retrieval service on other vendors' stock-quote video terminals was expanded in 1977 by the addition of a low-cost interactive service providing business and financial information for corporate users. By 1984 Dow Jones News Retrieval, as it was called, served 185,000 client terminals, having doubled its customer base each year since 1980. By 1988 it had added forty-nine databases; their offerings included medical and education information, an encyclopedia, text searches into 160 business publications and twenty regional and national newspapers, and airline reservation capability. The foundation was being laid for the interactive electronic edition of *The Wall Street Journal* that grew in paying subscribers through the 1990s and is so popular and profitable today.

While all the early technological strides and diversification moves were under way, the *Journal* continued its pursuit of editorial excellence, not only in its coverage of business but also in its reporting of national politics and other areas that served the readers' broader interests. Jerry Landauer, a tenacious Washington Bureau reporter, won the 1973 Drew Pearson Award and the 1974 Worth Bingham Award for his investigative reporting on Nixon's vice president, Spiro Agnew, and his finances—stories that capped four years of work. He was the first to disclose that the then–vice president was under criminal investigation for corruption. Another Washington reporter, Jonathan Spivak, won the American Heart Association's 1973 Howard Blakeslee Award for two articles—one about steps being taken to reduce heart-disease deaths and the other about controversy over the value and effectiveness of coronary bypass surgery.

In 1985, George Flynn died prematurely of cancer. He was a reserved, Lincolnesque figure. As we filed out of the church in his Illinois hometown after his funeral, Peter Brant, who had worked closely with George on our newsprint projects, said, "He was a business statesman."

I had promoted Bill Dunn, an Iowan, years before to vice president and general manager, and in 1984 to executive vice president. Like George, he had come up through the ranks at our printing plants. But he was different. He was a restless, keyed-up bundle of brains and energy. He relished being regarded as something of a loose cannon—personally, not professionally—as he tested the limits of displaying his independence. But he far outdistanced his peers at other publishing companies in building up our electronic information services and leading us into the digital age.

As Dow Jones prospered in these years, its stock price rose on the New York Stock Exchange. The stock's price-earnings ratio—the multiple of annual earnings per share by which the free market valued and priced each share—was higher than that of other publishing companies. I was sitting in an auditorium one day, waiting to be joined by my colleagues in making a presentation to a group of Wall Street securities analysts, when Bill Dunn came in the door. I got a kick out of overhearing one analyst nearby say to her neighbor: "Here comes the multiple."

CHAPTER 23

Four Dauntless Phillips Women

IN THE PHILLIPS HOUSEHOLD in the 1970s, Barbara was teaching, taking students to Europe, and starting a writing career. Our three daughters were moving through high school and into their college years and beyond, with adventures along the way that included a close encounter by Nina with a celebrated murderer.

All three daughters had begun their schooling at the Packer Collegiate Institute, a walk of about three blocks east of our Hicks Street house in Brooklyn Heights. Beside the As and Bs and generally laudatory remarks on their elementary-school report cards, there occasionally were comments like these on Lisa's March 1962 third-grade report card: "Lisa's mercurial, outspoken temperament has its advantages. She is an enthusiastic contributor to all our discussions. . . . Life will never be dull for Lisa. . . . The work is not too difficult for her, although she does make it unnecessarily complicated by insisting on her own point of view instead of checking with the book."

And on Leslie's kindergarten report that same month: "Leslie is an alert and capable little girl. Alas, she follows wrong leadership. . . . She thinks it funny to be flip, even impudent. . . . Leslie yawns all day, claiming that her sister keeps her from sleeping."

By 1971, Lisa had graduated from Packer's high school and had entered Middlebury College. Leslie in that year transferred to the Dalton School in Manhattan in her second year of high school. After graduating in June 1974 and going on to Colorado

College for one year, she transferred to Stanford. She graduated from Stanford in 1979, after taking one year off to accompany us to China and then work as a reporter on a newspaper in Noe Valley, a southern section of San Francisco.

Barbara, having earned her master's degree from New York University, began teaching high school English literature at Packer in 1971 and continued there through most of the seventies. On November 8, 1972, the chair of the English Department, Jane Rinden, wrote a report on sitting in on one of Barbara's classes of sixteen students: "Despite the fact that this was the last period of the day," she wrote, "the class was an exciting one. At times students could hardly keep their seats while waiting to be called on. . . . In her questions and comments, and in the supplementary information she offered the students, the great care of Mrs. Phillips's preparation was revealed. She knows how to stimulate students."

Nina transferred from Packer to the Chapin School in Manhattan when we moved from Brooklyn Heights to an apartment at 520 East Eighty-Sixth Street, with the two older girls away at college. Following her first year of high school at Chapin, in the fall of 1977, Nina transferred to the Madeira School, a girls' boarding school in McLean, Virginia, just outside Washington.

Before graduating from Middlebury, Lisa spent the winter and spring of 1974 in a "junior year abroad" academic program in Vienna. She wrote home that she had received an A in a crash course in German—"Of course, I wouldn't have stood for anything less." Her letter reported she had made four close friends in Vienna, "all girls, unfortunately." I visited Lisa in the spring, after a business trip to Germany, and sent a postcard to Nina at home, reporting "we are in a restaurant eating chocolate pancakes. . . . Lisa says you are the best letter writer." In April, Lisa and friends traveled by train through Italy—Florence, Venice, Rome, then on to Naples. They enjoyed the trip until, in Naples, one of her girl friends was attacked, and they fled back to Vienna.

Also in early 1974, Barbara and a fellow teacher, Barbara Winthrop, took a group of Packer high school girls to London on a winter-break trip. They saw original Shakespeare and Milton manuscripts at the British Museum, toured Canterbury and Stratford, Windsor Castle and Eton. And, of course, they shopped; Barbara bought a British woolen sweater for Leslie, a Sherlock Holmes cap for Nina. One girl, with previous psychiatric problems unknown to the teachers, had to be sent home after becoming homesick to the point of extreme despondency and threatening suicide if she was not allowed to go home. The group's other experiences were less threatening, though worrisome in other ways. "Two of the high school seniors have sneaked out with members of the hotel staff, sad-eyed Maltese," Barbara wrote to us. "And two headwaiters and one hotel manager have been propositioning Barbara Winthrop and me."

While Nina was at the Madeira School, I was invited to serve on the school's board of trustees, and I did so for several years. But on March 8, 1980, three months before Nina's scheduled graduation, she and her three suite mates, all student government leaders, were expelled. The headmistress had searched and found a few dried-up marijuana plant stems and a small smoking pipe at the bottom of a laundry hamper in their two-room suite, under the dirty clothes. The headmistress was Jean Harris. She expelled the girls on a Friday. Two days later, on Sunday, March 10, she drove to Purchase, New York, with a pistol and fired four shots at close range into her lover, cardiologist Dr. Herman "Hy" Tarnower, the so-called Scarsdale Diet doctor, killing him.

The three other girls' fathers and I appealed the expulsion. We argued (1) the punishment—expulsion, rather than a suspension—was out of proportion to the crime since it was a first offense and there was no evidence, and the girls denied, that they had smoked marijuana on the school grounds, and (2) the headmistress, as the Sunday murder demonstrated, had not been of sound mind when making the decision to expel the seniors. The school authorities, anxious not to relax discipline in the midst of their crisis, denied the appeal. We fathers then hired a Washington attorney to represent us. The upshot was that the girls could not return to school but were permitted to study for the final exams while home, take the exams, and if they passed, return to graduate with their class. That is what happened. Nina went on to Colgate University. Jean Harris was convicted and went to prison.

Up to that point Barbara and I had always admired Jean Harris. She was clearly high-strung, but she encouraged the Madeira girls to believe they could accomplish anything in life. That was exactly what Barbara emphasized to our daughters while they were growing up. Barbara had read Betty Friedan's *The Feminine Mystique* when it was first published, as well as Germaine Greer and other feminist writers. She was a fervent believer that women should be strong and independent and that there should be no barriers in our society to equal opportunities for women. She was an active worker on behalf of the National Organization of Women, its NOW Legal Defense and Education Fund, Planned Parenthood, and other organizations working for women's rights.

Nina, after college, went on to scout potential movie material for UA–Columbia Pictures, Tom Hanks, and then Sony Pictures. She eventually left the film business in order to have more time at home with Kate, Nina's and then-husband Kai Hedbabny's sweet and lovely daughter, while Kate was growing up. Nina earned a master's degree in special education (for children with learning disabilities) and taught first at Greenwich Academy in Greenwich, Connecticut, then at the Waterside School in Stamford, Connecticut, and later at the Stevenson School in Pebble Beach, California, all of them independent, or private, schools. Leslie, as mentioned in an earlier chapter, covered Congress and politics for *USA Today*, then became an aide to Senator Joseph Lieberman of Connecticut and communications director of the Senate Homeland Security and Governmental Affairs Committee. Lisa started as an intern at New York's Whitney Museum of American Art, then managed the Whitney's several branch museums and was a curator at the Whitney for many years. In 1999 she became the director of the New Museum of Contemporary Art in downtown New York. She raised $70 million to build a new building on the Bowery for the museum in 2007, the museum's first free-standing home. The year Lisa became the director of the New Museum—1999—was the same year Olivia and Savannah Phillips-Falk, Lisa and husband Leon Falk's frisky and fabulous twin daughters, were born.

CHAPTER 24

European Beachheads

IN THE EARLY 1970S, my colleagues and I at Dow Jones began exploring expansion into Europe's markets. Business and investments were becoming more international, as were the information needs of American and foreign readers. Because the *Financial Times* and the *International Herald Tribune* presented formidable competition in Europe, much more so than in Asia, we began by seeking to acquire established local-language European business newspaper publishers. When this produced more colorful adventures than successful ventures, we then proceeded on our own and began publication of a European edition of the *Journal, The Wall Street Journal Europe.*

The initial explorations were led by Don Macdonald, Dow Jones's chief marketing strategist and Asia point man, and Ray Shaw, who had spearheaded the news side of our first major overseas venture, the AP–Dow Jones Economic Report newswire service. Don first courted Jacqueline Beytout, owner of *Les Echos,* an influential French daily economic newspaper, and soon began negotiations to try to acquire it. Madame Beytout was often called "the groundnuts queen" because her first husband, when he died, had left her a fortune he made in Senegal growing peanuts—called groundnuts in Africa and Europe. She was quirky and unpredictable, but she took a fancy to Don. He went to Paris to negotiate; she came to New York to negotiate. It didn't take long for us to realize that her interest was more in the charming, smooth-talking Don Macdonald and in receiving an infusion of Dow Jones investment capital than it was in surrendering control over her newspaper or allowing us to persuade her to change her business operating methods in significant ways. We also realized that she would have made too volatile and unpredictable a partner if we had let her stay on, as she wanted. And so we bid her adieu and turned elsewhere.

Next, beginning in mid-1973, we explored a relationship with West Germany's Axel Springer Verlag, that country's largest publishing company. We began by proposing that we jointly launch a new German-language business daily, or jointly acquire and expand *Handelsblatt*, the principal existing German business newspaper. A meeting was arranged in early July 1973 with Axel Springer, the company's founder and controlling owner, at his original Hamburg headquarters, where his first newspaper, the *Hamburger Abendblatt*, was published. Bill Kerby, Don Macdonald, Ray Shaw, and I represented Dow Jones. The Springer intermediary in making these arrangements was Ernst Cramer, a likable German-born former officer in the American army, fluent in both languages. Shortly before we left for Hamburg, Cramer mysteriously but enthusiastically told us he had been instructed to urge us: "Think big, think real big."

In Hamburg, we met Axel Springer, who had built an impressive postwar media empire of newspapers, magazines, and broadcasting stations in West Germany. His papers controlled almost half the newspaper circulation in the country. They included *Bild*, a Berlin-based national tabloid with the country's largest circulation, and *Die Welt*, a serious full-sized newspaper respected in Germany and beyond, particularly for its analytical coverage of foreign-policy issues. Springer, then sixty-two, was a cordial and charming host at lunch. Very few other Springer executives were present. We began preliminary discussions. Then he invited us to continue our talks as his weekend guests at Schierensee, his historic country house and estate north of Hamburg. He preceded us by helicopter. Then Ernst Cramer and a driver, in two cars, took Bill, Don, Ray, and me north to Schierensee. Cramer and Springer's wife, Friede, were with us for the weekend, but no other Springer executives.

It was an unforgettable weekend, for several reasons.

The security on the approaches to the estate and inside the grounds was unusually tight. A violent left-wing German group, the Red Army Faction, calling its members "urban guerrillas" and also known as the Baader-Meinhof Gang, had bombed the Springer headquarters in Hamburg in May 1970, injuring seventeen, and had attacked other leading conservatives and businesspeople. Attempts had been made on Springer's life. In one instance, a booby-trapped bomb had been discovered inside one of his toilets, rigged to explode when the pressure of a body was detected on the toilet seat.

Springer showed us with pride his meticulous restoration of the main house, guesthouses, and outbuildings he had bought from the impoverished noble family that had owned the estate. Antique furniture, tableware, and rugs from the period of the main house's original eighteenth-century construction had been used to refurnish the house. And Springer's collection of faience, colorfully decorated glazed earthenware, of which he was immensely proud and for which he had full-color catalogs, was prominently displayed in the dining room.

As we sat outside on the stone terrace and chatted, he talked of his dedication to reconciling Germany and the Jews, his funding of projects in Israel, and the honors Israel had bestowed on him. The honors had been in recognition of his personal efforts and those of his publications, at his direction, to raise German public awareness of the realities of the Holocaust and to promote closer ties between West Germany and Israel. At other times he talked of recent dangers he had faced aboard his large sailing yacht in the Mediterranean when a howling gale bore down on them at Malta and they put out to sea to ride out the storm in open water. "I was hero," he said with a smile. He spoke, too, of other close brushes with danger: A Baader-Meinhof Gang attack had aimed to catch him at his summer home, on a private island he owned off the German North Sea coast, but because he fortunately had just left, he narrowly escaped the would-be assassins. They burned the house down.

Later, in Springer's study after dinner, it became obvious he had done his homework on us. He showed detailed familiarity with Dow Jones's history, structure, ownership, and the financial information publicly available in our annual reports—and with the backgrounds of each of us guests. It also became obvious, as Ernst Cramer had hinted earlier, that Springer's interest went far beyond starting or buying a German business newspaper with us. He had a grander alliance in mind. His vision was to combine our two media organizations as one means to bind Germany closer to America. He dreamed of a Germany that would be part of an Atlantic alliance. He was not enthusiastic about the alternative: Germany's future bound to other European states, some of whom he regarded as historically and morally weaker, in a European union. He proposed for starters that Dow Jones take a large minority stake in his publishing empire, and that the Springer organization be given a similar stake in Dow Jones in return. We agreed to exchange detailed financial information so that his proposal could be studied and seriously considered.

"America is the hope of the world, and particularly it is the hope of Germany," he said. He had studied several American publishers, he said, and had selected Dow Jones as the one most compatible in economic-political values and publishing philosophy. "I trust you," he said.

The following evening, after dinner, he took me aside and asked me to join him alone in a small, well-appointed windowless hideaway beneath a staircase. There were only two armchairs and a small table there. Asking me to sit beside him, he spoke again about how he had picked Dow Jones as his potential American partner only after a thorough investigation not only of our publications and our business but of our values and compatibility as well. He then turned peculiarly personal. Sensing that Bill Kerby was close to retirement and that I would be his successor, he said he wanted to regard me as a son, someone who could someday inherit on behalf of Dow Jones what he had built in Germany. His words were somewhat bizarre, yet touching. (As an aside: Springer did have one son, Axel Jr., a photographer. He committed suicide in 1980 at age thirty-eight.)

It would be easy to think that this appeal for an emotional connection was just a ploy from a manipulative deal maker, employing a variety of approaches in a negotiation, to seek to soften up and make more malleable the negotiator on the other side of the table. Perhaps. But I don't think Springer was being that cynical, that devious, that scheming. I believe he was a very idealistic individual, one who operated above the nitty-gritty and who truly was dedicated to achieving his vision of bringing Germany and the United States closer together in an Atlantic alliance. His idea of a publishing partnership of like-minded citizens was one means by which he said he hoped to advance that goal, and naïve though it may seem to some, I was inclined to take him and his declared purpose at face value. So were my colleagues.

We returned to the United States, after visiting with Springer a new headquarters he had built in Berlin. Back home, we won the Dow Jones board of directors' approval to seriously explore such a publishing alliance. I even put myself into a Berlitz total-immersion course for quick familiarity with the German language. But in the end, the alliance with Springer was not to be.

After the Dow Jones board approved active exploration of the Springer proposal, we received access to his organization's books and detailed, confidential operating reports. They increased our interest and enthusiasm. At Bill Kerby's request, I took charge of conducting a meticulous study under the code name "Project Julius." We developed a negotiating position, looking toward exchanging 40 percent of Dow Jones ownership for 40 percent of the Springer properties. Our board met again, in December 1973, and gave us authority to negotiate a deal with such terms. But then the plan began to unravel. Springer, unknown to us and unanticipated by us, appeared initially to have acted idealistically on his own without having first consulted and lined up the support of his key operating executives and board members. Though he was his company's controlling owner, he needed them—as we would—for the effective future running of the company.

We had met some of them on our earlier visit to the Springer building in Berlin. Springer had erected the building flush up against the Berlin Wall as a symbol of faith in the continued existence of a free West Berlin. It also clearly was a symbol of defiance of the Communist regime to the east, even though the inscription on the building read, "Not in Defiance But in Confidence." We had lunch in front of floor-to-ceiling windows that overlooked the barbed wire, the sentry watchtowers, and the strip of barren no-man's-land between them and the Wall. Present then was Peter Tamm, the company's chief operating officer and a former naval officer. He and the others seemed only aware then of the cover story: that we were there to discuss starting a new West German business daily with them.

But now, in late 1973 and early 1974, as I and some of my colleagues made several return trips to Schierensee, Hamburg, and Berlin to negotiate the larger enterprise, Herr Tamm sat across the table with his company's chief financial officer, "Dr. Prince Reuss"; Peter Boenisch, a former editor of *Bild*; and Ernst Cramer. Axel's son was present initially, as were others. Axel soon absented himself, making it clear that he had no intention of involving himself in the details of price negotiations.

Tamm and his colleagues were more than tough negotiators; we got the strong impression that they were antagonistic to the notion of diluting their authority with partners and thus were cold to the proposed transaction. We, for our part, grew increasingly concerned about the difficulties we would encounter working with company executives whose lack of enthusiasm was translating into hostility to the project. Later, a key director, the chairman of automaker BMW, weighed in, saying that certain tax considerations had been overlooked and now would mandate sharply increasing the price initially contemplated by both sides and going beyond the price parameters approved by our board. It was at that point that the negotiations broke down. Springer seemed to lack the will to go against the foot-dragging and not-so-subtle opposition of his own executives and board and thereby risk provoking open confrontation and revolt by them.

In a letter following the breakdown in January, hand-addressed to me personally and signed Axel, Springer said:

> One of the many frustrations in life is the fact that good things take agonizingly long to materialize. . . . Writing these

lines, I look down on the Wall and beyond. I am also looking forward to the American-German partnership which
we hope to create. And I know that in such partnership lie
hope and fulfillment of dreams. . . . I am confident that
Ernst's and Peter's visit will find a way to break the impasse
we seem to have reached. For, as far as I am concerned, the
goal remains, as I know it does with you.

Cramer and Boenisch flew to New York to try to resuscitate
the talks. Bill Kerby wrote a report to the Dow Jones board:

> Both were most apologetic about the first results and stressed
> both had strongly recommended the agreement. They were
> told it was up to them to sell their viewpoint and they now
> are armed with elaborate data sheets supporting our posi-
> tion. Phillips stressed it had been a mistake not to have the
> principal present at the key meeting. To this they agreed.
> Also he said that if there were further conversations both the
> principal and his outside financial advisor would have to be
> present. . . . To this they also agreed.

Cramer, on his return to Germany and after submitting his
report, wrote me saying a "summit meeting" was anticipated
"within the near future" in London.

But the opposition within the Springer hierarchy was too strong
to permit an agreement to go forward on reasonable terms. The
Springer dream remained only a dream. We turned our full
attention to stepping up the pace of the expansion we already
had begun in Asia, starting an Asian edition there in 1976, *The
Asian Wall Street Journal,* and using the lessons learned there to
lay the groundwork for entering Europe several years later with a
companion European edition, *The Wall Street Journal Europe.*

With that launch, in late January 1983, the *Journal* further
evolved into a truly global newspaper. It was now a paper serving
what was rapidly turning into a globalized economy, where businesspeople, investors, and other readers had interests that con-

stantly crossed national boundaries and who needed information and insights that no longer were limited to their own countries but instead were worldwide in reach.

We appointed Norman Pearlstine to lead the launch of *The Wall Street Journal Europe* and to serve as its first editor and publisher. Norm, a onetime *Journal* Tokyo Bureau chief whom Peter Kann had recruited as his managing editor when *The Asian Wall Street Journal* was launched in 1976, thus was experienced in the start-up of an overseas edition. He had gone from the Asian post to a job as an executive editor of *Forbes* magazine, based in Los Angeles, then had been persuaded, thanks largely to Peter's efforts, to rejoin the *Journal* as national editor in New York.

Now, assigned to start a European edition, he assembled a staff, planned news-coverage strategy to compete with the *Financial Times* and *International Herald Tribune*, worked up prototype pages, and moved into a newly leased publishing headquarters in Brussels. Printing was subcontracted to a Dutch newspaper with presses in Heerlen, The Netherlands, just across the Belgian-Dutch border.

In late January 1983, I and other New York executives joined Norm and his staff in Brussels, watched as the first issue was edited and assembled, then drove to Heerlen to be present for the initial pressrun. To our dismay, there was an electrical outage that plunged the printing plant into darkness and promised to block the press start. The platemaking and press crews did their preparatory work using flashlights and lanterns, while we observers wandered about nervously in this eerie light. With the help of standby generators and finally a resumption of power, the first issue of *The Wall Street Journal Europe*—the issue of January 31, 1983—did roll off the presses, even if a little late, and trucks sped the papers to distribution points throughout Europe. Champagne glasses were raised late that night in the Heerlen plant to toast this milestone occasion in *Journal* history. In coming years arrangements would be negotiated to send images of the European *Journal*'s pages by satellite to subcontractors' printing plants first in Switzerland, then outside London, then to other countries, to achieve broader and more timely day-of-publication delivery.

A few weeks after *The Wall Street Journal Europe*'s start-up, the Dutch managers of the Heerlen printing plant, who had been present that night to oversee and operate their presses, sent me and other *Journal* executives who had been present brass, kerosene-fed Dutch miners' lanterns, once in use in the coal mines near Heerlen. Some of us still have them as sturdy, beautiful mementos of that night when the lights went out, threatening to black out our opening-night pressrun and debut.

In subsequent years I was approached separately by *Washington Post* publisher Katharine Graham and *New York Times* publisher Arthur O. "Punch" Sulzberger, whose papers co-owned the *International Herald Tribune*, with proposals to share ownership of the *Tribune* and combine the European *Journal* with the *Tribune* in one, arguably stronger American daily in Europe. I always thanked them but said no. I was convinced that the two-thirds ownership by the *Times* and *Post* would always leave them in control, calling the shots on the newspaper's news, circulation, and advertising strategy, and that they would relegate the *Journal* to the role of provider of a beefed-up business section for their general-interest paper.

In late 1983 we moved the talented Norm Pearlstine back to New York as managing editor of *The Wall Street Journal*, leaving his deputy, John Huey, to continue his work in Europe as editor of the European edition. Paul Atkinson, a respected *Journal* advertising executive, was named publisher. In New York, as Norm succeeded Larry O'Donnell as managing editor, Larry became an associate editor. Fred Taylor, who had been executive editor, had left the paper. Norm clearly now was moving to take charge as the *Journal*'s top news executive. He would remain so and do an outstanding job of continuing to improve the paper and build its strength for many years, past my own 1991 retirement.

CHAPTER **25**

Publisher Pals

I JOINED AND BEGAN ATTENDING the annual conventions of the American Newspaper Publishers Association (ANPA) when I became president of Dow Jones in 1972 and then, in 1975, chief executive officer. The title chairman of the board was added in 1978 after Bill Kerby retired from the board. I served on the ANPA's board of directors from 1976 to 1984. Barney Kilgore always avoided the publishers' conventions, preferring those of the American Society of Newspaper Editors, saying of the publisher gatherings, "All they want to talk about is the price of newsprint." He had a point. In general, Barbara and I, too, preferred the company of the editors. But the key words there are "in general." We made many friends among the publishers. It doubtless was more than coincidence that those with whom we found common interests and the greatest congeniality were those who, by their actions, sometimes at great risk, had demonstrated that they never put their commercial interests ahead of their editorial obligations to the public.

High on that list was Katharine "Kay" Graham, publisher of the *Washington Post*. Our friendship ripened after we flew together to an ANPA board gathering at the Mauna Kea resort on the big island of Hawaii. Lying on the beach together between meetings, I was touched by her willingness to share personal confidences about the way her domineering mother—and sometimes her husband, the brilliant and charismatic Phil Graham, who suffered from bipolar disorder and eventually committed suicide—had habitually put her down. She spoke of how she still fought shyness, a fear of public speaking, and a feeling of inferiority even after she took over the *Washington Post* on her husband's death. In the years that followed she proved herself—and gradually gained confidence—by standing up, first, to holdover executives at the *Post* who tried to patronize her in the beginning, and then to the heaviest government intimidation pressures when she approved publishing the Pentagon Papers and later the Watergate reporting of Bob Woodward and Carl Bernstein. She subsequently disclosed, in her 1997 autobiography *Personal History*, some of the mother-husband slights and her feelings of inadequacy that we talked about that day on the Hawaiian beach and at other times. *Personal History* won a Pulitzer Prize for its merits, not least of which was its candor.

Barbara and I were among Kay Graham's summer weekend houseguests for several years at her Martha's Vineyard, Massachusetts, summer home and frequent guests at her Washington dinner parties. One day at Martha's Vineyard, fellow guests Bob Woodward and British Ambassador Peter Jay spent long hours walking the beach together. Woodward reported Jay had been seeking his advice on ending the notorious affair then in progress between Jay's wife, Margaret, and Woodward's friend and Watergate colleague Carl Bernstein. Margaret Jay was the daughter of former British Prime Minister James Callaghan. That evening, with Kay driving Barbara, Woodward, and me to a cocktail party, Kay said to Woodward: "I just cannot imagine Carl having an affair with Margaret. She seems so regal. He must think he's sleeping with the queen of England." To which Woodward replied: "Maybe she thinks she's sleeping with Disraeli."

Other Vineyard guests with whom we shared Kay's hospitality, as well as hours on the tennis court with her, on different summer weekends included Felix and Liz Rohaytn, he the Lazard Freres partner who engineered New York City's rescue from near-bankruptcy and later became U.S. ambassador to France; Ed and Judy Ney, he then head of the Young & Rubicam ad agency and later to become U.S. ambassador to Canada; Allan and Sondra Gotlieb, he the Canadian ambassador to Washington, she a novelist; Frank and Julia Daniels, he the owner-publisher of the *Raleigh* (North Carolina) *News and Observer*; and Frank and Jane Batten, he the chairman of Landmark Communications, owner of the *Norfolk Virginian-Pilot* and other newspapers, and founder of the Weather Channel. I enjoyed the company of these other guests and felt at ease with them not only because they were smart and engaging in conversation but also because they seemed down-to-earth and lacking in pretension, a contrast to the self-important blowhards sometimes encountered in all walks of life, including a few corners of journalism.

On June 30, 1987, Barbara and I attended Kay's seventieth birthday party. It was a big celebration, attended by hundreds and arranged by her four children, but primarily organized by daughter Lally Weymouth, who rented Washington's Departmental Auditorium for the occasion. Kay, though, supervised the guest list and seating arrangements. President Reagan brought his wine glass to the podium and toasted her with a Bogart imitation: "Here's looking at you, kid." Humor columnist Art Buchwald, one of the evening's eight toast givers, told the black-tie crowd, many from government and business, always wary of unflattering coverage in the *Washington Post*: "There's one word that brings us all together here tonight. And that word is *fear*." Former Secretary of State Henry Kissinger admitted that he "felt some trepidation when my former chief, President Nixon, called Kay in my presence with the suggestion that I instruct the *Washington Post* editorial board on the error of its ways. It was one of my least successful missions but as it turned out one of the most important events of my life. For out of that meeting grew a friendship which is one of the central facts of Nancy's and my life." Meg Greenfield, *Washington Post* editorial page editor and long one of Kay's closest buddies, talked of her boss's "outlaw" nature and "criminal mind." In her early days at the paper, she said, Mrs. Graham used to call her in midafternoon to sneak out to the movies.

In late 1980, after Ronald Reagan's election but in the interregnum before his inauguration, philanthropist and socialite Brooke Astor, a friend of Kay's, gave a dinner party at her New York apartment to introduce the president-elect and his wife,

Nancy, to New Yorkers "they should know." Kay gave a similar party for them at her Washington home. I surmised that it was on Kay's recommendation that Mrs. Astor invited Barbara and me, for neither of us had met her before.

We found Allan Gotlieb and his wife, Sondra, whom we had met as fellow houseguests at Kay's Vineyard home, to be both bright and delightful company, as did most of Washington's hosts at the time. He had been Canadian ambassador since 1981 and was to stay in that post until November 1986. We began a friendship and accepted several invitations to be with them as their guests at dinner parties at the Canadian Embassy, sometimes followed by movies. Doubtless we were part of what he christened his Public Diplomacy on behalf of Canada, but we liked them in any case.

Sadly, the Gotliebs' popularity in Washington fell off precipitously after March 19, 1986, when the press saw Sondra lose her cool and sharply slap the face of the embassy social secretary, Connie Gibson Connor, on the porch just outside the embassy front door. Ms. Connor was awaiting the arrival of Canadian Prime Minister Brian Mulroney and Vice President George H. W. Bush for a dinner party to showcase the prime minister but ostensibly to honor the vice president. The slap occurred, according to press reports of the incident, when the ambassador's wife stepped outside onto the porch and anxiously asked Ms. Connor the whereabouts of Richard Darman, whose power in the Reagan White House far exceeded that indicated by his title, deputy secretary of the Treasury. Told that he had rescinded his acceptance to dinner—and perhaps because she had counted his presence with the prime minister important to the successful dynamics and purpose of the evening—Sondra let fly at the messenger bearing this news, Ms. Connor.

Kay's service on the board of the American Newspaper Publishers Association—now known as the Newspaper Association of America—eventually led to her selection as ANPA's president. At a board meeting at a resort in Puerto Rico, she paid me the compliment of urging me, and getting some other ANPA leaders to join in urging me, to accept nomination as her successor a year or two after her term expired. But I told them I did not want to be ANPA's president: I had served as president of one of our industry's trade associations, the American Society of Newspaper Editors, and that was enough. And I was unwilling to have the time demands of the job cut into the work and responsibilities of running Dow Jones, as it surely would do.

Another publisher active in ANPA, Punch Sulzberger, the *New York Times* publisher, was a professional friend and colleague in those years and only became a personal friend after we both retired. He and his late wife, Allison Cowles, widow of Spokane publisher Bill Cowles, had moved to their house in Southampton, New York, not far from our Bridgehampton house. Barbara and I enjoyed dinners with them, postretirement, at both their place and ours, and continued to visit them after he became disabled, physically but not mentally, by a stroke. Punch was widely admired throughout our profession for having built the *Times* to new heights and for having courageously faced down the government in publishing the Pentagon Papers. But what attracted me to him in the 1980s was something else.

We were having breakfast together one morning in 1980 before ANPA convention sessions began when he said, "I just told John Oakes [then editor of the *Times*'s editorial page] that we were raising the price of the *Times* from twenty to twenty-five cents—thirty cents without the editorial page." I thought that anyone who could make a quip like that about his own paper was an all-right guy. I also credited Punch with appointing as his managing editor the abrasive yet brilliant A. M. "Abe" Rosenthal, by far the smartest, strongest, and most honorable editor I have ever known (with the exception of *Journal* editors, of course). Abe's news judgment was impeccable.

There were other publisher friends over the years from less prominent newspapers whom we saw as often, sometimes more so. They included the owner and publisher of the *Riverside* (California) *Press-Enterprise*, Howard H. "Tim" Hays, and his wife, Helen, and the part-owner and editor of the *Fredericksburg* (Virginia) *Free Lance-Star*, Charles Rowe, and his wife, MaryAnn. Barbara had worked as a reporter for the *Free Lance-Star* while she was attending Mary Washington College in Fredericksburg. When with the Hayses and the Rowes, we let down our hair more than with other publishers, and drank more, too. Unfortunately, the Hays and Rowe marriages broke up in later years.

Magazine publishers and some foreign publishers also were among my professional-life friends in that period. Malcolm Forbes was one of the former. He was a bigger-than-life extrovert, a born *Forbes* magazine promoter, a nonstop host to industry and media figures—and at the same time a warmhearted, gracious guy. I lunched with him periodically at the *Forbes* offices (where his famous Fabergé eggs were on display), sailed with Barbara and other guests on his yacht the *Highlander* to West Point or to welcome the queen of Thailand at a party in New York harbor, and went to his seventieth birthday party in May 1989 in a huge tent alongside his home in northwestern New Jersey. I brought our young daughter Nina to that party, where the highlight of the evening for her was when Malcolm introduced her to actress Elizabeth Taylor.

English publishers became friends also, work-world friends. Lord Drogheda, born Garrett Moore, was one of them. He was publisher of the *Financial Times*, then its chairman from 1970 to 1975, and he invited me on each of my trips to lunch at Bracken House, the *Financial Times* building that looked out upon the glories of St. Paul's Cathedral. Gordon Newton, the *FT*'s editor, often joined us.

Lord Drogheda was enormously worldly and at the same time quintessentially English, exuding the confidence and savoir faire of his class. While running the *Financial Times*, he served simultaneously from 1958 through 1974 as chairman of the Royal Opera House at Covent Garden.

When Drogheda retired in March 1975, he was succeeded by another of his class, the amiable Alan Hare. I continued my lunches with Hare on trips to London and at the same time continued to see Drogheda when he visited New York. Alan Hare, many years later, was replaced by a street-smart young publisher from the Midlands. He was a man who also invited me to Bracken

House for lunch on occasion, a man with a distinctly more modest background than that of his predecessors but a man whom the *FT*'s parent company, Pearson's, apparently thought better suited to the needs of the times. Alan Hare, related to Lord Gibson, Pearson's chairman, was not sent packing without a consolation prize. He was appointed chairman of the Château Margaux vineyards in France, a property that Pearson's happened to own. I hinted, facetiously, to Dow Jones's directors that it would be nice if our company bought a French vineyard to which departing chairmen could retire. There were no takers.

CHAPTER 26

Women on the Battlements

The Fight for Equality

IN 1973, SHORTLY after Dow Jones moved its Manhattan head-quarters from Broad Street to 22 Cortlandt Street, Edgar Roll, the company's circulation sales director, gave me and other members of the Management Committee a routine slide presentation in the executive-floor dining room. It showed circulation progress and forecasts for the *Journal* and the company's other publications. Projected on a screen at the front of the room were slides showing columns of comparative statistics, slides showing bar charts and pie charts, slides showing graphs. It was pretty dry stuff. Trying to lighten the mood, someone had prepared a final slide that showed a woman's bare derriere with the words "The End" stenciled on her buttocks.

I thought nothing of it.

Five minutes after I returned to my office, a delegation of women reporters trooped upstairs from the *Journal* newsroom and presented themselves in front of my desk. Someone had told them of the final slide in the circulation presentation. This was an example of blatant sexism, of putting down women as "sex objects," they protested. "By permitting it in your presence and condoning it," they said, "you were sending a signal to managers everywhere that such sexist behavior and attitudes were to be tolerated and were OK." I tried to assuage them by saying it was just a sophomoric effort to add a light touch to a dry statistical presentation, really was meaningless, not intended to be disrespectful, not reflective of company attitudes toward women. The delegation was not swayed and not amused.

My consciousness was raised that day. As the father of three daughters and the husband of an independent, feminist-minded wife, I thought I was sensitized to equal, respectful treatment of women in and out of the workplace. But my failure—and my colleagues' failure—to recognize the inappropriateness of that bare-bottom slide showed I needed the wake-up call.

We thought we were trying hard and making progress moving women into managerial jobs. In 1974 about 35 percent of Dow Jones's employees were women. They included Rose Carroll, *Barron's* magazine's advertising production manager; Pat Donnelly, head of the Circulation Sales Department's planning and analysis division; and Marge Cutter, managing editor of Ottaway Newspapers' *Traverse City* (Michigan) *Record-Eagle.* But I was aware that the progress was slower and skimpier than I and others wished.

"Your record of women in key news positions is nonexistent," Michael Gartner, a respected *Journal* alumnus, wrote to me on December 17, 1977. I had a practice of asking a few of the brightest *Journal* alumni to give me, from time to time, in strict confidence, no-holds-barred critiques of the paper and their ideas for improving it. These were journalists whom I regarded as among the best in the profession, whom I would have rehired in an instant had they been willing, who knew the paper well from the inside—and who now could appraise it critically with an outsider's objectivity and detachment. Mike Gartner was one of these. In 1977, nearly four years after he left the *Journal,* he was editor of the morning *Des Moines Register* and the afternoon *Des Moines Tribune* and later would be president of NBC News. Another alumnus who responded to my invitation to critique the paper was James Gannon, a sixteen-year *Journal* veteran and former political reporter in Washington.

Mike's criticism of my failure to promote women into key operating jobs was contained in a thoughtful, single-spaced, five-and-a-half-page appraisal of the paper, sent at my request. It went on to say: "You have no female bureau chiefs, no female news editors or assistant news editors, no females in positions of command." His criticism echoed what I was hearing from my wife, Barbara, at home: "It is not a pretty picture," she said. They were right. Mike made recommendations of specific promotions to correct the situation.

In the years that followed, women would become bureau chiefs in Boston, London, and other cities; assistant and deputy managing editors of the *Journal*; Dow Jones's vice president for staff development; and, a few years after I retired, publisher of the *Journal*. But we did not move fast enough or far enough to satisfy the women—or ourselves. Very few were ever represented in the upper reaches of management.

It was painfully ironic that this situation prevailed inside a company I was running—where I had the authority to change it—at the same time that my wife and I were active in trying to promote equal opportunity for women outside the company. Some might charge that not only was this ironic, it was hypocritical. I would dispute that. Barbara was active for years with the National Organization of Women's Legal Defense and Education Fund. She was active for even more years with Planned Parenthood and served on its regional boards. I fought for the admission of women into clubs where they had been excluded.

In the spring of 1980, a venerable Manhattan social club to which I belonged, the University Club of New York, was the setting of a tumultuous controversy over whether women should be admitted as members. I volunteered to speak for the affirmative side at a membership meeting to consider the issue. "Do you want to deny your daughters," I asked, "the same opportunities you and your sons enjoy here, dining among friends and participating in business and social networking?" After making other arguments, I wound up this way: "This club should be a leader, not a follower. Women are going to be welcomed into the city's and country's clubs where they are now excluded. It is inevitable. It is going to happen. Let's not be dragged kicking and screaming into the twentieth century. Let's get out front and lead the way."

The room erupted in boos. I told the gathering that I found it ironic that members of a so-called gentlemen's club should boo a fellow member with whom they disagreed. But the proposal was roundly defeated. *Newsweek* magazine reported the controversy and my role in it in an article, by Linda Bird Francke, on the battles then under way at many clubs over the admission of women. I resigned from the University Club, and also from Washington's Cosmos Club and Chicago's Chicago Club over the same issue. Some years later—of course—all eventually realized they were on the wrong side of history by trying to cling to an untenable, archaic custom, and they finally came around to admit women as members.

What's the explanation for how I could have failed to order the more rapid and more meaningful advancement of women at Dow Jones where, unlike the University Club, I did not need to wait on any majority vote? The chief explanation is that in organizations such as ours that had historically been made up mostly of men, the pool of experienced female candidates was small compared with today. The smaller the pool, the fewer the number, if any, who rose to the top to be considered viable candidates for high newsroom or corporate office. As a result, there were more qualified men available and competing for the top jobs. This same dilemma prevailed when we were searching for black candidates to promote to higher line jobs, with key operating responsibilities, as opposed to staff administrative jobs. This may well sound today more like a weak excuse than an explanation. It doubtless sounded in earlier times like a weak excuse to our women employees of that era and to Mike Gartner and others wiser than I, including my wife. But it reflects how the terrain appeared to me in the 1970s and earlier years. Later, as the pool of able, experienced women grew, the promotions grew, too.

At the end of the twentieth century and the beginning of the twenty-first, women did rise to high posts at the *Journal* and Dow Jones—though arguably still not as many and not as high as we would have wished. Joanne Lipman would be named deputy managing editor of the *Journal*, after distinguishing herself in the launch of the paper's Saturday edition; Alix Friedman also would become a deputy managing editor; and Dorothea Palsho would be vice president for circulation, even before I left. Other women, too, entered the higher levels of newsroom and corporate management, most notably Karen Elliott House, whom the Dow Jones board of directors appointed publisher of the *Journal* in 2002.

Karen's tenure was successful yet controversial, because her husband, Peter Kann, had succeeded me as Dow Jones's chairman and CEO. But her abilities had been widely recognized long before she married Peter in 1984, and he later wound up as her ultimate boss, behind several separating firewalls. She had won a Pulitzer Prize in 1984 for her Middle East reporting; she had been appointed assistant foreign editor in 1983 and foreign editor in 1984; *U.S. News & World Report* had tried to hire her away as its executive editor; I had appointed her vice president of Dow Jones's International Group in 1989. She became president of that group in 1995, in charge of all our overseas news and corporate operations. She had performed with distinction in each of these posts. And even way back in the years 1975 to 1978, when Karen was covering the Agriculture Department in the *Journal*'s Washington Bureau and Peter was just making his way back from Asia—she had joined the paper in 1974—her work had been outstanding enough to catch not only my attention but that of others. In 1977, when alumnus Mike Gartner had sent his *Journal* critique and improvement recommendations, his list of recommendations included this one: "I also would name a female to a bureau chief's post; my candidate would be Karen House, and my city would be Los Angeles."

With each Karen House promotion came a salvo of criticism leveled at Karen and Peter Kann and sometimes me by some media critic or Dow Jones insider over what some perceived as nepotism or personal-professional conflicts of interest, or both. The issue was a serious one and we considered it seriously. Its roots went back many, many years, before Karen or Peter's time.

Shortly after we opened a regional printing plant in 1963 at Silver Spring, Maryland, outside Washington, one of the men on the News Department proofreading desk there decided to marry a woman colleague working on that desk; I said one of them should leave and find work elsewhere. I sought to avoid the precedent, believing that in such cases if one employee were criticized or dismissed for poor performance, the spouse would harbor resentment and possibly quit, in either case depriving the company of the services of the second, more valued employee. The case was appealed to a governmental human rights commission—and Dow Jones lost. Thus ended the notion of not condoning employment of members of the same family. Over the years that followed, intraoffice romance and marriage flourished, and many employees' husbands and wives, sons and daughters, cousins and aunts followed them into the company.

Some of the criticism of Karen House's ascent was based on principle, and those critics had every right to question my judgment and, later on, that of the Dow Jones board of directors in promoting her while her husband held high office at the company. It was legitimate to ask whether we allowed situational ethics—a desire to retain two proven, highly valued executives—to trump what the critics viewed as sound policy. At the same time, a great deal of the criticism and anonymous sniping came from individuals who held personal grievances and grudges against Karen. She was tough-minded. She had little tolerance for laziness or incompetence. Her insistence on high performance was what made the operations she supervised successful. It was inevitable that the toughness that was one of her strengths would involve her in confrontations with the underperformers she criticized or dismissed, or with others with whom she differed on other issues.

Joanne Lipman, a deputy managing editor who left in 2005 to become editor-in-chief of Conde Nast's new *Portfolio* magazine, was a woman I liked and admired from the day she was hired in 1983 straight out of Yale and began turning in stories that caught many an eye. When *Portfolio* folded in 2009, a victim of the print-advertising collapse afflicting all newspapers and magazines, she wrote an op-ed piece in late October in the *New York Times*. Its theme was that "women haven't come nearly as far as we would have predicted twenty-five years ago. Somewhere along the line, especially in recent years, progress for women has stalled. And

attitudes have taken a giant leap backward." In the course of making that argument, Joanne painted a picture of *The Wall Street
Journal* in 1983 that I could not recognize.

"After graduation, when I first joined *The Wall Street Journal*,"
she wrote, "I could count the number of female reporters there
on one hand. The tiny ladies' room was for guests. The paper was
written by men, for men. It didn't even cover industries that were
relatively female-friendly, like publishing, advertising, and retail-
ing. When the newspaper finally did introduce coverage of those
sectors a few years later, most male reporters weren't interested.
So we women stepped up. . . . But we finally gained respect after
one of our number won a Pulitzer Prize for national reporting,
on the tobacco industry."

I was surprised, and disappointed, to read such historical revi-
sionism. Not that I thought our record was one to wear as a badge
of pride, or that a bit of hyperbole was necessarily out of place
in criticizing it, but I was taken aback by the number of misstate-
ments of fact that could be fit into so few sentences. I later read
a critique of the piece on "The NYTPicker," a website that says
it "reports on the internal workings of the [*New York Times*] and
comments on its content." It corrected in this way the same mistakes that struck me in Joanne's recollection of the treatment of
women at the 1983 *Journal*:

> Lipman must have quite a handful of fingers. In fact, *The
> Wall Street Journal* had a significant number of women report-
> ers throughout the 1970s and 1980s—including ones who
> covered banking, commodities, food, broadcasting, the
> stock market, and Hollywood. By the time Lipman arrived
> in 1983, the *WSJ* had been covering publishing, advertising
> and retailing—highly coveted beats—for years, with both
> men and women. And it had plenty of ladies' rooms, too.
> You doubt us? Just ask around the *NYT*. Plenty of former
> *WSJ* reporters and editors worked there in the 1980s and will
> confirm that Lipman's statement is deeply, totally false. Start
> with [*Times*] managing editor Jill Abramson or business edi-
> tor Larry Ingrassia. Lipman then claims that women "gained

respect" at the *WSJ* only in 1996 when Alix Friedman won the national reporting Pulitzer for her coverage of the tobacco industry. What about in 1983, when the *WSJ*'s Manuela Hoel-terhoff won the Pulitzer Prize for criticism?

In commenting on how journalists, who often probe the lives of others, often are quick to take umbrage when the spotlight of criticism is thrown on them, a wag in our profession once said: "Journalists don't have thin skins; they have no skins." I would plead guilty to that. What the Joanne Lipman episode illustrates, though, goes beyond my thin skin or women's issues. It demonstrates how even some of us at the top of journalism can get careless on occasion—and the need for us all to work hard day-by-day, every day, to continue to earn the readers' trust.

The issue of women's equality and respect for women in our society is broader than what was, and is, faced in the workplace. Sondra Gotlieb, mentioned earlier, a writer whom we knew as the wife of the onetime Canadian ambassador to Washington, wrote a series of columns about the Washington social scene in which she took the identity of "wife of." My own wife, Barbara, often—too often—was identified at various social and business gatherings only as the "wife of" her spouse, implicitly a mere appendage, less important, less a person of accomplishment in her own right. That was Sondra Gotlieb's point, of course. Most corporate wives, academic wives, diplomatic wives, and others are familiar with this second-class-citizen syndrome. Some don't mind it. Others do.

Barbara worked hard helping me in my career over the years, and not only as a counselor and sounding board. She hosted dinners at home in Chicago for visiting firemen such as then–executive editor Buren McCormack, dinners at our subsequent houses in Larchmont and Brooklyn Heights for colleagues and business associates from the Associated Press and other organizations, dinners later in Manhattan and Bridgehampton for other publishers, some Dow Jones directors and executives, and various Fortune 500 corporate chieftains. She accompanied me on many business trips and to Dow Jones board meetings in other cities,

acting as hostess. These contributions and her other achievements sometimes were recognized, sometimes not.

I recall vividly a summer dinner party given at Southampton's
Meadow Club in the 1980s by a corporate friend. Barbara's dinner partners were the president of a large investment-banking
firm, on one side, and on the other a prominent corporate raider
of that era. All through the dinner the two discussed deals, talking over Barbara the entire time. Not all, or even most, businessmen are this lacking in sensitivity and, for that matter, basic good
manners. But I recall enough other similar episodes to leave no
doubt in my mind that this was not an isolated case, either. Lesson learned: Being successful in business, or rising high in one's
chosen field, whatever else it might be, doesn't guarantee picking
up graciousness or even plain old common sense along the way.
If anyone ever thought it did.

Women's issues were not the only social issues that increasingly occupied us inside and outside the workplace. Black people,
then homosexuals were pressing for an end to discrimination on
the job and in our society at large. We recruited Don Miller as
vice president for Human Resources, the top personnel job. He
was talented. He also was African American. Black editors were
appointed as well. Some gay staff members were open about their
sexual orientation; others were not. We tried to be sympathetic to
their aspirations and to coverage of efforts to overcome discrimination based on race or sexual orientation.

In July 1994, after my retirement, I testified before Senator
Edward Kennedy's Senate Labor and Human Resources Committee in favor of a bill he had introduced, the Employment Non-
Discrimination Act of 1994, to extend federal bans on racial,
gender, and religious job discrimination to include discrimination based on sexual orientation. I testified that it was not only
morally right but also good business not to deprive American
companies and American society of the talents of any individual
just because he or she was gay. The bill never passed.

Our intentions at Dow Jones were good. Our accomplishments
were limited. As with women in the 1970s and earlier, the pool of

able, experienced black editors and professionals was small for historical and cultural reasons, not only within our company but throughout our industry. Newspapers competed to pirate proven black stars from each other.

"Family values" were first beginning to become a workplace issue, as employees pressed for, and largely succeeded in obtaining, more ample maternity leaves, flex time, and in some cases permission to work partly from home to permit parents to spend more time with their children. I recall one visit to the *Journal*'s Boston Bureau when, over dinner with staff members, a young new reporter, David Wessel, pressed me to consider paternity-leave time so new fathers could spend time helping with their newborn children. David eventually rose to be the *Journal*'s chief economics editor, based in Washington, and a regular guest on National Public Radio and other broadcast venues.

A leading figure in the women's movement, Betty Friedan, had a home in Sag Harbor, Long Island, not far from our vacation home, later our primary home, in Bridgehampton. Barbara, like many women, had been strongly influenced by her seminal book, *The Feminine Mystique*. We admired her work and accomplishments. She spent much of her time in Manhattan and teaching in Washington, but we saw her socially occasionally in the summer when she was in Sag Harbor, in the years before her health deteriorated. My most lasting memory was not of serious social and philosophical conversations with her, but of being taken by surprise by a comment she made one afternoon in her backyard at Sag Harbor. She had invited Barbara, me, and others to an informal outdoor luncheon. Standing around chatting with me beforehand, she volunteered, out of the blue: "I don't have anything against men. I like men. I like sex. The missionary position is my favorite position." I don't think her intention was to shock, though she did. Even icons can be human and unpredictable.

CHAPTER 27

Managing Growth

The Halcyon Years

THE 1980S WERE HALCYON YEARS at Dow Jones, particularly for the *Journal*. Its circulation in 1981 passed two million, largest in the nation. Advertising poured in faster than we could increase the page capacity of the *Journal*'s presses to accommodate it. Dow Jones's earnings soared. *Fortune* magazine's annual survey in 1984 found Dow Jones the second most admired company in America after IBM, and first in quality of its products and services. Other honors—both corporate and personal—were bestowed in the years leading up to celebration of the *Journal*'s centennial in 1989, with President George H. W. Bush and his wife, Barbara Bush, in attendance.

These were heady days. I was saddened, though, that some of those to whom I owed much did not live to see and enjoy all they had helped bring to fruition. One was the irrepressible Jessie Cox, matriarch of the Bancroft family, Dow Jones's controlling owners and descendants of Clarence W. Barron, who had bought the company from its founders in 1902. She died April 20, 1982, at the age of seventy-three, in a private dining room upstairs at "21," a favorite Manhattan restaurant of hers, where her family had gathered on the eve of Dow Jones's annual meeting. She was a Bostonian and a Red Sox fan. She rose that night, glass in hand, proclaimed to the assemblage, "What the hell is the matter with my Red Sox," then toppled over.

Jessie and her husband, Bill, had entertained Barbara and me when we were newlyweds in London, where she was the first American to be invited to judge events in the Commonwealth Horse Show at the White City Arena. Two warm gestures from that time endeared her to me. Soon after I married Barbara she took me aside and said, "You got yourself a good one." And when Barbara fell ill during one of Jessie and Bill's visits, Jessie took time to come around to our tiny apartment to visit and chat with Barbara, who was sitting up in bed. In the years that followed, we came to her home, the Oaks, overlooking Cohasset harbor, in Massachusetts, to brief her and her sister Jane on company affairs, to attend the fortieth birthday party she gave for her son Bill Jr., and, sadly, for the funeral of her husband Bill Sr. She was a longtime Dow Jones director, always supportive, always staunch in her defense of the *Journal*'s independence, with a backbone of steel and a sailor's salty tongue. She never once asked me to put something in the paper or keep something out on behalf of a friend or some other personal interest of hers. Nor did other members of the family over the years.

Another pillar of the company whose loss I felt deeply was Bob Potter, who died of cancer in 1988. He was Dow Jones's outside counsel and a director, a confidant of Kilgore's, then Kerby's, then mine. He was much more than a savvy legal adviser. He was wise, sensitive, and a friend. He was a Brahmin with a big heart and a common touch. He not only fought for racial justice in the United States and in South Africa but was not afraid to embrace causes that were the antithesis of what his colleagues at Dow Jones and his Manhattan friends thought "respectable"; he provided extensive and lengthy free legal aid to the Puerto Rican nationalists, part of the extremist movement that had tried to assassinate President Harry Truman.

In 1982, when a ruptured disc and perhaps stress gave me back pain that almost immobilized me at times, he sent me a letter that read in part:

> After the formal Executive Committee [of the board of directors] meeting on June 15, on my own initiative I discussed

with members of the committee my perception that your back had not appreciably improved over the past 15 months. We all agreed that it would be in the Company's interest, as well as your own, that you take a good long rest this summer and that you make full use of the Company's transportation facilities including the helicopter for weekends or other out-of-town trips. One thing the medics all agreed on is that driving or riding in a car for more than a short haul is the worst thing for a back.

You may resent my initiating this but I also have a selfish interest—in the autumn of my career as counsel to the Company I don't want to look forward to breaking in with a new publisher, having spanned two and a half so far!

Both Jessie Cox and Bob Potter had played important parts in transforming Dow Jones, in May 1963, from a privately owned company into a public one with shares available for purchase by outside investors. An underwriting team led by White Weld & Company, Goldman Sachs, and Stone & Webster Securities Corp. sold 110,000 shares of common stock to the public that May 28. The shares were tradable first on the over-the-counter market and then, starting in July 1976, on the New York Stock Exchange. The shares had not been liquid, or easily marketable, before; now members of the Bancroft family achieved liquidity and could easily raise cash when they wanted. Later, on June 30, 1986, each shareholder was issued a 50 percent stock dividend in the form of shares of a new Class B stock, each of which had ten votes and could not be transferred to anyone outside his or her family.

This was a controversial move. It was pushed initially by the Boston law firm of Hemenway & Barnes, longtime representatives of the Bancrofts, as a way to solidify Bancroft family control, block any takeover attempts, and permit the Bancrofts to sell portions of their common stock holdings to diversify—as they did in future years—without jeopardizing their control. It was a move endorsed by management and the board as a way to continue the Bancroft family's long record of zealous protection of the independence of the *Journal* and the company, in an era marked by increasing takeover activity by corporate raiders and others.

In those years and the years that followed, as the *Journal* and other parts of Dow Jones grew, the company's net earnings marched steadily upward, as did its stock price. Earnings in 1957, the year I became managing editor, were $3.6 million, on revenue of $31.4 million. By 1975, the year I became CEO, they had risen to $26.5 million and $237.8 million, respectively. In 1990, my last full year before retiring June 30 the following year, Dow Jones reported net earnings of $106.9 million and revenues of $1.7 billion.

Journal advertising was one of the main engines of this growth. Don Macdonald, who led the advertising sales team worldwide and had become vice chairman, suggested, in a lighter moment, yet seriously, a way to accelerate the growth. He said his friend Jack Cunningham, founder of the Cunningham & Walsh advertising agency, was willing to sell us his big schooner. We could entertain major customers and prospective ones in style afloat, as Malcolm Forbes and his *Forbes* magazine did so successfully with their yacht *Highlander.* I said no, thanks, as I recoiled from visions of spending my weekends hosting clients. Later I learned the beautiful wooden schooner's bow had subsequently developed dry rot. We might have lost some valued advertisers, to say nothing of our own necks, had the bow fallen off at sea while we were at the helm.

As late as 1964, the average size of the *Journal* was twenty-six pages. Barney Kilgore had always said he didn't want to see the paper exceed thirty-two pages; part of his formula for success was to keep the paper tight and selective, to sustain its appeal to busy readers. But several developments combined to break that size barrier. As business growth surged, new fields—from computers and other new technologies to emerging markets abroad and personal finance—cried out for coverage and became "must" reading for our subscribers. Competition was growing swiftly and expanding the boundaries of coverage as other publications recognized the appeal and importance to their readers of business stories, particularly when colorful business personalities and the drama of business battles were featured. All this required expanded news space and added pages. At the same time, advertising demand began outstripping *Journal* page capacity, so that capacity had to be increased and utilized. It wasn't a choice between increasing ad revenue and profits and staying small to please readers. The increased ad revenue was needed to finance the added reporters and editors required to satisfy our readers' expanded coverage needs and stay competitive.

By 1979 and 1980, some advertisers had to be turned away. By midyear 1980, extra units had been added to our presses and the Eastern Edition's page capacity increased from forty-eight pages to fifty-six, with the other regional editions going from forty- to forty-eight-page capacity. By mid-1981 the *Journal* again saw months when it was unable to accommodate all the advertising that businesses sought to run. Press units were ordered to bring capacity in all editions to sixty-two pages in 1983 and sixty-four pages in late 1984. The story of demand exceeding even the expanded capacity repeated itself again during part of 1983 and in some months of 1984, then again in 1985. Capacity was increased again, to eighty pages in 1986. And so it went.

We added a "second front page" and changed the *Journal* format to two sections in 1980, then three sections on October 3, 1988, to accommodate the expanded news coverage and the increased advertising. New international news pages were added in 1980, a daily op-ed page in 1981, with new liberal and conservative columnists, and expanded arts and leisure coverage in the fall of 1983.

The *Journal* and its staff continued to win Pulitzer Prizes and other recognition of the high quality of the paper's news and editorial-page coverage. Some examples: Editor Bob Bartley won a Pulitzer in 1980 for editorial writing, and in 1983 Manuela Hoelterhoff of the editorial-page staff earned one for criticism, for her insightful reviews of opera and other cultural events. In 1984 Karen House was awarded a Pulitzer for international reporting and Vermont Royster for commentary. In another two-Pulitzers year, 1988, Jim Stewart and Daniel Hertzberg shared one for their insightful coverage of the 1987 stock market crash and of insider trading in the securities industry, while Walt Bogdanich won another for revealing faulty testing by medical labs. By 1989, its centennial year, the *Journal* had won thirteen Pulitzer Prizes.

Stewart's and Hertzberg's prize was one in a long line of awards for *Journal* business coverage, including Ed Cony's first *Journal* Pulitzer for reporting, in 1960, for stories that "set off a general public reappraisal of business ethics." The business-reporting awards included a public service prize from Sigma Delta Chi, the National Society of Journalists, in 1977 for investigative reports on corporate bribery in the United States and abroad. Bogdanich's 1988 Pulitzer, on the other hand, was the latest honor bestowed on reporters broadening the *Journal*'s content. Jerry Bishop, for example, had won an American Medical Association Special Commendation in 1965 for his reporting on the ethics of medical experiments, and Dick Martin won an award in 1968 for stories on the battle against blindness.

Recognition came from other directions, too, not just in the form of awards. The *Washington Journalism Review* in 1981 published the results of a survey that found the *Journal* the most accurate in covering the government. Smithsonian magazine published a similar poll finding in 1983. A 1986 *Los Angeles Times* Gallup poll reported the *Journal* "the most trusted information medium" in the country.

In 1984, when *Fortune* magazine's annual survey of corporate reputations showed Dow Jones the second most admired company, overall, behind only IBM, *Fortune* also ranked us number one in quality of products and services, number three in quality of management, and second or third in three other categories— long-term investment value, financial soundness, and use of corporate assets. In the publishing and printing industry, Dow Jones was found to be the most admired, and number one in quality of products. For the survey, *Fortune* said it had questioned "8,000 senior executives, outside directors, and financial analysts" about 250 large corporations in thirty-one industry groups.

By 1988, Dow Jones still was ranked in the *Fortune* survey as the third most admired company on an overall basis, the second most admired in the country for the quality of its products and services, and the most admired in the publishing industry. This was the fifth consecutive year that *Fortune*'s survey had shown Dow Jones in such leadership positions. The survey conducted in 1991, the year I retired, showed us still ranked number one in the publishing industry for quality, though other corporations by then had replaced us among the top ten most admired companies in all industries.

Through the years, we tried constantly to avoid the pitfall of smugness and complacency that often accompanies success. In a January 16, 1987, Letter from the Publisher printed in the *Journal*, an annual Report to Readers that had become a tradition since I began the custom ten years earlier, I shared some of our improvement plans for the year ahead, then went on to say: "We also welcome . . . criticism. We know we can do better. . . . More important than any particular changes in content and organization is the constant effort by our editors and staff to maintain and reinforce the standards of trustworthiness and reliability on which our relationship with you rests. . . . We realize [our readers' trust] must be reearned, day after day and year after year."

I repeated this message, again and again, in newsletters to our employees, in meetings with reporters, editors, and Dow Jones executives, and in other forums. In similar venues and in frequent speeches inside and outside the company, I also repeated another message, as in this segment of remarks I made in early June 1985 in accepting, on behalf of the *Journal*, the Hubert H. Humphrey First Amendment Freedoms Prize from the Anti-Defamation League (ADL) of B'nai B'rith:

> Collectively, U.S. newspapers have vastly improved the extent and quality of their coverage over the past quarter century. . . . They have stressed care and balance as never before. They have gone on an orgy of self-examination and self-criticism that exceeds anything they have done in the past. We must do even more. We must do more to prevent our failing in the future, as we often have in the past, to

anticipate, to foreshadow for our readers some of the major trends in society.

It is distressing to look at our coverage in the 1960s of Northern racial tensions and later of campus unrest. We overlooked the smoldering fuses and moved in on those stories only when the explosions came. Many papers—not all—failed in the 1970s to alert their readers to the energy shortage that was in the making even before the oil boycott. Most failed equally in the 1980s to alert readers to the switch to an oil glut. Even those of us close to the scene failed to prepare our readers for the financial crisis that shook New York City in the 1970s and had such wide ripple effects. In the 1980s the crisis in the Social Security system was among the issues not sufficiently foreshadowed for our readers. The failure to anticipate such major news developments is one of the most crushing criticisms that deserve to be leveled at the performance of the press.

The ADL's Hubert Humphrey Prize was one of many honors bestowed on the *Journal*. Others, reflecting the *Journal* and Dow Jones's success, were bestowed on me personally in this era. I was given an honorary Doctor of Laws degree by the University of Portland (Oregon) and Doctor of Humanities degrees by Queens College, Pace University, and Long Island University. In 1981, *The Wall Street Transcript* selected me as "the best CEO in the newspaper publishing industry," giving me its gold award based on "interviews with industry executives, leading financial analysts, money managers, trade journalists, members of the academic community, and various professional sources." In 1986, *Financial World* magazine gave me its bronze award as second best CEO in the publishing, printing, and broadcasting industry, behind Thomas Murphy of Capital Cities/ABC Inc. (Not everyone shared these complimentary opinions. Years later, in May 2007, *New York Times* columnist Joe Nocera wrote that under my management, and that of my successor, Dow Jones was "the worst run . . . inept.")

I was inducted into the Information Industry Association's Hall of Fame in 1984. And in June 1988 the Center for Communication selected me as its Annual Award recipient. It was presented by CBS and then–"60 Minutes" correspondent Diane Sawyer and Thornton Bradshaw, former chairman of RCA Corp. and of NBC, at a Plaza Hotel luncheon. Bradshaw said the award was "for implementing global expansion efforts. *The Wall Street Journal* now extends around the world and is associated not only with business and finance, but with cultural and social issues as well. He is to be commended for his part in making the global village much more of a reality." Honors also came from, among others, the Deadline Club, a venerable association of New York journalists; the Beta Gamma Sigma national business fraternity; and the National Institute of Social Sciences.

As anyone who has received such personal honors knows, or should know if not taking him- or herself too seriously, some are given solely to recognize accomplishment and can be taken at face value, but many more are given because the donors pick recipients who they think can bring certain benefits to their institution. They want a speaker whose prominence or subject, or both, will interest their audience, be it a university's graduating class or a trade organization's membership. And, in a great many other cases, they want a speaker who they believe will draw a large enough paying audience to give a lift to their fund-raising. Be that as it may, and cynical as it may sound, the honors were welcomed not only for one's own ego but because they added luster and prestige at the same time to one's organization, its employees, and its efforts to expand its own businesses by heralding and further publicizing their strengths.

Dow Jones's growth and success in the 1970s and 1980s set the stage for two happy milestone celebrations. The first, in 1982, marked the one hundredth anniversary of the company's founding by Charles H. Dow, Edward D. Jones, and Charles M. Bergstresser, whose initial undertaking was delivering their handwritten financial news bulletins to Wall Street customers by messengers. The second celebration, in 1989, commemorated the centennial of *The Wall Street Journal*'s first issue on July 8, 1889. That first issue was four pages and cost two pennies. (In 1989, the cost was fifty cents a copy.)

In 1982, in observance of the centennial of the company's founding, we recommended, and the board approved, issuance of ten shares of Dow Jones common stock to each full-time employee with fifteen or more years with the company, as a gesture of thanks for their contributions to Dow Jones's success. Other full-time employees received five shares.

We also hosted "birthday parties" for employees in each of the cities in which the company had major offices. Company officers divided up the hosting responsibilities. In January, Ray Shaw and I were on hand to cut a birthday cake and make a few remarks of appreciation at a Houston party for sixty Dow Jones people and their guests at the elegant Hacienda de los Morales restaurant, with a mariachi band playing after dinner. Next day we were in Dallas for a dinner for 275 staffers and guests at the Texas Hall of State, a museum of Lone Star State history. The Los Angeles party was at the Dorothy Chandler Music Pavilion, the San Francisco one at the De Young Museum, the Washington one at the Corcoran Gallery of Art, the New York party at the Metropolitan Museum of Art, the one for Boston and Chicopee employees at Worcester's Mechanics Hall, a nineteenth-century guildhall. And so on, through the year.

Don Macdonald flew to London to officiate at the party there and lead the dancing. While chatting and dancing with London Bureau reporter June Kronholz, he memorably told her, "You are a piece of work." Taken aback by this in a feminist age, she replied, "I'm a *what?*"

When I spoke at these gatherings—and at different departmental meetings and retreats over the years—I often used similar texts, with modest adjustments to fit the particular audience and occasion. I figured that except for a handful of our Management Committee executives in attendance, no one there would have heard the earlier speeches, so why write an entirely new one for each occasion. I also often recycled the same warm-up jokes in my opening remarks. At one dinner gathering, Barbara was sitting at a table with several higher-echelon executives who had traveled out from New York with us. As I rose to speak, she saw them huddling together at the table, passing dollar bills back and forth. When she asked what they were doing, one said: "We're taking bets on whether Phillips will retell his penguin joke again."

One of the ways we later observed the 1989 centennial of the *Journal* was distribution of a special centennial edition that looked back at the last century but also featured forecasts for the next century by leaders from different walks of life. The edition included a piece by writer James P. Sterba on one hundred years' worth of mistakes. "Over the years, we've published words, phrases, sentences, headlines, and even entire stories that we wish we hadn't—stories that were painfully wrong, tasteless, careless, pretentious, or stupid," Sterba wrote.

He went on to recall that in 1960, for example, the *Journal* saw signs that Fidel Castro was losing his grip on power. In 1967 it foresaw Communist China fragmenting into a dozen regional pieces. One front-page story's lead sentence that got by layers of editors was atop an account of President Richard Nixon's relations with the top three auto manufacturers, and began this way: "Once upon a time, there were three pigs (who lived in Detroit) during the reign of Good King Richard." In 1980, Sterba reported, the *Journal* had quoted Alabama Securities Commissioner Thomas Krebs as saying that "throwing white-collar crooks in jail is more fun than choking chickens." Sterba added, "We didn't know that the latter phrase was a regional euphemism for male masturbation."

The high point of the celebration of the *Journal*'s one hundredth anniversary was a mammoth June 22, 1989, centennial party in New York in the high-ceilinged, beautifully designed Winter Garden. The Winter Garden was an arena-sized crossroads inside the World Financial Center, the building complex into which the *Journal* and Dow Jones had moved their headquarters in late 1985. Dow Jones executives and spouses mingled at the black-tie centennial party with the heads of hundreds of the country's major media, industrial, and financial companies. Barbara and I sat alongside President George H. W. Bush and his wife, Barbara. Others at our table included our longtime Brooklyn Heights friends GeeGee and Hamish Maxwell, chairman of Philip Morris, and Dick Fisher, CEO of Morgan Stanley. Roy Vagelos, chairman of Merck, was at our table, too; his company had headed *Fortune*'s "most admired" list. We had hosted him as a luncheon guest and had found him good company. Lionel Hampton and his band played throughout the evening. The president was the evening's chief speaker. He said, in part:

> This is an impressive audience. And as I look around, if anything catastrophic happened in the Winter Garden, the Fortune 500 would be lucky to keep in just the double digits. . . . In 1979, *The Wall Street Journal* became the largest circulation daily in the nation. But one rival complained that it was only because so many subscribers were at an age where they forgot to cancel. All kidding aside, *The Wall Street Journal* has a proud and enviable tradition. And although you deal in the world's most perishable product—news—polls have repeatedly shown that your paper is one of America's most trusted publications. A reputation like that can only be earned by adherence to your founders' pledge to always have the news "honest, intelligent, and unprejudiced." . . . Shortly after *The Wall Street Journal* was founded, 100 years ago, the Census Bureau declared that the "frontier" no longer existed in America. But *The Wall Street Journal*—you've proven them wrong—by advancing across ever new frontiers of technology and geography and innovation.

Twelve years later, on September 11, 2001, the Winter Garden would be destroyed as the twin towers of the World Trade Center, just across the street, came crashing down after terrorists rammed commercial airliners into the buildings. The Dow Jones and *Journal* offices in the adjacent World Financial Center were filled with debris and toxic asbestos dust and were evacuated, the office walls damaged and the critical, essential wiring smashed. The space could not be reoccupied until a year later, after extensive cleanup and renovation. Miraculously, no Dow Jones personnel were lost that day, though some had narrow escapes. My former assistant, Susan Chin, was in the World Trade Center, having just dropped off her son at a day-care center there; both got out unharmed. The *Journal*'s managing editor, Paul Steiger, was outdoors in the area when the buildings tumbled down, and hiked for hours to make his way many miles to uptown—hours when his colleagues, unable to contact him, thought he had perished. *Journal* editors assembled at a contingency communications center that had been prepared for emergency backup years earlier at our South Brunswick, New Jersey, office complex. Reporters phoned in eyewitness stories. And an incredibly complete paper was produced on schedule for the following morning, a historic professional performance, under the most trying conditions, that was recognized with a Pulitzer Prize.

If the *Journal*'s one hundredth birthday party in the dazzlingly decorated Winter Garden marked the climax of a heady couple of decades, the Winter Garden's destruction twelve years later, part of the momentous 9/11 national trauma, in a way also marked the end of easy times for the *Journal* and the start of the newspaper industry decline that would lead to the collapse of some of the country's most venerable journalistic icons. The Winter Garden, the World Financial Center that housed it, and our headquarters there all were cleared of debris and ready to be reclaimed and reoccupied a year later. The *Journal*, too, was to survive the industry's hard times and rise with renewed strength in future years.

CHAPTER 28

A Public Trust—and a Betrayal

"WE HAVE LONG REGARDED Dow Jones's corporate purpose as more than that of a business enterprise alone. The important role that our publications . . . perform in informing the public, in encouraging debate on national issues, and in education is a service to our society that we regard as a public trust."

This statement, from our company's 1975 annual report to stockholders and repeated in a February 1976 newsletter to employees, was one I made again and again over the years. I first made it, with considerable elaboration on "our common purpose," in a December 1972 employee newsletter shortly after I was named Dow Jones's president. I acknowledged that it sounded self-evident and even trite, but that didn't make it any less true. I repeated this theme in the years afterward, in a variety of forms and forums. The latter included public speeches, press interviews, and published letters to readers, as well as other messages to employees and stockholders. I added that profitability, of course, was essential to sustaining and improving the quality of that public service and to performing it with independence.

My colleagues and I also took pains to assure, in nominating new members for Dow Jones's board of directors, that they were aware of that philosophical underpinning of our business and could be counted on to support it as a corporate purpose.

Outside directors who served on our board during my watch ranged from corporate CEOs—such as Donald E. Petersen, chairman of Ford Motor Company; Richard D. Wood, chairman of Eli Lilly & Company; Rand V. Araskog, chairman of ITT Corporation; and Irvine O. Hockaday Jr., president of Hallmark Cards, Inc.—to educational and social leaders—such as Vernon E. Jordan Jr., former president of the National Urban League, who had become a partner in a prominent Washington law firm; and Rene C. McPherson, dean of the Stanford University School of Business. It was my practice, before inviting them to stand for election as a director, to invite them to a "news lunch" with our editors to discuss their businesses and their views on national issues.

These lunches gave us an opportunity to bring the conversation around to how well they thought the press was performing in covering business and the society as a whole. My antennae were alert for indications of whether we shared common principles or whether our guest harbored an antipathy to the press or a desire for the press to perform as a cheerleader for the business community or the interests of his or her own company. We thus tried to vet, or "audition," future board members.

We had differences and debates with board members over the years, but our directors all understood that they were on the board because we valued their business acumen and experience and that their role was not to try to shape news or editorial policy. During the time J. Paul Austin, chairman of the Coca-Cola Company, was a director, the *Journal* published a front-page leader by its Atlanta Bureau about the controversial role Austin's wife was playing in decoration of Coca-Cola's new headquarters building and in discouraging brown-bag lunches in the park outside. Austin said not a word, painful as the story must have been to him and his wife. Director Jim Riordan likewise never attacked our coverage of the company of which he was vice chairman, Mobil, when the *Journal* published stories about the company's tanker and real estate dealings with the sons of its president and chairman, respectively.

Vernon Jordan was not only a former civil rights leader but also a staunch Democrat and later an adviser and confidant of President Clinton. He was an advocate in discussions with me, and with editor Bob Bartley when they met at social functions, of what he viewed as more enlightened policies than the *Journal* embraced on issues affecting the black population in America and on other issues on the liberal agenda. Though his convictions were deeply felt, he was never personally hostile, nor did he threaten to resign when he failed to convert us.

None were stronger defendants of the independence of the *Journal*'s news and editorial columns in my years there than the members of the Bancroft family who served on the Dow Jones board during that period, as representatives of their family, Dow Jones's majority owners. Jessie Cox and her sister, Jane Cook, were outspoken guardians of the paper's integrity.

Their children and nieces and nephews—Bill Cox Jr., Martha Robes, and Bettina Bancroft Klink among them—succeeded them on the Dow Jones board during my time. They were equally supportive. They could have moved to place family members in the top executive jobs at the company, as has been the tradition with the Sulzbergers at the *New York Times* and the Grahams at the *Washington Post*. But the Bancrofts did not have the tradition, training, temperament, or inclination to run the company. I believe the company grew—and they prospered—under the kind of stewardship they maintained in part because they wisely supported and protected the independence of the people who were able to benefit from this environment in making the company grow. The growth was not only in revenues and earnings. The *Journal*'s reputation for quality and integrity, and that of its parent company, grew over the years also—and that was a source of justifiable pride not least for the owners.

Many years later, in the early 2000s, the growth in revenues and earnings were to stop, then reverse and decline, at least temporarily. In saying often that profitability was essential to improving the quality of our service to the public, I had always added that "conversely, it has been our experience that quality in our products, in turn, breeds profitability." With the rise of new media, and the migration of advertisers to those Internet sites, quality no longer assured profitability. The *Journal* and Dow Jones were not immune to the decline in financial fortunes that then afflicted all major newspaper publishing companies as the twenty-first century began. Dow Jones as a result was sold in late 2007 to Rupert Murdoch's News Corporation. But, in the years before and the years since, it and the *Journal*'s standards and reputation for quality and integrity were not compromised or diminished. They continued to grow.

When the day came when the *Journal*'s reputation was jeopardized, more than twenty years earlier during my years there, the blow came not from lapses by heavy-handed directors or owners, but by a breach of trust by a young reporter, one member of a news staff that shortly would number nearly six hundred. In early 1984 Norman Pearlstine, who had become managing editor in September the previous year, learned from the Securities and Exchange Commission staff that in October and November it had begun investigating unusual trading in the stocks of companies immediately prior to their mention in a *Journal* stock market column, Heard on the Street. It developed that thirty-four-year-old R. Foster Winans, who had been assigned to write that daily column, had made a deal with a Kidder, Peabody & Co. stockbroker to trade advance information on the contents of his column in exchange for a share of the trading profits.

Norm immediately put a team of reporters on the case to explore in detail how this leak of inside information had been perpetrated and what in Winans's personal history and psyche might have led him to commit such an offense. Norm played the resulting story in the lead position on page one. I confess my initial instinct had been to hope we could downplay the SEC investigation inside the paper. But I was wrong. Norm's instincts were exactly right. By reporting the story comprehensively and playing it prominently, he accomplished two important things: First, he showed our readers and the general public that we took our reputation for integrity and our responsibility to retain reader trust so seriously that when we had an ethics-violation scandal in our midst we would be the first to give our readers all the details, no cover-up. Second, he seized ownership of the story, leaving none of our dirty linen for competitors to be the first to hang out to dry and perhaps gloat over.

Pearlstine not only reacted the way a good editor should have. He also reacted in a way that only years later would be preached as sound crisis-management doctrine by business schools and consulting firms across the land. For a generation now "crisis-management experts" have been advocating this message: get the bad news out fast, get it out in full, don't dodge it or let it trickle out in dribs and drabs, lest you prolong the agony with each new revelation.

Winans was sentenced to eighteen months in federal prison on fraud and conspiracy charges. Then–U.S. Attorney Rudolph Giuliani prosecuted the case. Pearlstine continued his superb leadership of the *Journal* news-gathering operations until mid-1992, a year after I retired; he introduced expanded coverage of the media, the law, foreign affairs, and other areas of interest to our audience, and he greatly improved the paper's business coverage in general. The *Journal* soon recovered from the damage to its reputation dealt by the Winans episode. If one considers the size of the staff at the *Journal* and our other publications, it is a tribute to those people who put out these publications every day that the Winans scandal was one in a lifetime, despite the enormous temptations to make a lot of money acting on the information to which they are privy.

The *Journal*'s conflict-of-interest policy, codified when I was managing editor and fine-tuned further in the years since, prohibited reporters and executives from owning the stock of companies they cover, or engaging in short-term trading, or serving on the boards of companies the *Journal* or *Barron's* covers, or leaking advance information on the paper's contents, or engaging in a long list of other unethical or unseemly practices. The prohibitions extend to activities or relationships that even have the appearance of a conflict of interest, even if none actually exists. The Caesar's wife rule governs. The yardstick, when wondering if an action is proper, is to ask yourself if you'd be comfortable seeing it splashed across the front page of the next morning's newspaper. If the answer is no or is in doubt, we preached ad infinitum, then don't do it.

In my annual Letter to Readers, I emphasized that although we were grateful for their trust, confidence, and loyalty, we also recognized our need to reearn that trust and confidence day by day, every day. We knew it was imperative if the *Journal* was to perform its societal function as a trusted source of information on which readers and the public could rely in making critical economic and political decisions. This function in our society fell not to the *Journal* alone, of course, but to the press at large—a point I made often in public speeches in arguing the importance of a free press, even an imperfect press, in a democracy. A free press was not about the rights of the press so much as it was about the rights of the public, I emphasized.

I put forth this argument again and again in public forums over the years. I first did so at a lecture at the University of California, Riverside, on March 8, 1976, and later in accepting the Center for Communication's Annual Award at a luncheon at New York's Plaza Hotel in May 1988—and on many occasions in between. I said:

> When the Founding Fathers provided for a free press, when Jefferson and before him, John Milton, and later, John Stuart Mill argued for press freedom, they certainly never assumed the press would always perform well and act responsibly, would always know the truth and tell the truth. In light of the low-quality sheets of their day, they assumed we would have to suffer a goodly share of fools and rogues in the press.
>
> But they believed that through diversity, out of the vast welter of conflicting ideas that would be put before the public, the truth would emerge. And that it would emerge more effectively than through any efforts to impose standards of truth from the outside or through any other means yet devised. The evidence over two hundred years—at the local courthouse level as well as at the more cosmic levels of Vietnam and Watergate—is that the truth does indeed emerge in this fashion.

I said I believed our profession's raison d'être was the pursuit of truth that is successful through the diversity of its pursuit, if not through the perfection or responsibility of each and every individual pursuer. James Madison summed it up this way:

Some degree of abuse is inseparable from the proper use of everything, and in no instance is this more true than in that of the press. It has accordingly been decided . . . that it is better to leave a few of its noxious branches to their luxuriant growth than, by pruning them away, to injure the vigor of those yielding the proper fruits.

The alternative would be a doctrine of control and orderliness that the drafters of the Bill of Rights rejected.

CHAPTER **29**

The Digital Age

WHEN THE COMPUTERIZATION of news and information delivery first appeared as a speck on the distant horizon, Dow Jones moved quickly to explore and then harness it as a supplement to our newspaper-publishing business, not envisaging it as a substitute or successor business. The first major move, computerized retrieval of news and other databases, was pioneered by Bill Dunn and his colleagues. It was a brilliant success—and remains so. The second, later move, acquisition of a major global electronic supplier of real-time financial markets data, turned into a disaster.

The first steps into the digital age, taken in 1973, the introduction of a news retrieval service, were described earlier, in Chapter 22. By 1984, Dow Jones News Retrieval served 185,000 client terminals, having doubled its customer base each year since 1980. It continued its leapfrog growth in the decades that followed, a pioneer among publishers in charging its customers for its service and in profitability. It gave birth to *The Wall Street Journal* interactive online edition, the most profitable newspaper Web presence from its inception through the present day.

In early 1980, in recognition of the growing role being played by the electronic news-delivery operations, and by the Ottaway group's community newspapers, the Irwin book company, and other non-*Journal* activities, we reorganized Dow Jones's management structure. Up to then, throughout the company's history, it had been organized vertically: All news operations at the *Journal, Barron's*, the Dow Jones News Service, and other publications, such as the *National Observer*, reported to a single executive, the executive editor of Dow Jones Publications; the advertising and circulation sales departments of every publication reported upward to another single executive, the senior vice president for marketing; the production and engineering departments reported to another executive, and so on. Thus, none of these executives controlled or had responsibility for the profitability of any publication or news service. Only the two or three executives at the very top of the corporation had this responsibility.

Now we reorganized into a horizontal structure, with each major component of the company—each profit center—standing alone or with related enterprises. All their operating departments began reporting to a single executive who was responsible for their particular group and its profitability. We initially created eight stand-alone operating groups. There was a Wall Street Journal Group, later renamed the Business Publications Group; a Magazines Group that included *Barron's* and *Book Digest*; an Information Services Group that included the electronic enterprises— the original Dow Jones News Service, or ticker, and the new computerized information retrieval ventures; an International Group made up of the AP–Dow Jones international newswire services, the overseas editions of the *Journal*, and our investments in the *Far Eastern Economic Review* and the *South China Morning Post*; a Community Newspapers Group made up of the Ottaway papers; a Book Group synonymous with the Irwin company; an Affiliated Companies Group that supervised our newsprint-mill holdings and other equity investments; and an Operating Services Group that provided printing, engineering, delivery, and other services to the seven other groups.

In anticipation of this reorganization, Ray Shaw, who was forty-five and had been executive vice president, was elected president and chief operating officer in 1979; Peter Kann became associate publisher of the *Journal*, my deputy at the paper, and a vice president of Dow Jones; Don Macdonald was elected vice chairman of Dow Jones, responsible for the Magazine Group and the International Group; George Flynn was president of the Affiliated Companies Group; and Bill Dunn, who in 1977 had succeeded

Shaw as vice president and general manager at age forty-two, took on the additional titles of president of the Information Services Group and the Operating Services Group.

By 1986, the electronic publishing activities of the Information Services Group accounted for 15.7 percent of the company's operating earnings, more than double its 7.3 percent of just one year earlier. This was before counting the contribution of Telerate, Inc., the global electronic supplier of instantaneous real-time financial data in which Dow Jones took an ownership stake in the 1980s.

Dow Jones's involvement with Telerate dated back to 1978, when AP–Dow Jones became the marketing agent for Telerate products outside North America. Ray Shaw, who was supervising AP–Dow Jones, initiated this affiliation and was the lead player in nurturing our relationship with Telerate executives until he retired in 1989, after ten years as president. In 1985 Dow Jones purchased 32 percent of Telerate for $282.3 million. A business partner of ours, Oklahoma Publishing Co., bought another 20 percent that year for $177.5 million, bringing our combined holdings to a majority 52 percent. This came about because Ray Shaw, an Oklahoman himself, had developed a close personal and business relationship with Ed Gaylord, Oklahoma Publishing's CEO.

Sales and earnings of Telerate had grown at a compounded annual rate of more than 50 percent in the previous five years. In 1985 sales were $148.5 million and earnings $33.4 million. Telerate's continuously updated price data and news on U.S. Treasury securities, short-term corporate debt (called "commercial paper"), world money markets, foreign exchange, financial futures, and many other financial instruments were delivered to investors and professional traders via more than thirty thousand video display screens at securities and investment banking firms, commercial banks, corporations, and other financial institutions in the United States, the United Kingdom, and more than forty other countries.

We subsequently bought Oklahoma Publishing's holdings and increased our ownership of Telerate to 67 percent, then in

November 1989 increased our holdings to 92 percent through a tender offer to Telerate shareholders. In January 1990 we bought the rest, and Telerate became a wholly owned Dow Jones subsidiary. A transactional capability, in the form of a foreign-exchange trading service, was started by Telerate in 1989 and was acquired, too. We began assimilating Telerate into Dow Jones, as Dow Jones made the transition to becoming a leading global provider of instantaneous financial information. Some 50 percent of Telerate's revenue came from abroad. In 1990, 24 percent of Dow Jones's revenue came from its international operations, including Telerate's. The number of Telerate terminals in use worldwide totaled 89,300 at year-end 1990.

In 1989, Dow Jones's business publications, including the *Journal,* accounted for 29 percent of the company's operating income, and community newspapers 11 percent. The Information Services Group contributed 21 percent and Telerate 39 percent. In Dow Jones's annual report to shareholders for 1989, the Information Services Group's report of its activities and progress was, symbolically, the first of the different operating groups' reports to be shown—for the first time coming ahead of that for the *Journal* and other business publications.

We regarded the purchase of Telerate as a move to bolster our core business and our corporate mission: to supply high-quality news and information whenever, wherever, and by whatever means of delivery customers wanted. To help finance the purchase we sold some other businesses in which we had invested earlier. It was a redeployment of assets. At the start of 1988 we sold the Richard D. Irwin book company to Times Mirror Corporation, which later resold it. Its growth had slowed, and it was not central to our core business and mission. In January 1989, we sold our stake in Continental Cablevision, realizing a capital gain of more than $164 million. That was a tougher decision, for Continental was growing rapidly and we knew its future was bright.

Among the considerations in the Continental sale were these: Though Continental had positive cash flow—more dollars flowing in than out each year—it was reporting losses on its books because of accounting rules governing depreciation and other noncash considerations. If we increased our ownership to more than 25 percent, accounting rules would have forced us to show its losses and large, growing debt as part of our own financial results. We, as a publicly owned company whose stock was traded on the New York Stock Exchange, believed shareholders would not react well to such heavy downward pressure on Dow Jones's reported earnings, likely resulting in losses, and to such growing debt. We were sure the Bancroft family, always averse to significant debt, would not take kindly to that—or to incurring the yet larger amounts of new debt that would have been required to buy the remainder of Continental that we did not yet own. Nor did we think they would accept large additional borrowings to buy the remainder of Telerate if we did not sell off other assets to help finance that move.

There was another, equally or more important consideration at the time. We would have liked to have kept Continental and its cable properties as long-term parts of Dow Jones, contributing earnings and strategic benefits on into the future. However, it became hard for us to envisage the entrepreneurial, immensely talented Amos "Bud" Hostetter and his team—who valued their independence and on whom we were totally dependent to keep running Continental—becoming part of a larger corporation and giving up their existing growth methods in favor of building profits and limiting debt. I believed they wanted to build up the company by their ongoing methods in order eventually to cash in by selling it for a huge capital gain, rather than operating it for annual profits over the long term. Sell it for a capital-gain bonanza they later did, in a deal with AT&T. Bud and his top executives, after a brief tenure with the purchaser, retired wealthy. AT&T later resold the parts of Continental.

Our 1990 Dow Jones annual report to stockholders, commenting on the Telerate acquisition, said: "It is management's view that the distinction between print and electronic information delivery will diminish over time and that Dow Jones increasingly will be offering the public complete business information packages delivered in a wide variety of forms."

This summed up the vision—a prescient one, I believe—that motivated our acquisition of Telerate. We hoped to extend our existing leadership in electronic publishing (and in print) by acquiring a much more diversified, worldwide digital content distributor. We saw this as positioning Dow Jones to grow as the dominant provider of business and financial information in both print and digital form, the traditional and the new, futuristic media delivery vehicles.

It did not work out that way. In the years ahead, Telerate's competitors—Reuters and Bloomberg—grew faster and increased their share of the market at Telerate's expense. Telerate's revenues and earnings continued to grow into the mid-1990s, then reversed. In Dow Jones's annual report to shareholders for 1996—my last year on the board of directors following my 1991 retirement as an officer and employee—the company said:

> Dow Jones Markets (formerly known as Dow Jones Telerate) has been a major contributor to the company's revenue and earnings for several years. As recently as 1994, when the operating income of the business publishing segment was under pressure, strong growth in the financial information services segment (of which Dow Jones Markets is the largest component) kept overall results on an upward path. In 1996, that situation was reversed as the operating income of the Markets unit declined.

The handwriting was on the wall and subsequently Dow Jones sold Telerate, at a huge loss.

The seeds of that failure were planted years earlier. It is often said that success has many claiming to be its parents, while failure is an orphan. There is enough responsibility for Telerate's failure to go around and be shared by many, certainly including me. My diagnosis of what went wrong is this:

1. I, and my associates, underestimated the difficulties of managing a very complicated new business, one alien to our expe-

rience and beyond our ability at the time to understand fully the intricacies of its operations. We were well aware that this was widely regarded in management doctrine as a major potential pitfall, but we believed the strategic objective of the acquisition was important and we could do it. We bought Telerate in steps over several years, rather than all at once. One reason was to give us a period of time in which to familiarize ourselves with Telerate's business from the inside, get to know the key Telerate executives better, and keep the Telerate management in place.

2. I, and others, underestimated the difficulties the cultural differences between our two companies' personnel would pose in assimilating Telerate into Dow Jones. This, too, was a recognized potential pitfall we thought we could skirt. Neil Hirsch was Telerate's founder and CEO. He had brilliantly built a business first by recognizing and filling a need for then-nonexistent instant, reliable price quote information on government securities and commercial paper, as corporate short-term debt instruments were called. Neil and his colleagues had what I called a trader's mentality, like many of the Wall Street traders they served, whose business led them to haggle over every quarter of a point or eighth of a point price spread. They tended to want to negotiate or argue every issue—even down to something as seemingly minor as observing the no-smoking rule during Dow Jones board meetings. At other times, some of Neil's subordinates would agree to a request—only to then go their own way—or report progress that was less than we earlier had been led to believe was occurring. Our purchase of Telerate's stock at the time the acquisition was completed made many Telerate executives very wealthy. That personal security removed one important underpinning of the future motivation of at least some of them and their willingness to take direction. Carl Valenti, Bill Dunn's protégé and deputy and a technology wiz, was moved into Telerate as its president to work with the existing Telerate executives; later in the 1990s Ken Burenga, by then Dow Jones's president and chief operating officer and a keen, technology-savvy manager, moved to Telerate to try to improve its performance.

3. We clearly recognized from the start some of the principal elements that would have to be added to Telerate's offerings to keep it competitive with Reuters and Bloomberg. Among them: historical pricing data essential to analytical tools software and other decision-making aids we needed to add and expand; expanded transaction capabilities; risk-management analysis functions; and other new offerings to keep pace with a fast-expanding and evolving marketplace. These and network modernization and upgrades required capital. Some of these improvements were added, many were not, or at least not in sufficient measure. I recall asking regularly, before I retired from the company and afterward while still a director, whether these functions were being developed as speedily as we had been told they would be. I recall the executives at Telerate assured me, along with Peter Kann and other Dow Jones executives, that they were. Having retired in 1991, I cannot say for certain what occurred in the years afterward that caused Telerate to fail to stay competitive and to lose market share to others. I can only speculate.

I believe that some of the Telerate executives, while successful in building the firm's offerings in the company's early phases, were not as well equipped or as driven as their competitors to adapt to the swiftly evolving demands of customers for analytics, transactional services, and other new products. I believe that this also proved to be beyond the capabilities, training, and experience of the Dow Jones executives assigned to the task, hard as they worked at it and talented as they were. Dow Jones invested substantially under Burenga in improving Telerate's products and services, but in retrospect it appeared to be too little too late. I wondered if, in earlier years, Telerate executives—not just the holdovers, but those transferred from Dow Jones as well—limited spending on new projects to maximize earnings, and at the same time felt discouraged from asking to borrow large amounts of capital for investment because of the known historic reluctance of Dow Jones, its board, and its owners to carry large debt obligations. (The company's long-term debt, from a high of $719 million at year-end 1989, the time of the Telerate merger, had been paid down to $229 million by the end of 1997.)

I am sure others have speculated on whether my successors could have managed Telerate more successfully than they did, to have it survive and prosper. Or whether the story would have ended differently if Ray Shaw and Bill Dunn had not left the company. We will never know, but my guess is that it would not. Ray retired from the company in 1989 to join his sons' business in North Carolina. Bill Dunn quit shortly afterward, effective January 1991, when he was not named my successor as CEO. Ray had developed the strongest ties to Neil Hirsch and the other Telerate executives, and he was a sound businessman. Bill Dunn had the keenest understanding of the technology. But they, too, given the areas in which they had been trained and experienced, would have been sorely challenged to fully understand and deal with Telerate's rapidly changing markets and to cope with the parameters of Telerate's key executives' abilities and personalities.

There were some who believed that Telerate's failure weakened Dow Jones to the point where Dow Jones and the *Journal* had to be sold. Others said it proved journalists made poor chief executives in this day and age. I don't buy either argument. As recently as 2000, Dow Jones's stock price stood at an all-time high of $76 a share. What brought about Dow Jones's subsequent share price decline, earnings erosion, and sale in late 2007 were the same tectonic shifts that brought down newspapers generally across the country (and all other newspaper-related stocks): mass migration of readers and advertisers to the Internet, compounded by recessions, with consequent collapses in advertising and other revenues. Once-great names were driven into bankruptcy—the *Chicago Tribune*, the *Los Angeles Times*, the *Philadelphia Inquirer*, the *Minneapolis Star-Tribune*, and others. All were burdened by debt when bad times arrived for them, and all were run by business executives supposedly more qualified than those who had come from the ranks of journalists. Even the *New York Times*, the *Washington Post*, and *USA Today* were substantially weakened.

The *Journal* was fortunate to be bought by an owner, Rupert Murdoch, who, whatever his other sometimes controversial qualities, believed in newspapers and was willing to invest heavily to build the *Journal*'s quality and competitiveness. The *Journal* is rare among newspapers in emerging from its trials as strong and respected as it is today.

CHAPTER **30**

Russia

THE 1980S, HEADY YEARS of *Journal* expansion at home and abroad, also were years of far-ranging overseas exploration with colleagues and friends. The 1981 trip through China with Barbara and Dow Jones companions, my third China visit, was followed in 1983 by travel with Barbara, daughter Nina, and Dow Jones executives to Brussels, Berlin, and then on to the Soviet Union. It was our first trip to Russia, and the cold war still was under way. The next year we went aboard the Dow Jones Gulfstream 3 jet with *Journal* editors to the Middle East—Israel, Saudi Arabia, and Jordan—soon after Israel's incursion into Lebanon in its attempt to expel Palestine Liberation Organization fighters there who had been launching raids across the border into Israel. That Israeli-Palestinian conflict and broader Middle East confrontations were to continue, in multiple forms over the years, to this day. Between those and other business trips were vacation travels with family or friends—through Kenya, India, Greece, by sail through the Aegean and Ionian Seas, and also through Turkey, Scotland, southern France, the Caribbean, and often back to where Barbara and I had begun life together, England.

The 1983 trip to western Europe and the Soviet Union began in June. We had scheduled a Dow Jones board meeting in Brussels to give the directors and their spouses a firsthand look at operations of the newly launched *Wall Street Journal Europe*. Some of us flew to Brussels on the Dow Jones plane, its first transoceanic flight. Company policy forbade Ray Shaw, the company's president, and me from traveling on the same plane, so he and his wife, Kay, flew over commercial. Over the Atlantic Ray suffered chest pains and trouble breathing. He was hospitalized in Brussels upon landing. A few weeks later, after being flown home on the company plane, he underwent successful heart bypass surgery at a New York hospital.

We went forward with the board meeting and related activities, though all were saddened and concerned that Ray was absent, undergoing hospital tests. I presided at a dinner given by the board for the Brussels staff and invited guests at a historic, high-ceilinged former palace rented for the occasion. The board meeting the following day and luncheon afterward took place at another beautiful rented palace, this one in the Belgian countryside. There was a side trip that some took to Bruges.

Then, later in the week, with the board activities concluded and as Ray and Kay were flown back to New York, several of us went east to Berlin, for a brief stopover before going on farther eastward behind the Iron Curtain to start a previously planned visit to the Soviet Union. Our group, in addition to Barbara and Nina, included Norm Pearlstine, *The Wall Street Journal Europe*'s editor and publisher; Bob Bartley, the American *Journal*'s editorial page editor, and his wife, Edie; Karen House, then assistant foreign editor; Seth Lipsky, the European *Journal*'s editorial page editor; and David Ignatius, then a *Journal* correspondent knowledgeable about the Soviet Union. Berlin had been transformed in the thirty-four years since, as a correspondent, I had first flown into the blockaded, shattered city aboard a C-47 military cargo plane carrying coal, part of the Berlin airlift.

Berlin in 1983 still was a divided city. The infamous wall the Communists had built in 1961 to seal off their East Berlin from West Berlin would not come down until November 1989. The German capital would not move back to its historic seat in Berlin until reunification of East Germany with West Germany in 1990, with the transfer from Bonn of all the government ministries and the Bundestag, or parliament, not completed until 1999. But by the time of our visit in 1983 most of the wartime ruins were gone from West Berlin, that part of the city had been rebuilt, commerce was thriving, and the city had become a mecca for artists. Our hotel, the Kempinski, was glitzy, modern, and luxurious. We dined on Berlin's famed thoroughfare, the rebuilt and now glistening Kurfürstendamm. At the head of the avenue loomed the Kaiser Wilhelm Memorial Church, bombed out but left unrepaired as a memorial to the death and destruction the city had known.

When we arrived in Moscow a few days later we passed another memorial, this one marking the farthest point of the German Army's World War II advance, just on the western edge of the city. We were met by David Satter, whom Bartley and Lipsky had employed to accompany us as our translator, so we would not be dependent on the accuracy of Soviet translators. Satter, a former Rhodes Scholar, had been the *Financial Times*'s Moscow correspondent from 1976 to 1982; from 1982 to 1988, Bartley used him as a special correspondent, writing articles on the Soviet Union for the *Journal* editorial and op-ed pages.

Yuri Andropov was the Soviet leader at the time, general secretary of the Communist Party. He had been chief of the KGB, the secret police, and had been instrumental in putting down the 1956 Hungarian uprising and invading Czechoslovakia in 1968 to prevent loosening of Soviet control there. These were the post-Stalin years; Andropov's predecessor was Leonid Brezhnev, and his successor when he died in February 1984 would be Konstantin Chernenko.

David Satter and David Ignatius helped arrange interviews with Soviet Foreign Ministry officials and other midlevel authorities. Satter arranged for us to meet with dissidents he had known while stationed in Moscow as a correspondent. We met one such woman in a park, away from possible listening devices; we met another in his cramped apartment. They criticized their government's domestic and foreign policies and told us some of the antigovernment jokes making the rounds in Moscow: "After Brezhnev returned from India, where many people had traditional red dots painted in the center of their foreheads [as religious, caste, or social symbols], he told friends that everywhere he went, people he talked to would tap the front of their heads and say, 'You're missing something here.'" I figured the dissidents with whom we talked must have been mild ones, tolerated by the regime, for surely the government's pervasive surveillance apparatus knew exactly where we went each day and could easily observe with whom we met.

Our hotel was worn and threadbare, with a babushka-clad woman on duty on each floor observing (and undoubtedly reporting) our comings and goings. But the borscht in the dining room was good. Plenty of potatoes and cabbage, too, even if meat and other more imaginative dishes were in little evidence then. The streets, the Muscovites' apartments, the stores were even shabbier, living conditions harsh, consumer goods supplies meager and low quality. One could sense repression in the air, citizens fearful and reluctant to express opinions or engage foreigners in conversation.

Except, that is, at the officially sanctioned interviews that had been arranged for us at government ministries, at the Academic Research Institute of the USA and Canada, and elsewhere. There we encountered a different problem, one of our own making. At the latter institute for the study of trends in America, for example, Satter translated as the Russians around the table responded to our questions and asked questions of their own, always in predictable, programmed mouthings of the Soviet party line and party doctrine. But Satter did not stop with conveying translations. He would become emotional and infuriated by some of the Russians' comments and would immediately heatedly dispute them, challenging our hosts to explain what he perceived as falsehoods in their party-line statements and contradictions he saw in Soviet policy positions and actions. I had to quickly rein him in. His critiques usually were valid, but we were not there to sit and listen to him take on the role of chief challenger and debater. We were there to hear firsthand the Russians' perspectives on the future of Soviet-American relations and how disputes at various world friction points might be resolved, or at least defused. I certainly did not want our translator preempting our role and our prerogatives when it came to questioning and responding. I in effect told him to stick to translating and skip the adversarial role.

We were in Moscow for another reason as well. We sought Soviet permission to open the *Journal*'s first Moscow news bureau. Word of success in this quest came one night when my colleagues surprised me by hosting a fifty-seventh birthday party for me in a restaurant's private dining room. They invited a number of Russian officials, and some came. After various toasts, and after Seth Lipsky presented me with a handsome black Persian lamb's wool Russian Astrakhan winter hat, a Soviet Foreign Ministry official came over and told me they would grant us a Moscow Bureau.

"But we will have to receive in return permission to open another Soviet news bureau in Washington," he said. I asked why, since the Soviet news agency Tass and other Russian organizations already had bureaus there. His reply: "So that when we expel you for something you write, and your government retaliates by closing one of our bureaus, we will still have the same number we have now." He went on to muse, "Maybe we will ask for a Washington Bureau for a Soviet ecological publication." I asked why that was. "It would be fitting reciprocity," he replied, "because you represent the sharks of Wall Street."

The Russians were not known for their sense of humor. I remembered Henry Kissinger remarking on that at John Diebold's dinner in 1971 when Kissinger compared the Russians unfavorably with the sophisticated Chinese he had dealt with on his trip to prepare for Nixon's breakthrough visit to China. Yet here in Moscow I had just heard two witty cracks within two minutes from a Soviet bureaucrat. And earlier we had heard dissidents tell the Brezhnev jokes making the rounds. Those were the last jokes we heard on our visit, however.

Our *Journal* group went on to Leningrad, which today has reverted to its historic name, St. Petersburg. There we stayed in the old but still plush Astoria Hotel. We toured the Hermitage Museum and other former czarist palaces and, most moving of all, the Piskariovskoye Memorial Cemetery. Here, in this large parklike memorial, in mass graves beneath the grass, lie half a million civilians who perished during the World War II German siege of the city. Many were victims of air and artillery bombardments, but most died of starvation and disease. The German siege lasted nine hundred days, from September 8, 1941, to January 27, 1944, during which time all the city's land links to the outside world were blockaded. Only a trickle of supplies could be brought in across Lake Ladoga, frozen in winter.

From Leningrad we flew to the far south to Tbilisi, capital of Georgia, the Soviet republic where Stalin was born. We spent several pleasant days there and in the surrounding countryside before ending our Soviet Union trip. Barbara and I returned home by way of southwest France, where we joined old Brooklyn Heights friends to relax and rest up aboard a barge traveling the Canal du Midi. The friends with us also were our longtime vacation companions GeeGee and Hamish Maxwell, Carol and Ted Reid, and Connie and Donald Reich. We ate cassoulet in Castelnaudary where the dish reputedly originated, toured the medieval fortress city of Carcassonne—and I spent a large part of the time prone on a deck chair or in my bunk trying to throw off a bad chest cold, incurred no doubt from the past few weeks of nonstop traveling.

One might wonder what we accomplished in Russia. We broke no news while there. We came away with few new insights. We saw and heard pretty much what we had expected. Yet we carried away impressions and personal observations that all added up to "the feel of the place," this lair of America's longtime cold war adversary. We would be better equipped in the future to recall and see in our mind's eye the city streets, the people, the offices of power, the countryside, and other places we previously could only try to imagine, in a vacuum, for they were such abstractions. The following year, 1984, we would carry away similar benefits from a multination tour in the Middle East.

Our repeated requests to interview the top Soviet leaders had been denied while we were in Moscow, but four and a half years later, on December 9, 1987, after Mikhail Gorbachev had come to power in the Soviet Union in March 1985, I did have an opportunity to participate in an interview with him when he came to Washington to confer with President Reagan.

The media-conscious Soviet leader, who had introduced a policy of *glasnost*, or openness, invited thirty of America's top editors, publishers, and broadcasters to a highly unusual meeting with him at the Soviet Embassy. We sat around a long, green-felt-covered conference table and, for ninety minutes, listened to his criticism of the U.S. press and shot back questions on Soviet human-rights abuses, nuclear missile deployment, and other issues. It was a tough and sometimes testy exchange. "You're indulging in storytelling about America, calling it a shining city atop a hill and saying everything is beautiful," Gorbachev lectured us. Citing broadcast reports that he was building a $30 million vacation cottage, he said, "That's evil smelling. That's what the press sometimes does."

When the session ended late in the afternoon, I hurried back to the *Journal*'s Washington Bureau office, sat beside the typewriter of a bureau reporter, Gerald F. "Jerry" Seib, and went over my notes with him while he "collaborated" with me and banged out a story on deadline. It ran the next day on page two under my byline. The *Washington Journalism Review*, in an account of the meeting written by the *Los Angeles Times*'s Michael Wines the following March, said "Phillips . . . wrote by far the best account of the session." But since the Gorbachev meeting produced very little in the way of fresh news or insights, and I was rusty, I would have had a hard time under deadline pressure eking out a respectable story from the material at hand were it not for Seib's skill.

"Spokesmen have cloaked the summit in smiles," we wrote in our lead, "but Gorbachev gave a group of U.S. media executives an impassioned, combative, and sometimes defensive lecture." The story reported he accused the American press of portraying the Soviets as enemies and of profiting from sensationalism. "A lot of people think only of profits, and the rest is unimportant," we quoted Gorbachev as saying. "The leaders in this area should think not only of profits but of universal human relations." The Soviet leader told the gathering, our story said, that he wanted to cut "propaganda" from the peace talks between our countries, and then he remarked, "That's what you people are all about."

Gorbachev said he had turned down scores of interview requests because questions always focus on Jewish emigration, internal power disputes, and the Soviet war in Afghanistan. Asked whether the recent Soviet-U.S. agreement on intermediate-range nuclear missiles was motivated by political weakness, he responded, "Your favorite information is information that is not objective. You're inspired by the gossip."

The Soviet leader obviously considered the news media molders of American public opinion, and by hosting this meeting and getting his message to American media leaders, he must have felt he was getting it to the public. For my part, personally, the chief benefit of the Gorbachev meeting, similar to the benefit of our earlier trip to Russia, was that it produced "a feel" for the Soviet leader, firsthand impressions helpful in sizing him up and seeing him in my mind's eye in future years.

CHAPTER **31**

The Middle East

IN 1984, THREE YEARS before Gorbachev's visit to Washington, Jerry Seib had been the *Journal*'s Middle East correspondent when Barbara and I, Peter Kann and Karen House, and Bob and Edie Bartley visited Israel, Saudi Arabia, and Jordan. Jerry and his wife, Barbara Rosewicz, also a *Journal* reporter, shepherded us around, arranged interviews, and were both good company and helpful authorities on the background of the region. A little over two years later, at the end of January 1987, Jerry Seib was being held in Tehran's notorious Evin Prison by Iran's radical Islamic regime, and his companions on the 1984 trip were working feverishly, and thankfully successfully, to get him out.

Before we departed for the Middle East on November 19 of 1984, we spent time with Prince Bandar bin Sultan, Saudi Arabia's longtime and influential ambassador to Washington and a nephew of King Fahd. Karen House, the *Journal*'s foreign editor then, and previously its State Department reporter in Washington, knew Bandar well. He invited us to a reception at the Saudi Embassy, where no alcoholic drinks were served. He then invited just a few of us from the *Journal* to dinner at his home in McLean, Virginia, where Scotch, bourbon, vodka, wine, and the like were plentiful. When I inquired about the discrepancy, he said: "The embassy is the king's house." Bandar arranged for permission for us to visit his kingdom and was there in Saudi Arabia to facilitate appointments and otherwise smooth the way for us during our visit.

In contrast to 1951, when the Saudis refused me a visa when they realized I was Jewish, this time they were pleased to host me and my *Journal* traveling companions. They obviously were anxious, as were officials in Israel and Jordan, to try to promote sympathetic, or at least well-informed and understanding, coverage of their countries in the American press. That would be helpful, they must have calculated, to their efforts to influence U.S. policy makers to take positions friendly to their nations' interests. We had no illusions about why we were warmly welcomed.

In November of 1984 we flew in the Dow Jones Gulfstream 3 jet first to Jerusalem. We stayed in the King David Hotel, toured the city's historic sites, then went on to Tel Aviv for interviews. Yitzhak Rabin, then defense minister and a leader of the Labor Party, had us to lunch in an austere dining room, around a bare wooden table, with several of his aides and generals. Rabin later would become a martyred prime minister, assassinated by a right-wing zealot in 1995 for trying to make peace with the Palestinians.

The Israelis arranged for us to drive northeast to visit the Golan Heights, the disputed, much-fought-over strategic high ground on the Syrian border. It had been Syrian territory until the Syrians lost it in 1967 in one of the several wars Israel's Arab neighbors had fought—and lost—with Israel. We drove north along the Jordan River valley in a battered VW minibus with our escorts, Lieutenant Colonel Renan Gissin, of the Israel Defense Force, and Rafi Horowitz, a government official and former Israeli army officer. We passed through bleak desert, then communities where irrigation nurtured citrus groves, vineyards, melons, tomatoes, and, farther on, cotton. We neared the cobalt-blue Sea of Galilee, with eucalyptuses on its banks. Then ahead loomed the basalt heights of Golan.

After our minibus climbed two thousand feet to the top of this forty-five-mile-long plateau strategically commanding the Jordan and Hula valleys, we arrived at a tattered and worn-looking camouflaged field station on the Heights, home to Tank Battalion Oz. Three-man, Israeli-built Chariot tanks, surrounded by shells, were deployed nearby. The battalion commander, a twenty-seven-year-old major, took us to join his young soldiers for a chicken lunch in their mess hall, complete with toilet paper for napkins. It was Thanksgiving Day in America; this was our Thanksgiving dinner, though it was an ordinary midday meal for our hosts— Thanksgiving not being a holiday outside our own country. But for us it was a special occasion, in a setting that grew increasingly grim once we left the tank battalion's encampment.

We went on to Outpost 109, a maze of fortified trenches and bunkers perched on a bleak, rocky hilltop overlooking the Syrian plain. Damascus was only forty-five miles away. It was lonely, barren, and cold there atop the Golan Heights, far from the warmth of the farmland below. A chilling wind was blowing through a labyrinth of tunnels and gun emplacements. They were manned by reservists. Their commander was Captain Meir Waxman, who for eleven months of the year was a computer salesman.

The captain took us "downstairs," through a steep tunnel to a room carved into the earth, where we all sat around a table and talked. There were a few tattered paperbacks there and a battered television that occasionally picked up "Bonanza" and evangelical programs from Christian Lebanese stations. The captain said "never again" as he recalled what happened here on Yom Kippur in 1973. Before the 1967 war, he said, generations of Israelis in the Kibbutz Ein Gev farm community below grew up in bunkers, constantly being shelled by the Syrians on the Heights. And, he added, fishermen couldn't go out on the lake without being bombarded. Just seven years later, in view of soldiers at this outpost, Syrian tanks moved from their normal training positions on the plains below and broke through a pass to the Heights, threatening northern Israel and its crucial water supply. That Syrian attack was beaten back, and the Syrians never retook the Heights they lost in 1967.

Later, at sundown, as we gazed out from the cold trenches at Syrian territory far below on one side and Israeli farmland far, far below on the other side it was brought home dramatically to us how whoever held these Heights easily commanded the surrounding lands. And how, in earlier years, Syrian artillery bombardments from here could make the land below untenable for the Israelis. The Israelis were determined now not to let their lands there be held hostage again in such fashion.

Driving back to Tel Aviv after dark, most of the passengers in our weather-beaten minibus dropped off to sleep. But not the colonel, Renan. In the clear night, under a bright star hanging low in the sky, a sign appeared that said "17 kms. to Nazareth." Another sign appeared, "Megiddo, 10 kms." Renan spoke into the darkness of the bus. "Megiddo, that's Armageddon, you know, where the Bible says the end of the world will be." Barbara asked, "Do you think it will happen soon?" Renan stirred from his lethargy. "Not as long as the Israelis hold Megiddo," he said. (Barbara subsequently wrote a lively account of our Golan Heights experience for the *Journal*'s op-ed page, under the byline B. A. Thomas, her maiden name.)

From Israel we flew in the Dow Jones plane to Saudi Arabia— by way of Egypt, since the Saudis would not authorize any direct flights to their country from Israel. In the Saudi capital of Riyadh, Bandar had set up an interview with his father, Prince Sultan bin Abdul Aziz, the minister of defense and one of the sons of the legendary founder of modern Saudi Arabia, King Abdul Aziz. We also were invited to dinner at the home of Sheikh Ahmed Zaki Yamani, the longtime petroleum minister and driving force in OPEC, the Organization of Petroleum Exporting Countries, which set oil production quotas, and hence prices, at that time.

After dinner, Yamani beckoned me to sit next to him on an overstuffed couch in the large living room, a room occupied at one end by a sizable indoor swimming pool. He told me his hobby was reading palms, and he asked if he could read mine. As he examined my palm, he began telling me things about my nature and character that were so on target that I was dumbfounded at first. Then it struck me that Barbara had been seated next to him at dinner. He obviously had subtly steered the conversation so as to draw out these details.

Our Saudi hosts gave the men in our group souvenir desert-tan Arabian robes and headpieces, and the women head-to-toe black abayas, or burkas, and veils. We tried them on in one of our hotel rooms in Riyadh, photographed each other in this local attire, and decided we could easily mingle with the street crowds and be taken for Arabs. We did visit the local souk, or market, one night, but not in disguise.

From Riyadh we flew east in the G3 to the oil fields at Dharan, on the Persian Gulf. Bandar met us at a military airbase nearby, an air defense command center. He was very proud of having trained as a fighter pilot. He showed us around the radar monitoring screens and other workings of the command center and told how fighters had been scrambled from this base a few weeks earlier to turn back Iranian jets that had violated Saudi air space. Someone else complained that, near the kingdom's western frontiers, Israeli pilots sometimes flew over the Saudi border and dumped out garbage.

Later, we flew west for a quick visit to the old commercial crossroads city of Jeddah, on the Red Sea. The mayor entertained us at dinner along with the CEO of the American company Waste Management Inc., and his wife. The Saudis in Jeddah had contracted with Waste Management to get rid of their trash and sewage. Next day, on November 29, we flew off again, to neighboring Jordan and its capital, Amman.

Jordan's King Hussein was alive and in power then, married to an American, Queen Noor, daughter of the former CEO of Pan American Airways. Karen House was on good terms with the king, having cultivated him as a prime source for the Middle East stories that had earned her the Pulitzer Prize. The day we arrived he invited us to tea with him at his palace, atop a hill overlooking the capital. The winding road to the palace was guarded by military checkpoints at almost every turn. Jordan had a large Palestinian population, many of whom were living in refugee camps, having fled from Syria, Iran, and, most recently, Israel during the Arab-Israel wars. They had tried to seize the Jordanian government, and their uprising had been put down violently by the king.

As we wound up our discussions with Hussein, his chief of staff invited us to have dinner with him later that evening in a private dining room at a downtown restaurant. We thanked him, agreed to see him then, and, later on, gathered in the room at the restaurant. Toward the end of the meal, we discussed the recent Israeli pursuit of Yassir Arafat's PLO into Lebanon, which ended with the PLO moving its infrastructure to Libya, only temporarily as it turned out. It was then that the king's chief of staff, commenting on Israeli bombing and shelling of certain civilian apartment complexes in Beirut, said: "The Israelis don't care about children." That was a bit much for me to leave unanswered.

"When the PLO adopts a strategy of emplacing its weapons and warriors in apartment complexes, trying to use civilians as shields, who is it who doesn't care about children?" I asked. "When the PLO provokes the Israeli move against the PLO's Lebanon sanctuaries by sending raiding parties across the Israeli border to attack not only soldiers but also schools and hospitals, who is it who doesn't care about children?" These were documented, well-reported cross-border attacks that had been going on for years during that period.

Barbara whispered to me, "Calm down. He's our host." But I didn't care about that at that point. I was not going to let that typical Arab-states party-line remark go unchallenged.

The next day we drove south and toured the temples and caves of an ancient civilization at Petra, then flew home to New York on December 2, 1984.

A little over two years later, in early 1987, our traveling companion and the *Journal*'s Middle East correspondent, Jerry Seib, was being interrogated in an Iranian prison. On a ten-day reporting trip at the Iranian government's invitation, he and fifty-six other foreign journalists had visited Tehran and toured battle areas of Iran's six-and-a-half-year-old war with Iraq. Then on a Saturday, the last day in January 1987, he had been arrested and imprisoned. The official Islamic Republic News Agency said he was being held as a "spy of the Zionist regime." It didn't help that the Iranians jumped to the false conclusion that, with a name like Seib, he was Jewish.

Peter Kann and I went to Washington Monday, February 2, and saw Secretary of State George Shultz, to ask for any help the U.S. government could provide in obtaining Jerry's release. He told us what we already knew and expected: the U.S. government had no influence with Iran, since it had broken off diplomatic relations with Iran in 1980, following the hostage crisis during the Carter administration. The U.S. Embassy in Tehran had been occupied then by Islamic militants, with Iranian government approval, and U.S. diplomats held prisoner for many long months. Shultz thought, and we agreed, that the wisest course now would be for the American government to keep a low profile lest a public confrontation aggravate the situation and make it harder for the Iranians to make concessions. Though the United States had no leverage with Iran, Shultz promised to ask the Swiss and other third-party governments to try to intervene on Jerry's behalf.

It was primarily the effort mounted by *Journal* foreign editor Karen House and her colleagues on the paper's foreign staff that, happily, resulted in Seib's release after four days. We and Karen had been told by experts on Middle East politics that if we were to obtain his release, it had to be done quickly. With every passing day, they argued, the position of the radicals within the Iranian government who wanted to hold onto him and stage a show trial would harden. It would be increasingly difficult politically, these authorities argued, for moderates in Tehran who might be amenable to his release to make their case against opponents once the latter got dug deeply into their positions.

With this warning that urgency was essential, Karen and others worked the telephones day after day and night after night to try to enlist the help of government officials, diplomats, and businesspeople they knew in countries such as Turkey, France, Japan, Pakistan, South Korea, and elsewhere who maintained good relations with Iran and might exert influence there. Because of the time differences around the world, Karen pursued these efforts through the night, when it would be daytime in Asia, for example. We had briefed Shultz on these efforts, and he agreed they were the best hope of getting through to the Iranians. Karen and her colleagues assembled documentation of Seib's Kansas Catholic background, birth, education, and life history—including clippings to demonstrate his past impartial writings on Iran and the Middle East—and transmitted copies to the third parties to use in trying to convince the Iranians the charges against Seib were baseless.

Finally, on the Wednesday after his Saturday arrest, Jerry was ordered expelled from Iran and released to the care of the Swiss Embassy, much to our relief and, much more important by far, to his and his wife Barb's relief and that of their families. He was put on a Swissair jet to Zurich and arrived there Friday, February 6, his thirty-first birthday. I issued a two-sentence statement thanking "the many public and private individuals in many countries whose support and assistance made his return possible." Jerry, after being reassigned to Washington, went on in later years to become the *Journal*'s Washington Bureau chief and, subsequently, assistant managing editor and Washington executive editor.

What a blessed outcome his 1987 release was in contrast to the tragic ending in early 2002, long after I had retired from Dow Jones, of the abduction in Pakistan of Daniel Pearl, the *Journal*'s South Asia Bureau chief. He was seized not by a government entity, as in Seib's case, but by Islamic terrorists affiliated with Al-Qaeda. Pearl was beheaded after about four weeks in captivity.

CHAPTER **32**

Winding Down

IN THE MID-1980s, in anticipation of retirement in 1991 at age sixty-five, I began to think about whom I would recommend to the Dow Jones board as my successor as company CEO. The years of management transition that followed, mostly years of prosperity at the company, also brought for me bouts of national presidential politics voyeurism, proximity to two aircraft emergencies, and eventually fun-poking retirement parties.

In executive sessions of the Dow Jones board, with other management directors excluded, I had periodically discussed management succession "in case I got hit by a truck." Now, as we moved toward the late 1980s and my retirement date grew closer, those discussions became more than theoretical. Ray Shaw and Peter Kann were the obvious leading choices to succeed me. Bill Dunn and Norm Pearlstine also were considered.

Ray was president and chief operating officer of the company, an experienced and able businessman who had started as a newsman. He had gone through heart bypass surgery and his future health prospects were a question mark. Peter Kann was sophisticated and worldly, closely involved with running *Journal* operations at home and overseas, and had participated in the company's management decision making for years. Both men had performed exceedingly well in all their previous assignments, possessed proven ability and judgment, were sensitive to the company's ethical values, and were well liked and respected throughout the company. Dow Jones's board members and the company's majority owners all agreed with my assessment that both men had the qualities to be effective future leaders of the company.

Bill Dunn, brilliant as he was in pioneering our production and electronic activities, was a volatile personality who barely disguised his resentment of what he regarded as the *Journal*'s privileged, superior-acting News Department. Norm Pearlstine, equally brilliant, did not yet have as wide-ranging corporate experience as Ray or Peter, and was doing such a magnificent job leading and improving *Journal* news coverage that I was reluctant to move him out of that role.

Then one morning in late 1988 Ray Shaw walked into my office and shocked me by taking himself out of the running. He said he planned to retire early, at age fifty-five, on March 31, 1989, to move to Charlotte, North Carolina, to spend more time with his family. I was convinced that the real reason was an unspoken one: concern by him and his family that the pressures and stress of the CEO's responsibilities would risk return of his heart ailment in aggravated, life-threatening form. Only later did I come to believe I was wrong in my reading of his prime motivation.

Ray's two sons and their growing families were living in Charlotte. His wife, Kay, already had moved there, and Ray was commuting on weekends. It doubtless had been family considerations that prompted Ray's decision. Health concerns may have been a factor—he subsequently underwent a second bypass operation—but he did not let that slow him down. Shortly after retiring, he and his sons, in partnership with his old friend Ed Gaylord of Oklahoma Publishing Company, bought and ran American City Business Journals Inc., a chain of small, locally oriented business weeklies. They expanded the number of papers and later, in 1995, sold the company to the Newhouse family's Advance Publications, continuing to manage the group for Newhouse. Ray lived a full life until 2009, when he died suddenly at age seventy-five from allergic shock following a wasp sting.

Peter Kann had been associate publisher of the *Journal* since late 1979, a member of the company's board of directors since 1987, and had been elected executive vice president of Dow Jones (along with Bill Dunn) in 1985. He also had served as president of the company's International Group and its Magazines Group since that year. Now, in preparation for his taking on my responsibilities when I retired, I turned over to him in January 1989 the jobs of publisher of the *Journal* and editorial director of Dow Jones publications. And subsequently in October 1990, on my recommendation, the board elected Peter president and CEO effective January 1, 1991. We announced this on October 17, 1990. I had been CEO since March 1975. I remained chairman until my retirement June 30, 1991, after forty-four years with the company. I stayed a member of the board until April 1997, at which point I had reached the mandatory retirement age for directors of seventy.

The management transition thus was completed smoothly in mid-1991. Peter went on to provide Dow Jones and the *Journal* with able, talented leadership in the years that followed. There were critics of his management, and subsequently mine, but the company remained essentially strong, until the years after 2002 that brought the hemorrhaging of advertising revenue and the flight to the Internet that afflicted the entire publishing industry and left the future of all newspapers in question.

In the years just prior to mid-1991, as I prepared for and moved through the steps of our management transition, several other developments were taking place in my professional and personal life. I was participating in my final acts, some ceremonial, as CEO. These included presiding at the *Journal*'s centennial party in 1989, as described in Chapter 27. I also attended my last Democratic and Republican presidential nominating conventions, political events that took place every four years and that I had often attended with the *Journal*'s Washington Bureau coverage team—sometimes with Barbara—for a very long time. I also attended Gridiron Club dinners in Washington, which I had been attending for many years at that point. And I was close by at a moment of near-tragedy in 1991 when Dow Jones's helicopter, with eight people on board, made an emergency landing in New York's East River. On the personal level, I began planning what I would do after retirement.

Dow Jones had owned a twin-engine Sikorsky helicopter since the early 1970s. It was used to ferry personnel between our Manhattan headquarters, our sprawling three-building Princeton, New Jersey, office and printing-plant campus, the Chicopee, Massachusetts, office and printing complex, Ottaway community newspapers' headquarters in Campbell Hall, New York, and occasionally Boston, Washington, and other locations. It carried up to six passengers and a crew of two, including pilot Sandy Kaplan, a veteran of helicopter action in Vietnam.

On April 16, 1991, it took off with a full passenger load from the Wall Street heliport at Pier 6 in lower Manhattan, bound for the Princeton offices. Shortly after takeoff one of its engines failed. Sandy brought the craft down in the middle of the juncture where the East River flows into New York harbor, then deployed the flotation devices with which it was equipped. Police harbor patrol boats soon surrounded the crippled aircraft. The river was turbulent with its fast current and the wake of passing ships. For half an hour, as the frightened passengers waited crammed inside, the police worked to stabilize the downed helicopter so that it would not tip, take in water, swamp, and sink, as some other helicopters that had crash-landed in the river had done. Finally, one by one, all aboard were taken off safely into a rubber police dinghy.

I was in our headquarters building a few blocks away, at 200 Liberty Street, when I received word of the accident. I went to the pier and watched as ambulance crews checked the rescued men and women, releasing all but one, who was hospitalized for treatment of hypertension. A few weeks later Sandy Kaplan sent his rescued passengers, as well as me and some others, a memento: T-shirts on which was imprinted a photo—copied from the April 17 *New York Times*—showing the half-submerged helicopter, surrounded by harbor patrol craft and police officers in a rubber dinghy working to secure lines and stabilize the aircraft. Beneath the photo were the words "Dow Jones Yacht Club."

The only scare I personally experienced while flying on company business came in late October 1989. The San Francisco Bay Area had been struck on October 17 by an earthquake that registered 7.1 on the Richter scale. It collapsed a section of the San Francisco–Oakland Bay Bridge, led to widespread power outages, and caused twenty-seven fires including a major blaze in the Marina district, where an apartment building sank into a lagoon; 63 people were killed in central California, 3,757 injured, and 12,000 left homeless. A couple of days later I flew to San Francisco in the company plane to do what I could to offer comfort and support to our many affected employees in the area.

A *San Francisco Chronicle* poll later showed three out of every four residents admitted they had emotional problems since the quake. I found the reporters and commercial department personnel in our San Francisco office badly shaken up. Some told of cowering in door frames during the quake, a location said to be safer than others when parts of buildings were collapsing. Others told of losing homes in the Marina district. Later I drove south to our Palo Alto printing plant and heard similar stories. I tried to drive west to our Ottaway newspaper in Santa Cruz, on the coast and close to the epicenter of the earthquake, but the road over the mountains was damaged and closed. Only emergency supplies were being permitted through.

Flying home, we were over the Rocky Mountains when pilot Greg Miller announced over the intercom that the Gulfstream had lost power in one of its two jet engines. There were rugged mountains all around and no level place nearby to land, but Miller skillfully kept the plane aloft until, about twenty or thirty minutes later, he made an emergency landing at the Salt Lake City, Utah, airport. I saw fire trucks and ambulances lined up along the runway as we made our approach and came in to land. As our wheels touched down, with power in only the left engine, the plane skewed to the right and skidded off the runway and into the mud. No one was hurt. The plane stayed behind waiting for repairs and a replacement engine, and I took a commercial flight back to New York later that day.

Excitement of a different, milder variety came from attending national political events at the invitation of the *Journal*'s Washington Bureau. I attended presidential nominating conventions not as a member of the working press (although those were the credentials we were given), but as an interested observer. I spent my time schmoozing with editor and publisher friends from other publications and the networks, being included at some meetings *Journal* reporters arranged with political figures, following the convention proceedings from the press gallery, but mostly watching admiringly how our reporters and editors together planned each day's coverage and worked late into the night under deadline pressure to get carefully reported, skillfully crafted, distinctive stories into the next day's papers. I had first sat in the press section at a political convention back in July 1948, when the Democrats meeting in Philadelphia nominated Harry Truman. It was perhaps fitting that as I neared the end of my journalistic career I was at another Democratic convention, in July 1988, at the Omni Coliseum in Atlanta. I felt I had come full circle, so to speak.

The convention nominated Massachusetts Governor Michael Dukakis, with Texas Senator Lloyd Bentsen as his running mate. But to me the most memorable event of the week was the opening-night speech by a young Arkansas governor, Bill Clinton. He was regarded as a comer in the party and thus given a prized speaking spot. Clinton's speech was a disaster—not just in my opinion but also in the opinion of most of the press corps and most of the delegates. He spoke way too long. There not only was no brevity, there was no judgment or selectivity; he indiscriminately rolled off a laundry list of every new program he and the party favored—on and on and on for more than thirty minutes.

I came away convinced, as were many others, that Clinton was finished as a prospect for national office. But four years later he was back as the Democrats' candidate—successful candidate—for president. It was one of the many times he earned the nickname "the comeback kid."

A few weeks after the Democrats' Atlanta convention I was at the Louisiana Superdome in New Orleans for the August 15 to 18 Republican convention that nominated George H. W. Bush. He would go on in the fall election to defeat Dukakis. And in 1992 he would in turn lose to Bill Clinton.

Aside from my 1948 visit to the Democratic convention in Philadelphia and my work at the Democrats' 1956 Chicago convention when I was managing editor of the Midwest Edition there, I began attending both parties' conventions on and off starting with the Republican 1968 convention in Miami that nominated Richard Nixon over Nelson Rockefeller and chose Spiro Agnew as his running mate. In the presidential election year before my final conventions in 1988, Barbara and I had attended the Democrats' July 1984 convention in the Moscone Center in San Francisco.

We were in the hall when Queens Congresswoman Geraldine Ferraro, the first woman to be nominated by a major party for such high national office, accepted the party's nomination for vice president on the ticket headed by Walter Mondale, the Minnesotan who had served as vice president under Jimmy Carter. There was much cheering, flag-waving, and applause, to which Barbara contributed. Barbara wore a pin that read "Jane Wyman Was Right." Jane Wyman, an actress and earlier wife of Ronald Reagan, had divorced him. But in the election in the fall of 1984, the Mondale-Ferraro ticket went down to defeat and Reagan was reelected president.

Our daughter Leslie was at the convention that July as part of the *USA Today* reporting team. Outside the convention hall, Barbara and I, sometimes with Leslie, went to parties given by editor Henry Grunwald and *Time* magazine, Al Neuharth and *USA Today*, Kay Graham and her *Washington Post* and *Newsweek* magazine, the *New York Times*'s Punch Sulzberger, and Gene Patterson, then of *Congressional Quarterly*. We socialized with our longtime friends Tim and Helen Hays, owners of the Riverside, California, *Press-Enterprise*, and went to dinner at Oakland's celebrated Chez Panisse restaurant with Leslie and *Journal* colleagues Al Hunt and his wife, Judy Woodruff, Bob and Edie Bartley, and Norm Pearlstine.

In late March 1988, the same year I attended the Democratic convention in Atlanta and the Republican convention in New Orleans, Barbara and I were Washington Bureau Chief Al Hunt's guests at President Reagan's farewell appearance at the Gridiron Club banquet in Washington. This, too, as well as the Gridiron dinners to which Al invited me in 1991 and in the subsequent year when he became the club's president, struck me as another closing of the circle. The 1988 dinner came thirty years after Barney Kilgore had taken me as his guest to my first Gridiron white-tie-and-tails banquet and show in 1958, soon after I became managing editor.

At the 1988 dinner, the last at which Reagan would appear before leaving office, Nancy Reagan won a standing ovation by singing "Thanks for the Memories," with lyrics of her own. Referring to former White House chief of staff Don Regan, with whom she famously clashed and got him fired, and Soviet leader Mikhail Gorbachev's wife, Raisa, with whom she had a testy encounter or two, Mrs. Reagan sang, in part:

> Thanks for the memories,
> Of all the times we had,
> The happy and the sad,
> Looking back, Don Regan doesn't even seem so bad . . .
> That Soviet Mona Lisa,
> Otherwise known as Raisa,
> She said to me, "Would you like to see my MasterCard and Visa?"
> Thanks for the memory.
> Oh, it's been so swell,
> Not always happy, that's granted,
> The Congress raved and ranted,
> The right wing became disenchanted.
> In spite of it all we had a ball,
> Thanks for the memories.

New York Governor Mario Cuomo, speaking on behalf of the Democrats, said he remembered being introduced to Reagan by New York Senator Patrick Moynihan. Cuomo said that Moynihan began, "'Mr. President, I'd like you to meet—' Before he could finish the president looked over at me and said, 'Oh, you don't have to introduce us. I know Lee Iacocca well.'" That was followed by some self-deprecation by Cuomo: "Bob Novak and others have said of me that I'm insular, that I trust only my inner circle. Well, Bob, that too is false—I don't trust the people in my inner circle. I don't trust enough people to *have* a circle."

As the show wound its way toward midnight, Reagan said: "I understand your motto—The show must go on—and on, and on. Nancy and I thank you for inviting us. We just didn't know we were supposed to stay overnight."

Among the *Journal* guests with whom we were seated that night were NBC anchor Tom Brokaw on Barbara's right, former *Journal* Washington Bureau Chief Alan Otten on Barbara's left, Federal Reserve Chairman Alan Greenspan on my right, and Arkansas's then governor, Bill Clinton, on my left. A few days before the dinner, David Shribman, then our Washington Bureau's chief political reporter, had dropped me a note at Al Hunt's request with four paragraphs of background on my seatmate, Clinton. His note said in part:

> I'm certain that you will find Governor Clinton to be good company. My most enduring memory of him was at the National Governors' Association annual meeting last summer in Traverse City, Michigan—political reporters get to go to the most glamorous places—when he went on stage and played the jazz sax with members of the Four Tops music group. Governor Clinton is young (forty-one years old) and is one of the rising Democratic stars in the South. He won election in both his last two terms with landslides of more than 63 percent. He was first elected in 1978 at age thirty-two and then, like Governor Dukakis, became a convincing political figure on the strength of his comeback from humiliating defeat. He's a Rhodes Scholar with a politically active wife, Hillary, a lawyer who has played a big role in education reform in Arkansas.

That evening's encounter with Clinton came four months before I heard his disappointing speech at the Atlanta nominating convention. I don't recall the conversation at the Gridiron dinner being any more substantive than small talk about the show, the Arkansas economy, and the candidates of both parties campaigning for nomination at the coming summer conventions. I certainly had no sense that I was in the presence of a future president. And I'm certain I made no lasting impression on him.

The following year, 1989, I was back in Washington in February at the Sheraton Carlton Hotel, presiding for the last time at one of the Dow Jones board meetings we periodically moved to the nation's capital. We were meeting there that month to give our directors the opportunity to interact with leaders of the new administration—in this case the incoming George H. W. Bush administration—and to get firsthand our Washington Bureau members' insights and impressions of the changeover in government and what it might mean for the political, economic, and foreign policy outlook.

From Monday, February 13, through Wednesday there were meetings of board committees and of the full board interspersed with a big reception for government, political, and media guests; a dinner for Washington Bureau members and their spouses; and breakfasts, lunches, and other morning and afternoon gatherings to which Al Hunt and his colleagues had invited Washington officials to speak to our directors and their spouses and answer questions. Those who participated in these private sessions included Federal Reserve Chairman Alan Greenspan, White House Chief of Staff John Sununu, Senate Minority Leader Robert Dole, House Majority Leader Thomas Foley, and National Security Adviser Brent Scowcroft. There also was a briefing session with a panel of *Journal* reporters.

Among our guests that week was Ralph Nader, the consumer advocate. He wrote me a cordial thank-you letter afterward in which he said, in part: "In meeting and talking with Bob Bartley, I noticed he had no horns, and he managed to print my long lingering letter to his editorial page that same week. . . . Please give my regards to your wife whose observations indicate that there is no party line at *Wall Street Journal* gatherings."

A month after the 1989 Washington meeting, my predecessor as CEO, and longtime friend and supporter, Bill Kerby, died at eighty-one. His daughters asked me to deliver the eulogy at his memorial service at Brooklyn Heights' Grace Church, on Hicks Street opposite where we and our families had both lived years before. I was pleased to have a chance to express publicly and to his family the deep admiration and affection I had felt for Bill over the more than four decades since he had hired me.

Another career circle was closed two years later, in mid-1991, with my own retirement from Dow Jones. That June was another month for sentiment. My colleagues gave Barbara and me a retirement party and roast June 7 in the River Club's ballroom. Joan Konner, the first woman dean of Columbia University's Graduate School of Journalism, and her television producer husband, Al Perlmutter, gave an intimate retirement dinner earlier in their Central Park South apartment; we were surrounded by beach mates, tennis mates, and other friends from the newspaper world. In June, thanks to Al Hunt's string pulling, a letter with good wishes and congratulations came in from President Bush, and Senator Patrick Moynihan inserted a tribute in the June 13 Congressional Record. Bush's letter, undoubtedly drafted by Hunt, said among other things: "You must be a great politician too— otherwise, you would never have been able to handle *The Wall Street Journal*'s editorial page and Washington Bureau!"

The June 7 company dinner, with our daughters there, pretty and in their best dresses, brought together for toasts and roasts Dow Jones editors, executives, and directors and their spouses as well as Bancroft family members and a few outside business associates. My administrative assistant for twenty-three years, Karen Cuddy, made a witty and moving toast, as did veteran directors Vernon Jordan and Jim Riordan, AP President Lou Boccardi, *Journal* editors Norm Pearlstine, Paul Steiger, and Bob Bartley, Bill Clabby from the electronic-publishing side, Don Macdonald, and representative Bancrofts. All poked good-natured fun at me before saying warmhearted things about our shared experiences.

They were followed by a film, narrated by my colleagues, that was mostly a clever roast, with a tribute at the end. It had been assembled with the help of old family photos supplied, unknown to me, by Barbara. It drew a good many laughs, not least from me.

Bill Clabby, narrating "The Early Years," contended I had "financed [my] honeymoon on Dow Jones's expense account." Later, in a segment titled "The Sportsman," Clabby showed clips of me skiing, sailing, fishing, playing tennis, and swimming, and said, "You know what they say about a 'Jack of all trades, master of none'? He's the best example of that when it comes to sports, I want to tell you."

Norm Pearlstine said, "Actually, there is a Warren Phillips cult in the newsroom and a number of people have studied his every move in an effort to figure out how to get to the top." The camera then swung to the newsroom to show reporters and editors at work—each one wearing bushy black fake eyebrows and fake black moustaches mimicking mine. Ray Shaw was captured saying, "Once Phillips got hold of a joke he'd tell it from New York to Hong Kong to Heerlen [in the Netherlands] and back to New York—and it never got any better. But he'd always be guaranteed one group of people would think that joke was funny as hell, and that group would be the Management Committee."

As Peter closed the evening with his trademark graciousness, a gentleman rolled a huge black motorcycle—too big to fit into the elevator—down the stairs and into the River Club ballroom. It was a retirement gift. I had never ridden a motorcycle or expressed the slightest interest in one. But, as the saying goes, it's the thought that counts.

Amid the toasts at the earlier retirement party Joan Konner and Al Perlmutter had given Barbara and me, Punch Sulzberger had presented me with another farewell gift, a company plane to use in my retirement. It was a toy plane on which he had pasted the words "Wall Street Journal."

During all this celebrating and congratulating there were a few, more serious summing-ups that looked back at my fifteen years as CEO. Some of the milestones were summarized in a report prepared at the board of directors' request by Jim Soderlind, vice president for planning, and Ken Burenga, the general manager who would serve as president under Peter Kann. These milestones also were included in a June 28, 1991, memo to the staff from Kann. These summaries mentioned revenue growth in my

CEO years from $200 million to $1.7 billion; net earnings growth from $20 million to more than $100 million "even in the midst of recession"; transformation of the company into one with a strong international presence it did not have before and a strong presence in electronic publishing, often called in those days database publishing; growth of the *Journal* from a one-section paper with 1.4 million circulation into a three-section paper with a global circulation of 2 million; and all the while promoting "quality above all, integrity," and other high standards and values.

Years later, on January 30, 2005, the *New York Times* credited me in an article on page two of its Sunday Business section with "presiding over the most successful financial era in the history of Dow Jones & Company."

CHAPTER **33**

Bridge Works

Two Second Careers

RETIREMENT, DREADED BY many in our society, brought for me and Barbara fresh adventures, the recapture of the deed to our own time, and an even closer relationship. We not only had more time to spend together, but at her suggestion we started a new business together: Bridge Works Publishing Company, an independent book publisher. For the two of us, it developed into a second career.

At the time I retired in mid-1991, this possibility had not yet occurred to us. I had made a list of "postretirement projects" that I intended to undertake. It included learning to cook, mastering my new motorcycle, teaching, and continuing to work on behalf of the nonprofit boards on which I served. These included the Public Broadcasting Service and Columbia University.

On February 12, 1992, my mother died, at the age of ninety-two, from a staph infection contracted at a Queens hospital where she was being treated for congestive heart failure. At the time, I was teaching as an adjunct professor at Columbia's Graduate School of Journalism. In the fall semester that year I taught at Harvard University as a Lombard Fellow at the John F. Kennedy School of Government. The mission of the Joan Shorenstein Barone Center there and its graduate students was to examine the intersection of the press and politics. The title of my course was The Changing Press: The Effects of Economics, Technology, and Societal Change on Its Public Mission. I opted to live with students at Lowell House Tuesdays through Thursdays, the days I spent in Cambridge teaching and meeting with students. The discussions and other interactions with the Columbia and Harvard students, and their bright, probing questions, gave me the fresh feeling of youth again.

During 1992 Barbara came up with the idea that we start a small press to publish quality fiction and nonfiction. Here was a chance for us to work together in areas of shared interest from our earlier professional lives—the world of words, the world of ideas, and the world of writers with lively minds. We sought advice from others knowledgeable about independent publishing. George Gibson, later to be publishing director of Bloomsbury USA, and David Godine, publisher of the respected literary imprint bearing his name, were among them. Later Bill Henderson of Pushcart Press, and Judy and Marty Shepard of Permanent Press, shared their experiences and advice with us, too. We persuaded National Book Network to be our distributor, the start of a long and productive relationship not only with NBN but also with its parent company, the Rowman & Littlefield Publishing Group, and its savvy and dynamic president, Jed Lyons. Susan Hayes, former production boss at Little, Brown, became our freelance production chief, working from Boston, and filled that important role with us with skill and dedication for two decades.

Our first book, published in the spring of 1993, was the memoirs of a small-town Maine newspaper editor—an instant success that helped launch Bridge Works's reputation nationally. The author, Alexander "Sandy" Brook, a Yale graduate and wartime navy fighter pilot, had tired of a job on Wall Street after World War II and had bought a rundown weekly, the *Star*, in Kennebunk, Maine. He improved and expanded it, building it into a prize-winning crusader for open government and environmental responsibility in the face of awesome political and commercial pressure. Sandy had the knack for taking the reader beneath the seemingly placid surface of a small town and turning the dramas there into colorful prose. When Barbara discovered Sandy in 1992, he had sold the paper and was living in Sag Harbor, Long

Island; she heard him read from his manuscript at a local writers workshop and recognized its promise, and we published it under the title *The Hard Way: The Odyssey of a Weekly Newspaper Editor.*

"Easily one of the best books ever written about journalism," the *Washington Post* said in its review. The *Baltimore Sun* called it "the stuff of newspaper legend." The *Los Angeles Times* said it was "an almost mythically perfect tale." And so it went—in 165 reviews in newspapers, magazines, and wire services from coast to coast. "Important reading for anyone concerned with journalism," said the *New York Times*. And this from the Associated Press: "Compelling. . . . One epic battle after another, each a Homeric struggle."

We published three other books that first year, one of which was *Goodbye, Friends,* a collection of Barbara's short stories, some of which had been published earlier in literary journals such as *Ascent* and in the *East Hampton* (New York) *Star*. "O'Henry-like endings," said the *Houston Chronicle* in its review. "Absorbing . . . honest portrayals of the conflicts many women face," said the Scripps Howard News Service. And bestselling author Susan Isaacs called *Goodbye, Friends* "a first-rate collection, short stories that appeal to both the head and the heart." David Brown, producer of such films as *Driving Miss Daisy* and *The Player*, said, "*Goodbye, Friends* reflects, with daring insight, women's dilemma in our rapidly changing society. . . . These are masterful stories."

Our second year won Bridge Works more recognition. *The Prince of West End Avenue*, a first novel by Alan Isler, was a finalist for the National Book Critics Circle Award for fiction and won the National Jewish Book Award. It was republished in editions in Britain, France, Germany, the Netherlands, Italy, Portugal, Spain, Finland, and Sweden. It was described by the *Los Angeles Times* as "rich and complex. . . . Supremely original." The novel, about a German refugee living in a New York retirement home, a man whose family perished in the Holocaust, "displays a sharp and original wit," the *New York Times* review said. "Gradually, though, *The Prince of West End Avenue* emerges as a paradoxical tale of how to make peace with an unbearable past and the sin of pride."

Author Alan Isler, a former Queens College English professor, had been unable to interest publishers in his manuscript and it was gathering dust on his shelf when a mutual friend urged Barbara to take a look at it. She did, she recognized Isler as a rare talent—and upon publication of his novel, many around the world were captivated by his talent as well.

Another first-time author we published in 1994 was Tom Perrotta. Alexandra Shelley, who worked with Barbara for many years as a freelance editor, brought his manuscript to us. They had been classmates at Yale. When we published his *Bad Haircut: Stories of the Seventies*, the *Washington Post* raved: "Wonderful stories . . . cumulatively more powerful than any coming-of-age novel read recently." Said the *Hartford Courant*: "Stories, like those of J. D. Salinger, based on the kind of truth that spans generations." Perrotta went on to write successful novels at larger publishing houses—novels that included *Election* and *Little Children*, which were made into movies. Janet Maslin, writing in the *New York Times* in 2000, called *Bad Haircut* "his first and still best book. . . . Unassumedly brilliant." As with *The Prince of West End Avenue* and many subsequent books, we sold rights to *Bad Haircut* to a big-time publisher, in these two cases Penguin and Berkley, respectively, to reprint the works in paperback, which Berkley did through multiple subsequent editions over the years.

Barbara, as editorial director and copublisher of Bridge Works, was responsible for finding and choosing the authors we would publish and then working with them on editing their manuscripts. I, as the other copublisher, was responsible for production, marketing, selling subsidiary rights, and flackery—seeking reviews. As it became obvious that Barbara had the eye and the judgment for picking winners, Bridge Works's recognition and reputation grew.

American Bookseller magazine, a publication of the American Booksellers Association, said in a full-page profile in its November 1995 issue that "for a house that's averaged only five titles a year, Bridge Works has had more than its share of winners. . . . An amazing record." It praised Barbara's "track record for picking winners" from the more than one thousand submissions we received each year. In a 1997 profile in the Fort Lauderdale, Florida, *Sun Sentinel,* the Rowman & Littlefield Publishing Group's president, Jed Lyons, was quoted as saying: "This is absolutely the most phenomenal success story in small literary publishing since Algonquin emerged in the early eighties. . . . Barbara has exquisite taste." Other admiring profiles of Bridge Works appeared in the *Kansas City Star*, Long Island's *Newsday*, the *Hartford Courant*, *Publishers Weekly*, the *Southampton* (New York) *Press*, the *New York Times* in December 2003, and in other publications.

The psychic income far exceeded the dollar income. Some years we made a small profit; other years we incurred a small loss. Sales of subsidiary rights for foreign translation, U.S. paperback reprint, and film options gave our finances a boost. *Patty Jane's House of Curl*, a first novel by Lorna Landvik, over which Alexandra Shelley, and Barbara too, labored long and hard, was our greatest revenue producer. U.S. paperback rights were sold to Ballantine Books, with a $47,500 advance from them on future royalties; a German publisher bought German-language rights with a $67,500 advance; and an additional $22,000 came from the Quality Paperback Book Club. All told, more than $135,000 worth of subsidiary rights were sold before the book, the author's first novel, was even published. This was accomplished by Michele Rubin and Maja Nikolic, both of Writers House Inc., in New York, our longtime agents for subsidiary rights sales.

USA Today called *Patty Jane's House of Curl* "fun and funny, spiked with tragedy and sad times." The *Dallas Morning News* characterized it as "the story of women who were lucky enough to find a place where they could not only talk, but be heard." Other rights were sold for British and Spanish editions, and for audio and large-print editions. Sales of all licensed paperback and foreign editions exceeded more than a quarter of a million copies.

Of the more than one hundred titles we published in Bridge Works's first nineteen years of existence, not all were financial successes. *Zip Six*, a novel by Jack Gantos, was praised by the *Boston Globe* as a "raw yet paradoxically exhilarating prison novel," but it failed to sell well. Gantos, a former federal prison inmate himself, went on to win the National Book Award for children's fiction. Rosemary Aubert's *The Feast of Stephen*, the second in a five-book mystery series she wrote for us, won Canada's 1999 Arthur Ellis

Award for best mystery. Some of the books in her Ellis Portal series—starting with *Free Reign*, which the *New York Times* called "a smart, suspenseful whodunit"—were translated into Chinese and Japanese, as well as German and French. Sharon Rolens's *Worthy's Town* was a finalist for the 2000 Barnes & Noble Discover Great New Writers Award, but nonetheless was another that did not sell particularly well. Kristina McGrath's *House Work* and Ann Mohin's *The Farm She Was* were among the *New York Times*'s Notable Books of the Year in 1994 and 1998, but they did not set any sales records.

In 2000, as we grew older and failed to develop a viable succession plan for Bridge Works, we sold the company to the Rowman & Littlefield Publishing Group but continued to run it. In 2005 we returned to publishing books ourselves, independently. The latest, published in November 2010, is a novel of intrigue amid the war in Afghanistan, written by Elliott Sawyer, a decorated officer who fought there with the 101st Airborne Division. In addition to print editions, we also have published our titles as e-books in recent years.

As the early years of the twenty-first century unfolded, book publishing became a more difficult business, as had that other print-publishing industry so familiar to us, newspapers. Book publishers still sometimes managed to do well with nonfiction works on current events, celebrities, cooking, spirituality, and business subjects, and how-to books on topics ranging from investing to conducting romantic relationships. But for all publishers, industry-wide, quality fiction, our specialty, became harder and harder to sell in self-supporting quantities.

What are the reasons for that? Quality fiction, sometimes called literary fiction, excels in exploring character development and the complexities and vagaries of life. The audience for such thoughtful fiction always had been a limited one, made up mostly of well-educated readers. Our view, and that of others, is that now, in an era of declining educational standards, there are fewer adults interested in reading fiction about life's complexities and nuances and more who are attracted by the excitement and entertainment they find in science-fiction fantasies, vampire stories, novels originally written for children such as the Harry Potter series, and popular mass-market novels with one-dimensional characters. These are the novels selling best.

A contributing element is that as newspapers and magazines fell on hard times, they drastically reduced space allotted to book reviews. Quality fiction, and small publishers, suffered and lost much of their past access to the public through newspaper and magazine pages as editors were forced to practice triage, usually using their much-reduced space for the highest-profile books.

These trends, combined with our advancing age, led Barbara and me to slow down from publishing thirteen or fourteen titles a year to perhaps one a year—and to find time for other activities. Barbara keeps on as a dedicated tennis player and gardener in Bridgehampton and, in winter, in Palm Beach. I have become addicted to competitive croquet. And we enjoy the company of our children and grandchildren at every available opportunity.

Daughter Lisa, her husband, Leon Falk, and their twins, Olivia and Savannah, come out to their Long Island weekend house nearby in Wainscott almost every weekend. The New Museum of Contemporary Art, of which Lisa is director, continues to gain more admiration and recognition with each passing year. Leslie, in Washington, continues as communications director of the Senate Homeland Security and Governmental Affairs Committee, as her daughter, Lola, continues to grow and thrive. Nina, having moved to California with sixteen-year-old daughter Kate, divorced Kai in 2010 but soon recovered from that difficult time, and now teaches elementary grades at the same Pebble Beach school that Kate attends. Kai's understanding and supportive parents live nearby in Carmel. In addition to vacation visits with us in Bridgehampton and Florida, they all assemble with us for what has become an annual tradition—gathering to spend the Christmas-through-New Year holiday period together in rented family cottages at the Moorings Village, a resort at Islamorada, in the Florida Keys.

The family was and remains happy, despite a few rough patches over the years. Barbara and I are happy. Looking back, we have much to be thankful for—and we are.

Epilogue

DOW JONES AND *The Wall Street Journal* were bought at the end of 2007 by Rupert Murdoch's News Corporation. Murdoch has invested heavily since then to expand the *Journal's* coverage. It's debatable whether the paper's long-treasured independence has been "lost," but there is no sign to date that its integrity has been compromised. Dire predictions that Murdoch would use the *Journal's* news columns to advance his commercial and political interests have not come to pass in the years since the acquisition. He is smart and has commented often on how foolish it would be to risk the credibility on which the paper's success has always been founded.

As perhaps the sole survivor who worked closely with the man who did most to build the *Journal*, the legendary Barney Kilgore, under whom I served as managing editor, then executive editor, I have reflected often over the years on the similarities and differences between the two men, Murdoch and Kilgore. I believe Barney would have appreciated many of Murdoch's qualities, even if not all. Were it not for the criminal and ethical lapses disclosed in 2011 inside News Corporation's British newspapers unit—even if not known or condoned by Murdoch himself—the two men might well have respected each other, maybe even liked each other.

Kilgore was not one to crave power or participate personally in politics, as Murdoch has sometimes been accused of doing, or to use his publications to those ends, as Murdoch has done with some of his. Kilgore was not one to use sensationalism to sell newspapers, as Murdoch has done with some of his mass-market, popular publications—and which led to the British tabloid wrongdoing scandal that engulfed him and News Corporation in 2011 and, as this book went to press, caused several top executives to resign. There was nothing in Kilgore's actions or persona that would ever draw the demonization that has so often been directed against Murdoch, even before the British phone-hacking scandal.

That said, and those deep differences aside, I believe the two shared many attributes that might have drawn them to each other. Murdoch, like Kilgore, is a visionary and a builder. Both changed the media landscape as innovators. They made their mark as entrepreneurial publishers, strong leaders, strong-willed and creative. And both shared an enduring love of newspapers, a passion that far transcended what one might feel for an ordinary enterprise that existed solely to make money.

Is the *Journal* better now under Murdoch or worse off than if it had stayed independent under Bancroft family ownership? Perhaps it is presumptuous of me to offer judgments, given the length of time I have been retired and out of touch with involvement in active, day-by-day journalism in a changed world. Yet my belief is that the answer clearly is that the *Journal* is better today— and its readers and the general public are the beneficiaries of that. Considering the economic hard times that have beset all newspapers, the *Journal* would have been drastically cutting staff and news space now, as other newspapers have been doing, had Dow Jones remained a public corporation, under Bancroft family control, its shares traded on the stock exchange. In contrast, Murdoch's faith in newspapers has led him to invest heavily in enlarging the *Journal*'s staff and expanding its coverage. Circulation has grown, while that of other papers has declined.

Has the paper improved? Without question, yes, if compared to what it would have been if economic hard times had taken their toll. Compared to earlier times, some readers and journalists argue the answer is open to debate. My answer still would be yes, the paper is better, though I would rate it a closer call. As coverage and display of general news has been expanded, the *Journal*'s distinctiveness has been reduced somewhat and it has grown to look more like other newspapers. The paper's signature leaders and investigative and interpretive stories still are there, but most are not flagged, to set them apart for the reader from stories less researched, less developed, sometimes less important.

On the other hand, major news and continuing stories of significance—the American banking bailout and related economic crises, the Gulf oil spill, the 2011 Egyptian and Libyan revolutions, and spreading Mideast unrest, for example—have been reported as well as any in the *Journal*'s history and, in most cases, in more timely and thorough fashion than the performance of competitors. Coverage of government, politics, international news, sports, and certain metropolitan areas, such as New York, is more comprehensive than before. The *Journal*'s online presence has been vastly improved. And the *Journal* has added to its weekend edition a new section, Review, that is cerebral and superb, appealing to thoughtful subscribers both new and old. Its other new weekend section, Off Duty, also is appealing; it's hip and addresses many aspects of leisure life and the business of living.

Yes, the *Journal* has changed. Everything changes over the years—in life, in business, and in journalism. The *Journal* was steadily evolving throughout its history. It would have changed more in the future, whoever the owner. These changes have been a net plus. Rupert Murdoch is not a young man, so a big question remains: will his successors remain as devoted to quality journalism at the *Journal*, and what will be the nature of change under their stewardship?

For now, though, *The Wall Street Journal* remains strong, through parlous times. Few other newspapers can say that. It continues to serve its readers and the nation well. That cannot help but be a source of satisfaction, even pride, for all who ever were associated with building its reputation and strength. It certainly is for me.

Selected Glossary of
The Wall Street Journal Titles

Managing Editor, Midwest Edition: Supervised news coverage by the news bureaus in that region. Also had authority over other, non-news departments on those rare occasions when interdepartmental issues had to be resolved instantly, on deadline, when there was insufficient time to consult New York headquarters. Managing Editor of Pacific Coast Edition and other regional editions had similar responsibilities.

Managing Editor: Directed news coverage, had day-to-day operating responsibility for the paper's content outside the editorial pages, and was responsible for hiring, firing, and assigning beats to staff members.

Executive Editor: The person to whom the managing editors of the *Journal* and other Dow Jones publications reported. Responsible for news department policies and budgets. Represented the news department in management discussions of interdepartmental issues.

Editor: Directed the staff and content of the opinion pages of the *Journal* and, at times, the arts pages. Was responsible for shaping editorial policy and expressing it vigorously in the daily editorials. Carried no authority over the news staff and content (except when William H. Grimes first held the title) and was synonymous with editor of the editorial page.

Publisher: Responsible for the paper's direction and smooth operations, growth strategies, policies, standards, and relations with its customers and the general public. The person to whom all the paper's chief departmental executives reported, either directly or at times through the general manager. Most of the time, but not all, Dow Jones's CEO concurrently held the position of *Journal* publisher.

General Manager: The person to whom all top department heads reported and who resolved interdepartmental issues. When an executive without news background held this post, the jurisdiction would include advertising, circulation, production, finance, and administrative departments but would exclude news and editorial.

Business Manager: A mostly honorific title bestowed to raise the prestige of someone already running several departments, such as operating services (production) and information services (electronic products and services).

Editorial Director: A mostly honorific title bestowed on a former top news executive to indicate that, although the person had assumed business responsibilities and titles, his or her previous experience still entitled the individual to weigh in on the editors' discussions and decisions.

Executive Vice President: A deputy to the president, already responsible for a group of operating or administrative departments.

President: The chief operating officer of the company and, at times, the company's chief executive officer, or CEO. The heads of all operating and staff, or administrative, departments were responsible to the president, who was responsible for the smooth operation of the company, its strategies, budgets, policies, and future planning, and new start-ups and acquisitions.

Chairman of the Board: Usually also the company's chief executive officer, or CEO. The president was responsible to the chairman, the two worked closely together, and the chairman's duties often overlapped those listed above for the president. In addition, the chairman planned board of directors meetings and agendas, chaired the board meetings, and handled relations with the company's principal owners and other shareholders. The president and chairman both dealt with other outside constituencies—governmental bodies, Wall Street analysts, the press, legal challengers, public-responsibility advocates, and the public at large.

Vice Chairman: An honorific title bestowed in 1979 on Don Macdonald, already in charge of all marketing, international, and magazine operations at that time.

Selected Chronology

This table is intended to help the reader trace the jobs performed over the years by the individuals mentioned in this book. The year the name first appears in each column is the date he or she was first appointed to the post. In most cases it can be assumed the individual remained in that position until a new appointee's name appears lower in the column. In a few cases a new appointee's name does not appear because he or she does not figure in the text; examples would be the omission of McWethy's successors in column one and Kilgore's predecessors in the last two columns. The table thus does not pretend to be a complete history of *Journal* and Dow Jones executive appointments, but only a guide to the timing of the appointment of editors and other executives included in this book.

	Managing Editor, Midwest Edition	Managing Editor	Executive Editor	Editor	Publisher
1941		Kilgore		Grimes	
1943		Kerby			
1945		McCormack	Kerby		Kilgore
1949					
1950		Gemmill			
1951	Bottorff		McCormack		
1954	Phillips	Bottorff			
1956					
1957	McWerthy	Phillips	Bottorff		
1958				Royster	
1961					
1964					
1965		Cony	Phillips		
1966					Kerby
1970		Soderlind; Taylor	Cony		
1971					
1972					
1973					
1975					Phillips
1976					
1977		O'Donnell	Taylor		
1979				Bartley*	
1983		Pearlstine			
1985					
1988					
1989					Kann**
1990					
1991		Steiger	Pearlstine		
2001				Gigot***	
2002					House

* Carried the title of editorial page editor from 1971
** Was associate publisher from 1979
*** Title is editor of the editorial page

General Manager	Business Manager	Editorial Director	Executive Vice President	President	Chairman of the Board
Kilgore					
				Kilgore	
	McCormack				
			Kerby		
McCormack					
Bottorff			McCormack	Kerby	Kilgore
Phillips		Phillips			
			Phillips		
				Phillips‡	Kerby
	Dunn				
					Phillips
Shaw					
Dunn			Shaw		
				Shaw	
			Kann; Dunn†		
		Kann			
Burenga				Kann§	
			Burenga	Burenga	Kann

† Until 1991
‡ CEO added in 1975
§ Also CEO

FURTHER READING

Brayman, Harold. *The President Speaks Off the Record.* New York: Dow Jones Books, 1976.

Kerby, William F. *A Proud Profession: Memoirs of a* Wall Street Journal *Reporter, Editor and Publisher.* Homewood, IL: Dow Jones–Irwin, 1981.

Rosenberg, Jerry M. *Inside* The Wall Street Journal*: The History and the Power of Dow Jones & Company and America's Most Influential Newspaper.* New York: Macmillan, 1982.

Royster, Vermont. *My Own, My Country's Time: A Journalist's Journey.* Chapel Hill, NC: Algonquin Books, 1983.

Scharff, Edward E. *Worldly Power: The Making of* The Wall Street Journal. New York: Beaufort Books, 1986.

Tofel, Richard J. *Restless Genius: Barney Kilgore,* The Wall Street Journal, *and the Invention of Modern Journalism.* New York: St. Martin's Press, 2009.

Wendt, Lloyd. The Wall Street Journal*: The Story of Dow Jones and the Nation's Business Newspaper.* Chicago: Rand, McNally & Company, 1984.

INDEX